Evaluation Practice for Collaborative Growth

Evaluation Practice for Collaborative Growth

A Guide to Program Evaluation with Stakeholders and Communities

Lori L. Bakken

OXFORD
UNIVERSITY PRESS

Oxford University Press is a department of the University of Oxford. It furthers
the University's objective of excellence in research, scholarship, and education
by publishing worldwide. Oxford is a registered trade mark of Oxford University
Press in the UK and certain other countries.

Published in the United States of America by Oxford University Press
198 Madison Avenue, New York, NY 10016, United States of America.

Library of Congress Cataloging-in-Publication Data
Names: Bakken, Lori L., author.
Title: Evaluation practice for collaborative growth : a guide to program evaluation with
stakeholders and communities / by Lori L. Bakken.
Description: New York, NY : Oxford University Press, [2018] |
Includes bibliographical references and index.
Identifiers: LCCN 2017057063 (print) | LCCN 2017059395 (ebook) |
ISBN 978-0-19-088538-0 (updf) | ISBN 978-0-19-088539-7 (epub) |
ISBN 978-0-19-088537-3 (pbk. : alk. paper)
Subjects: LCSH: Evaluation research (Social action programs)
Classification: LCC H62 (ebook) | LCC H62.B2865 2018 (print) | DDC 658.4/013—dc23
LC record available at https://lccn.loc.gov/2017057063

9 8 7 6 5 4 3 2 1

Printed by Webcom, Inc., Canada

CONTENTS

PART THREE: Conduct

PREFACE

Practitioners across professions are continually faced with funders' growing requirements for information that demonstrates a program's worthiness of financial support and value to those it serves. Low programming budgets often prohibit small organizations, especially nonprofits, from hiring professional evaluators to address these requirements, so practicing professionals must have some level of understanding and ability to design and conduct a program evaluation.

This book provides a resource for readers who want to build their capacity for program evaluation and be guided through its seemingly daunting and elusive process. Therefore, this book is for those who develop or coordinate programs and work with people, partners, and communities in disciplines such as public health, social work, education, environmental sciences, and community development. It provides a fundamental understanding of program evaluation concepts, strategies, and practices while maintaining a focus on those that have been most useful to me and my collaborators. It, therefore, fills a unique gap among other books on program evaluation through its focus on basic concepts, simple writing style, familiar examples, and practical tools.

Throughout the book, I encourage readers to collaborate and partner with a program's key stakeholders during the evaluation process so that the final product is both useful to and used by them. Collaborations and partnerships in evaluation can trigger disagreements and controversy among stakeholders with competing interests. So, this book prepares readers for some of the ethical and political challenges that may be encountered when conducting a program evaluation and provides strategies for how to handle them in today's complex sociopolitical environment. At times, the book's contents may seem a bit advanced for those who are not specialists in evaluation. Some advanced concepts are intentionally incorporated to build a reader's evaluation capacity and avoid misapplied concepts, oversimplified approaches, or easy strategies that reduce the accuracy of information and potential power of evaluation.

Although this book is designed and written as a resource for practitioners, it can be used to support courses, workshops, and other capacity-building efforts in which practitioners (e.g., nonprofit directors or program coordinators) and students learn to develop, conduct, and lead a collaborative program evaluation. The book's contents are applicable in disciplines such as community psychology, community leadership, education, public health, social policy, citizen science, environmental sociology, and agroecology. Prior knowledge of evaluation is not assumed; however, readers who have knowledge or skills related to research, program planning, or data analysis may find some of the book's contents easier to grasp than novice readers.

BOOK'S CONTENT AND ORGANIZATION

The book is organized into four major sections. Chapters One through Four provide readers with the foundational knowledge and skills necessary to plan and lead or facilitate a collaborative program evaluation. Chapters Five through Nine represent the "doing" steps of an evaluation; in other words, the components of an evaluation that prepare readers to answer an evaluation's questions and achieve its purpose. Chapter Ten describes various ways of reporting and disseminating the evaluation's findings. The final chapter of the book describes emergent trends in the evaluation field and what new knowledge and tasks are suggested by them. Although this book is structured in parts that reflect the evaluation process, each chapter was written to stand on its own for those readers who want to skip to chapters that are of most interest to them. Readers will find worksheets, organizational tools, references and illustrations throughout the book that will facilitate their evaluation efforts.

Evaluation competency is best acquired through education and experience. I welcome readers to build and enrich their competence, confidence, and capacity to do a collaborative program evaluation so that they are better prepared to meet requirements for information, make important decisions about a program, and learn about ways to improve a program using an evaluation's findings.

MY EXPERIENCE

This book reflects my nearly 30 years of experience as an internal and external evaluator. I have evaluated educational and, to a lesser extent, service programs both locally and nationally. Most recently, my experiences have provided me with opportunities to work more closely with nonprofit organizations and community residents. In doing so, I have worked alongside Cooperative Extension educators, community developers, coalition coordinators, nonprofit directors, and social workers who have been inspirational in their efforts to evaluate the programs they develop and provide. These experiences and relationships have been some of the most rewarding of my career and they have motivated the capacity-building emphasis of this book.

My practice philosophy advocates collaboration and stakeholders' involvement in all phases of evaluation planning, implementation, reporting, and dissemination; it continually emphasizes practices in which one plans an evaluation during a program's planning process. My work draws from a range of evaluation approaches, including objectives-based, program-oriented, participatory, decision-oriented, expertise-oriented, and systems evaluation. I have performed both retrospective and prospective program evaluations using qualitative, quantitative, and mixed-methods approaches. As an academic, I encourage scholarship and evidence-based practice; therefore, I often have integrated program evaluation with educational research in ways that are fruitful and informative to both practice and the field more broadly. It is through this book that I share these experiences and highlight the tools and strategies I have found to be most useful when conducting program evaluations.

ACKNOWLEDGMENTS

The author would like to acknowledge the individuals without whose help and encouragement this book would not have been written. I would like to thank David Follmer who encouraged me to realize a career goal and supported me throughout the process. Thank you for your kind support and patience as I struggled with the ebbs and flows of writing.

Thank you also to Cynthia Jasper, who wouldn't let me forget that this effort was important for a variety of reasons and encouraged me to stay on task. My husband, Curtis Olson, is always a believer in me and constant supporter of every task to which I set my mind. Curt, I really appreciate your unending faith in me and my abilities to get the job done. Thank you for being by my side during this journey. I also wish to thank my parents, who have been anxiously awaiting my announcement that this book is complete. I suspect they look forward to sharing their daughter's accomplishment with family and friends. Last, I wish to thank all the students, collaborators, and colleagues who inspired me to write this book and kept me engaged as a lifelong learner. Their questions, challenges and ideas were never ending and helped me to create a book that is better because of them.

ABOUT THE AUTHORS

Dr. Lori Bakken, MS, PhD, Professor, University of Wisconsin-Madison, has over 25 years of experience leading and conducting evaluation studies in the medical, public health, and education fields. The early part of her academic career focused on evaluating and improving laboratory performance in medicine and public health. In 1995, her focus shifted to designing, implementing, and evaluating educational programs to improve the quality and quantity of clinical research conducted in the United States. Over the next decade, she developed one of the nation's first and highly successful education and career development programs for clinical researchers and established a National Institutes of Health-funded research program to study the career development of clinician-scientists. In 2010, she joined the University of Wisconsin (UW) School of Human Ecology's faculty and assumed the role of an evaluation specialist for the University's Cooperative Extension Services. In this role, she began working more closely with community and nonprofit organizations, thereby expanding her rich experiences and expertise in evaluation. In 2013–2014, Dr. Bakken took a brief leave from the UW to serve as the Director for Teaching and Research in Education Outcomes Assessment for the Center for Continuing Education in the Health Professions at the Dartmouth-Hitchcock Medical Center and Dartmouth College. Following a productive year at Dartmouth, Dr. Bakken returned to the University of Wisconsin-Madison, where her studies currently focus on evaluations that utilize systems thinking and collective approaches to demonstrate organizational and community impact. She is also interested in how gatekeeping influences inclusive evaluation practice, specifically at the intersections of food security and health. Dr. Bakken is a member of the American Evaluation Association and she holds degrees in Medical Technology (BS, 1980), Medical Microbiology (MS, 1991), and Continuing and Vocational Education (PhD, 1998) from the University of Wisconsin-Madison.

Vikram Koundinya is an Evaluation Specialist in the Department of Human Ecology at the University of California (UC)-Davis and UC Cooperative Extension. Vikram's research focuses on program evaluation, needs assessment, and other extension educational processes. His teaching includes Evaluation Capacity Building of UC Cooperative Extension and UC-Davis colleagues in the form of workshops, webinars, educational materials, and one-on-one consulting. Prior to joining UC-Davis, he served as an Evaluation Specialist at the Environmental Resources Center of University of Wisconsin (UW)-Extension, where he worked with extension educators and project partners to plan, develop, and implement evaluation of agricultural, conservation, natural resources, and environmental programs. Before joining UW-Extension, Vikram worked as a postdoctoral fellow at the University of Connecticut and Iowa State University, supporting the evaluation of agricultural, extension, and economic development programs. He holds a bachelor's degree in Agriculture from A.N.G.R. Agricultural University in India, and master's and doctoral degrees in Agricultural and Extension Education from A.N.G.R. Agricultural University and Iowa State University, respectively.

Evaluation Practice for Collaborative Growth

PART ONE

Prepare

Program evaluation is as much a process as a way to make decisions about a program's need, value, worth, or fidelity. Therefore, an adequate background and preparation for conducting an evaluation of a program is essential. The time and energy you invest in preparing for a program's evaluation will go a long way toward its success and utility to stakeholders. Chapters One through Four equip you with the mindset, knowledge, and skills you will need to adequately prepare for a program evaluation. These preparations include thinking like an evaluator; understanding your role in an evaluation; conducting the evaluation using high standards of professional, inclusive, and ethical practice; and communicating and negotiating with stakeholders to determine the evaluation's purpose, use, and questions. This part of the process provides you with the clues and information you need to select an evaluation approach. There are multiple approaches to evaluation, and it is important that you understand their philosophical underpinnings and theoretical foundations in order to select one or more of them to guide the evaluation appropriately. You also will learn that some programs are not necessarily ready to be evaluated, so you will acquire the background needed to determine whether to proceed with a program evaluation. You also will be given guidance on preparing an evaluation proposal so that the agreement among you and the evaluation's stakeholders is very clear. Collectively, these four chapters will prepare you for the next phase of the process, which is to determine the details of the evaluation's design.

CHAPTER 1

Thinking Like an Evaluator

In today's world of accountability, it is becoming increasing important for social science practitioners to evaluate the programs and interventions they develop and implement. Moreover, government agencies and foundations that typically fund these programs are increasingly requesting that social science professionals demonstrate their programs' impacts on and values to communities through evidence-based practices. An evaluation skillset, therefore, is essential for practitioners in service-related fields, such as education, nonprofit management, social work, or public health (Davis, 2006).

Although external evaluators often are called upon to perform this service, social science practitioners must develop requisite knowledge and skills to engage in evaluation practice. By doing so, the internal capacity of their organizations and respective fields for evaluation is enhanced (Stevenson, Florin, Mills, & Andrade, 2002). Active participation in evaluation activities increases a sense of ownership, which promotes greater use of evaluation results in the decision-making and program implementation processes; thereby, facilitating successful outcomes (Hoole & Patterson, 2008; Mercier, 1997). Consequently, practitioners who incorporate evaluative thinking into daily professional practice experience and acknowledge the benefits of evaluation (Taut, 2007). By building the capacity of practitioners to conduct evaluations, sustainable practices of informed decision-making and action planning are created, which, in turn, foster high-quality, effective public services (Preskill & Boyle, 2008).

With that background, let us take a moment to engage your evaluative thinking skills. Suppose you and a group of friends were given two types of freshly baked chocolate chip cookies and asked to pick the one you liked most. What criteria would you use to select your favorite cookie? Do you prefer crispy cookies or soft ones? Do you like them loaded with chocolate chips? Do you prefer a nice, rich buttery flavor over a less rich cookie? Do you prefer chocolate chunks over small chocolate chips? How might you nego-tiate differences of opinion among your friends? How would you assess each cookie so your personal biases don't interfere with your judgment about the best cookie? What evidence would you collect and how would you collect it to determine which cookie is the best? As we go about our daily lives, we are con-stantly using evaluative thinking to assess various things and phenomenon that we encounter in our daily world. Cookies are just one example. We use these skills when we purchase groceries, buy a new car, determine whether we need or want to learn a new skill, select a life partner, and so on. We apply these same thinking patterns when we evaluate programs. It's just that programs and interventions in the social sciences are a more complex, because they involve people and communities.

This book will expand your evaluative thinking skills and guide you through a four step evaluation process. It is designed to provide you with a fundamental understanding of evaluation approaches, methods, tools, and practices so that you will become more proficient at evaluating your own programs and interventions. This chapter begins by introducing you to a few basic evaluation concepts using an example from everyday life. I will then use these same concepts to shift your thinking about program evaluation from an isolated activity to an activity that is intricately intertwined with program planning.

PURCHASING A CAR: AN EXAMPLE OF EVALUATION IN EVERYDAY LIFE

When was the last time you purchased a car? What did you do before you de-cided which car to buy? What type of information did you use to decide among several makes and models of cars? Why did you purchase the type of vehicle you chose? As you think about the answers to these questions, I envision a process not unlike my own. It goes something like this.

I decide that I like the nine-year-old mini sport utility vehicle (SUV) that I currently own, but it is time that I purchase a new one. As models change over time, I also decide that I want to explore similar vehicles made by other manufacturers. I begin my thoughts with a few ideas about the car's features. I like the fact that SUV's sit higher than regular cars and have more cargo space. I also like the way they can accommodate my recreational gear (e.g., skis, bikes, kayaks). My current SUV has a standard transmission of which I am growing weary, so I decide I also would like an automatic transmission. My current SUV is dark green, which shows dirt, so I would like to get a lighter-colored car, preferably beige. I also am getting older, and I like the standard features that come with many midsized cars—air conditioning, power door locks, CD/MP3 player, etc.—so I keep these features on my wish list.

At this point, I have given some thought to the type and features of the vehicle I am looking for, so I go online to compare models that have these features. While online, I also look at prices, maintenance costs, and features that are standard on each make and model. I also like my cars to have a "small" feel because I am a petite woman, so I look at the overall dimensions of each vehicle. "Perks," such as built-in cargo racks, also are factored into my comparison because these features can be expensive and make a difference in the overall purchase price.

After comparing models and narrowing my selection to two vehicles, I decide to test drive each of them. During my test drive, I transcend steep hills, navigate tight corners, and accelerate quickly to interstate speeds. I notice that one of the models feels a bit underpowered, but it has that smaller feel for which I am looking. It is also a bit less expensive than the more powerful model, so I consult a few of my friends and acquaintances who own that model to get their opinions on the model's performance. After pondering the information, I decide to begin my negotiations with a salesperson. Let's pause now and think about the process thus far and what I have done.

I determined the *criteria* for my vehicle purchase when I decided that I wanted a beige SUV with an automatic transmission and cargo capacity to accommodate my recreational activities. Each of these features (i.e., beige color, automatic transmission, and cargo capacity) is a criterion that ultimately would help me to compare models and make a decision, or *judgment,* about the car. When I did the online comparison, I collected *evidence* to facilitate my decision and acquired information about each vehicle's cost, maintenance, and features. I collected additional evidence about the vehicle engine power when I did the test drive and consulted the opinions of friends and acquaintances. In summary, I collected *evidence* and compared it to my *criteria* to make a *judgment* about the vehicle I intended to purchase.

Evidence, criteria, and judgment are the basic elements of every evaluation, and you use these concepts every day as you go about your lives. You are evaluators when you purchase fruits and vegetables in the grocery store, select a physician to oversee your health care, meet a new neighbor, or taste a friend's chocolate chip cookies just out of the oven. If you do it every day, why does it seem so foreign and difficult when, in your professional roles, you are asked to evaluate the programs you or others develop? The answer to this question is multifaceted. First, a social science practitioner's language, knowledge, and skills for evaluation practice typically have not been developed. Second, as an interdisciplinary field, the evaluation field has grown tremendously in recent years and in doing so, it has adapted highly rigorous and sophisticated approaches, methods, and tools. Although this book will not cover the evaluation field in any depth (other textbooks do that very well), it will provide you with an overview of program evaluation, so you can incorporate some evaluation practices in your programming efforts and build your personal capacity to work with professional evaluators.

MAJOR COMPONENTS OF AN EVALUATION PROCESS

Over the years, the evaluation field has expanded and become increasingly sophisticated as the questions and problems being addressed by programs and interventions have become more challenging and expansive in scope. The approaches, methods, and tools that evaluators use also have expanded as the field shifted from objective-based approaches to those of complex systems. This book takes you through a four-part process of *preparing* for, *designing, conducting,* and *reporting* an evaluation (Figure 1.1).

Within this process are multiple tasks and activities that will require your attention. The preparation and design for an evaluation are the most time-consuming parts of the process, but they are critical to an evaluation's success. In order to set the stage for subsequent chapters and provide you with an overview of program evaluation, in the remainder of this chapter, I briefly describe the basic activities and tasks that are part of an evaluation.

Prepare

The first step in preparing for any evaluation is to be certain you have the requisite background to plan and conduct the evaluation. This background includes knowledge of the professional and ethical standards that guide

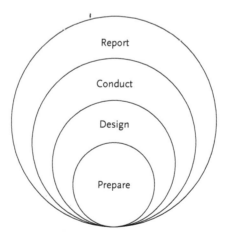

Figure 1.1. Four-step Evaluation Process.

evaluation practice, competencies needed to conduct an evaluation, and skills to build and maintain partnerships and collaborations throughout the evaluation process. It is also important to know about the various perspectives and approaches that guide an evaluation's design. Evaluation approaches are driven by the philosophies or world views that both you and your stakeholders bring to the process. Will your approach be based on program goals and learning objectives? Will your approach be theory driven? Will it advocate participation of all relevant stakeholders? Does the approach need to be designed in a way that will aid decision-making? The answers to these questions will become apparent as you engage with key stakeholders to gain an understanding of the evaluation's context, purpose, and questions.

This part of the preparation process requires conversations with several individuals or groups of people who have a stake in the program or its evaluation (i.e., stakeholders). An examination of a program's context also necessitates visits to locations and communities in which the program is provided. Therefore, the preparation needed to design and conduct an evaluation is a time-intensive process that requires strong listening skills, excellent communication, abilities to successfully negotiate, keen observation, and patience. Often, the language and processes familiar to evaluators are unfamiliar and may feel intimidating to a program's stakeholders; therefore, it is best to avoid jargon and explain concepts in ways that facilitate understanding. For example, evaluation concepts such as, desired or expected "outcomes", are more easily sought with questions such as, "What change do you expect or is likely to happen as a result of your program?" It often takes a series of several conversations with key stakeholders to acquire the information necessary to evaluate a program. A worksheet I sometimes use to guide these conversations is presented in Box 1.1.

Once acquired, this information should be conveyed back to stakeholders in order to reach a mutual understanding about how a program is to be evaluated. Other considerations that are important in the preparation process are a clear understanding of everyone's role in the evaluation, cultural norms and practices, protection of individuals and groups who will participate in the evaluation study, and adherence to evaluation principles and standards (American Evaluation Association, 2004; Yarbrough, Shulha, Hopson, & Caruthers, 2011). It is often helpful to conduct an evaluability assessment (Wholey, 2004) to be certain that critical elements of the preparation process are discussed.

Your early conversations with stakeholders should attempt to ascertain the evaluation's purpose, use, goals, and guiding questions. The *purpose* can be determined with the questions, "Why would you like to do this evaluation?" By asking the question, "How will you *use* the findings from the evaluation?" you can establish stakeholders' intended *use* for the evaluation's results. Evaluation questions can be determined with the question, "What would you

Box 1.1. PROGRAM LOGIC QUESTION GUIDE

EVALUATION-RELATED QUESTIONS

1. What program are you evaluating?
2. Why are you evaluating this program?
3. How will you use findings from this evaluation?
4. What goals are you trying to achieve by evaluating this program?
5. Who cares about the evaluation's findings?

PROGRAM-RELATED QUESTIONS

1. In what ways do you hope participants will change as a result of this program? Immediately (i.e., knowledge, attitudes, and skills)? In one to three years (i.e., application of knowledge and skills or behavioral changes)?
2. In what ways (expected or unexpected) do you hope programming efforts will change your organization? Your community? The folks you serve?
3. How will your program achieve the immediate changes stated in Question #1?
4. What evidence will you have to demonstrate that the program was implemented as planned?
5. What resources (community, human, organizational, financial, etc.) are available for programming efforts that lead to the desired changes (refers to Questions #1 and #2)?
6. What are some of the stakeholder assumptions that may influence the program's design, implementation, or goals? Can these assumptions be validated through scholarship or other "credible" sources?
7. Should planners and evaluators consider other potential changes to program participants, the organization, or community that may be suggested by scholarship, professional groups, or others and have not been considered in answers to Questions #1–5?

like to learn from this evaluation?" or "What questions do you have about your program?"

Often, program directors have specific goals that they would like to achieve through an evaluation, such as building staff capacity or becoming more competitive for grants, so it is helpful to know these as well. They also may need an evaluation to inform new programming efforts. Needs assessments (Queeney, 1995; Wambeam, 2015) coupled with environmental scans (Simerly & Associates, 1987) are useful for addressing this purpose.

In practice, stakeholders often have difficulty articulating or conveying the questions they would like answered by an evaluation. It is through your preparatory conversations with them that you acquire information that will allow you to pose some initial evaluation questions that are refined in the design process. When you have a thorough understanding of the program's and evaluation's context and purpose, as well as stakeholders and their questions, you can select an evaluation approach or combination of approaches that will guide the evaluation's design and answer the evaluation questions.

Design

Your chosen approach for the evaluation will guide you toward specific details of the evaluation design. These design elements are determined through a process that engages as many stakeholders as possible to refine and prioritize the initial evaluation questions that guide the evaluation's design. I would like to pause for a moment to emphasize my point that *an evaluation's purpose, use, and questions determine an evaluation's design.* Once the questions are clearly determined, you can articulate a general study design. Questions that begin with "How . . . ?" "Why . . . ?" or "In what ways . . . ?" are typically process-related and signal qualitative designs. Questions that imply comparisons or program effectiveness, such as "Is my program successful?" or "Does my intervention reduce parental stress levels?" typically call for quantitative designs. Questions related to the fidelity of the program often suggest a qualitative approach. Common to our age of accountability are questions such as, "What are the long-term outcomes or impact of the program?" These questions often require more complex quantitative or mixed methods designs. This is not an exhaustive list of evaluation questions you will encounter in your experiences as an evaluator. Evaluation questions vary by stakeholders and context. Some basic designs often can be applied to answer them, but the context of the program will undoubtedly make each design unique and possibly more complex. Other design elements include instruments used to collect data, determining from whom or what source data will be collected, plans for tracking and storing electronic data, and finally, analytical plans that describe data analysis in detail. The details of these study designs and data collection tools and strategies are covered in Part II.

Conduct

When you have a clear plan for the study design, data collection, and analysis you can begin the evaluation. It is important that you have a well-thought-through plan before you conduct your evaluation study; otherwise, your evaluation may be fraught with unnecessary challenges and problems. Good

planning is essential to avoid the pitfalls brought on by factors such as unnecessary or insufficient data collection, unclear expectations, lack of sufficient
resources, and other issues that may rob you of valuable time and support.
For example, you may have difficulty recruiting participants for an evaluation
study or obtaining their consent, so it is important to mentally walk through
your evaluation plan in order to be prepared for any setbacks that may be
encountered along the way. Not all pitfalls can be anticipated, so an evaluator
must remain open and flexible to changing the initial plan if necessary. Your or
your team's job is to ensure that all information collected is complete and accurate (Yarbrough et al., 2011). Evaluation participants should be clear about
the purpose of the study and how you will use their information. They also
should be informed that their participation is voluntary, and that they can
withdraw from the evaluation at any time. When appropriate, participants
should provide written or oral consent to participate in a study (see Chapter 2
for more information). Once information is collected from study participants,
you can analyze data according to plan. Because your analyses often reveal
unexpected findings, it may be necessary to perform post-hoc analysis or interview additional participants.

Report

Reporting the evaluation's findings marks the final step in an evaluation
process. This is a great time to get stakeholders more heavily involved. They
are essential for interpreting data and presenting it in a form that will be
readily understood and used. The reporting step is also a time when conflicts
may arise between you and the program's stakeholders who may have been
surprised by an unanticipated negative finding and wish to withhold the
information from written or oral reports. When this happens, it is important that you remind stakeholders about the standards for evaluation and
the importance of integrity. It is also helpful to emphasize the evaluation
as a way to learn about a program and improve its performance and quality.
Finally, when a written report is prepared, be sure to include an executive
summary that highlights the evaluation questions and the answers gleaned
from the evaluation. Chapter 10 will provide you with more details on how
to organize and present an evaluation's findings to various stakeholder
groups.

The final chapter of this book brings the evaluation process full circle
by preparing you for some of the challenges you may be faced with as you
are asked to evaluate programs in the context of complex social or political
environments. Chapter 11 covers emergent trends in evaluation that include
systems thinking and approaches to evaluation (e.g., developmental evaluation), contribution models, and social justice and inclusion.

PROGRAM PLANNING AND EVALUATION

Evaluation provokes anxiety among programmers and other stakeholders for a variety of reasons. These reasons include lack of knowledge, skills, and language regarding evaluation; one's inability to transfer that knowledge when obtained; lack of confidence to apply the skills needed to do an evaluation; an apparent lack of time to get the job done; inappropriate planning; fear of being held accountable or losing a program; and the overwhelmingly complex nature of some programs. These are very good reasons to get anxious about evaluation, but many of them can be avoided with advance planning, appropriate knowledge and skills, support from and coaching by an experienced evaluator, and strong interpersonal skills (King & Stevahn, 2013).

This section stresses the importance of planning an evaluation as part of a program planning process. Why is it important to plan an evaluation as part of a program planning process instead of waiting until the program has been implemented? Let's suppose I wanted to have a barbeque for 30 to 40 friends and family members. I would need to purchase sufficient groceries to feed them or hire a caterer. I also would need a backyard space and seating to accommodate them. Additionally, I would want to purchase beverages—summers are hot—and be sure that I had utensils, plates, cups, and condiments. If I decided to make the food myself, I also would have to allow adequate time to prepare and store the food in advance. What if it rains? I should probably have a backup plan that includes shelter. Evaluation planning is very similar in that you need to be sure you have the resources and skills to conduct an evaluation, given its scope. You also will need a backup plan or flexibility when things don't go as expected, such as insufficient or skewed participation, missing survey responses, or delayed meetings with stakeholders. Your goal is to conduct an evaluation in a timely manner so that you can deliver its findings in an appropriate time frame. You also want to be sure that the evaluation findings actually deliver answers to the evaluation questions. Without some careful planning, it is easy to get off target or expand the evaluation's scope in a way that originally was not intended.

Several program planning models include evaluation as part of the overall planning process (Caffarella, 2002; Donaldson & Kozoll, 1999; Sork, 2000). As a point of reference, I would like to propose one particular model for helping you to think about evaluation on the "front end" of program design, development, and implementation. Rosemary Caffarella in her book titled, *Planning Programs for Adult Learners* (Caffarella, 2002), discusses the *Interactive Model of Program Planning* as one that reflects the typical nonlinear process by which most programs are planned. Central to this model are 12 components of a program planning process that can begin with any one of these components and often changes in contour, content, and size (p. 21). Moreover, planners often multitask and perform many of the model's components simultaneously. One of these components is "formulating evaluation plans." The important point to my emphasis on program planning as an interactive model of multiple components, including evaluation, is that evaluation planning is part of a program *planning* process. An evaluation should not be planned the day before the program is implemented or when all the participants have gone home. I cannot emphasize this point enough, so I will say it again. *Evaluation planning should be done as part of a program planning process.* Like all rules, this rule has some exceptions, which I will address in the last chapter of this book when I talk about developmental evaluation and systems approaches.

SUMMARY

This chapter has engaged your evaluative thinking, introduced you to some fundamental evaluation concepts, and provided you with an overview of the process for conducting an evaluation. The remaining chapters of this book will assume that you are planning your evaluation as part of a program planning process and emphasize only components of an evaluation plan that are imbedded in that program plan. To begin this journey, Chapter 2 will describe the requisite knowledge and skills for a successful program evaluation.

REFERENCES

American Evaluation Association. (2004). *Guiding principles for evaluators.* Retrieved from http://www.eval.org/p/cm/ld/fid=51

Caffarella, R. S. (2002). *Planning programs for adult learners: A practical guide for educators, trainers, and staff directors* (2nd ed.). San Francisco, CA: Jossey-Bass Publishers.

Davis, M. (2006). Teaching practical public health evaluation methods. *American Journal of Evaluation, 27*(2), 247–256.

Donaldson, J. F., & Kozoll, C. E. (1999). *Collaborative program planning: Principles, practices, and strategies.* Malabar, FL: Krieger Publishing Company.

Hoole, E., & Patterson, T. (2008). Voices from the field: Evaluation as part of a learning culture. In J. Carman & K. Fredericks (Eds.), *Nonprofits and evaluations: New directions for evaluation, 119,* 93–113.

King, J. A., & Stevahn, L. (2013). *Interactive evaluation practice: Mastering the interpersonal dynamics of program evaluation.* Thousand Oaks, CA: Sage Publications, Inc.

Mercier, C. (1997). Participants in stakeholder-based evaluation: A case study. *Evaluation and Program Planning, 20,* 467–475.

Preskill, H., & Boyle, S. (2008). A conceptual model of evaluation capacity building: A multidisciplinary perspective. *American Journal of Evaluation, 29*(4), 443–459.

Queeney, D. S. (1995). *Assessing needs in continuing education.* San Francisco, CA: Jossey-Bass Publishers.

Simerly, R. G., & Associates. (1987). *Strategic planning and leadership in continuing education.* San Francisco, CA: Jossey-Bass Publishers.

Sork, T. J. (2000). Planning educational programs. In E. R. Hayes & A. L. Wilson (Eds.), *Handbook of adult and continuing education* (pp. 171–190). San Francisco, CA: Jossey-Bass Publishers.

Stevenson, J. F., Florin, P., Mill, D. S., & Andrade, M. (2002). Building evaluation capacity in human service organisations: A case study. *Evaluation and Program Planning, 25,* 233–243.

Taut, S. (2007). Defining evaluation capacity building: Utility considerations [Letter to the editor]. *American Journal of Evaluation, 28*(1), 120.

Wambeam, R. A. (2015). *The community needs assessment workbook.* Chicago, IL: Lyceum Books, Inc.

Wholey, J. S. (2004). Evaluability assessment. In J. S. Wholey, H. P. Hatry, & K. E. Newcomer (Eds.), *Handbook of practical program evaluation* (2nd ed., pp. 33–62). San Francisco, CA: Jossey-Bass Publishers.

Yarbrough, D. B., Shulha, L. M., Hopson, R. K., & Caruthers, F. A. (2011). *The program evaluation standards: A guide for evaluators and evaluation users* (3rd ed.). Thousand Oaks, CA: Sage Publications, Inc.

Acquiring Requisite Knowledge and Skills

Chapter 2 describes a fundamental skill set needed to practice evaluation ethically and responsibly. I begin by describing the various roles of an evaluator in planning, implementing, and reporting an evaluation. These roles have implications for the ways you will conduct an evaluation and use the various tools and skills needed to function in a professional manner. Evaluation standards and principles are described that will guide your professional work and practice, regardless of your role in an evaluation. These standards also help to guide you through difficult challenges when negotiating with stakeholders who may not agree with your approaches or the findings of an evaluation. As a vital part of those standards, evaluators are expected to uphold ethical practices and protect those involved in the evaluation or program being evaluated. Competencies for ethical practice are a single part of a set of competencies that are necessary to practice effectively and efficiently. Effective communication and negotiation skills are another essential component of an evaluator's competencies and are used often in the course of an evaluation. These skills are most effective when used with integrity, honesty, and from a perspective of reciprocal learning that helps to model and build capacity among the organizations we work with and serve.

ROLES OF EVALUATORS

Evaluators can occupy a variety of roles in planning, conducting, and reporting an evaluation. They often are brought into an organization or community setting as an *external* and objective "eye" for a program. For example, a funder who requests an external evaluator to oversee the collective evaluation activities of several grantees. An organization also might employ an external evaluator to evaluate an existing program or help to design an evaluation for a program in the planning stage. *Metaevaluators* are external evaluators who evaluate the evaluation activities of a program or set of programs. Typically, this role is used for accreditation or reaccreditation of existing programs. External evaluators also may help to build evaluation capacity within an organization or oversee a set of evaluation activities conducted by the organization's staff. Evaluators can serve as *coaches* for staff who have acquired some evaluation skills and need support as they further develop their skills. Program staff can serve as evaluators of their own programs, too. In this role, staff are *internal* evaluators. Many of you likely consider yourselves to be in this role. Sometimes, staff are internal to an organization and asked to evaluate programs that are not of their own development. They, too, are referred to as internal evaluators. In participatory evaluation practice, also known as collaborative inquiry (Cousins & Whitmore, 1998), evaluators engage key stakeholders to the extent possible and throughout the evaluation planning, implementation, and reporting processes. When doing so, an evaluator's role is typically *facilitative* in nature.

As facilitators, evaluators *bring a structure for engaging clients and stakeholders*, grounded in their evaluation methodology (e.g., planning meetings or conducting interviews, focus groups, and surveys); *contribute to the potential effectiveness of teams* by offering them accurate and reliable data that are easy to understand and use in making decisions and improving programs and organizational performance; and *remain independent*, aiming to include different perspectives in the evaluation without taking sides (Catsambas, 2016, p. 20). According to Catsambas (2016), "good facilitation of the evaluation process increases client engagement and buy-in, fosters a safe place for honesty, and creates a neutral space for airing different views with an impartial and independent evaluator" (p. 20). "Good facilitation" is not easy, however, especially when group tensions and disagreements are high, and we are trying to facilitate transformative change (Mertens, 2009). These situations require you to be self-reflective, self-knowing, effectively communicative, and culturally competent. Self-understanding and awareness, in addition to facilitation skills, allow you to confront differing viewpoints, un-silence marginalized voices, and remain neutral as you manage difficult interpersonal and group dynamics in evaluation. You, therefore, must be a confident individual who lives up to professional standards of practice and exercises effective interpersonal skills.

EVALUATION STANDARDS

Over the years, practitioners and researchers in the evaluation field have developed important standards for professional and ethical evaluation practice. *The Program Evaluation Standards* (Yarbrough, Shulha, Hopson, & Caruthers, 2011), now in its third edition, were created by the Joint Committee on Standards for Educational Evaluation and are applied broadly across the field. These standards are grouped into five major categories that provide a foundation for professional evaluation practice; namely, utility, feasibility, propriety, accuracy, and accountability.

The *utility* standards stress the importance of an evaluator's credibility and skills to involve stakeholders throughout the evaluation process as they clarify and negotiate the purpose(s) of an evaluation, understand and make explicit stakeholder values, provide useful and relevant information, provide timely and accurately communicated reports, and maintain a neutral posturing during the conduct of an evaluation. Above all, this set of standards emphasize the importance of the evaluation's utility in providing information that can benefit its stakeholders. The *feasibility* standards stress the importance of assuring that sufficient resources are available to conduct an evaluation in a timely manner, managing the evaluation in ways that will maintain its progress and provide appropriate feedback to stakeholders, and carefully considering the political and cultural context of the evaluation. The *propriety* standards speak to the importance of inclusive participation, formal agreements, respect for human rights, clarity and fairness in addressing the stakeholders' needs and purpose for the evaluation, and transparency throughout the evaluation's conduct. This set of standards also addresses conflicts of interest and the importance of conducting an evaluation in a fiscally responsible manner. The *accuracy* standards emphasize the need and importance for valid and reliable information; sound design and analysis; precise data collection and tracking; clear and explicit reasoning, communication, and reporting; and interpretation of findings relative to the context of the evaluation. Finally, the *accountability* standards are intended to assure the overall quality of an evaluation through precise and detailed documentation and internal and external evaluation of an evaluator's work (i.e., metaevaluation). This last standard often is addressed through committees formed by an evaluator and stakeholders to monitor the evaluation and assure that these standards are continually maintained. It is also not uncommon for external evaluators to be requested by funders as a part of grant awards.

The evaluation field also is guided by the *American Evaluation Association's Guiding Principles for Evaluators* (American Evaluation Association, 2004), which support ethical evaluation practice. The first principle, *systematic inquiry*, highlights the importance of conducting systematic, data-based inquiries in order to ensure the accuracy and credibility of information obtained from sources. This principle also highlights the importance of clearly and correctly communicating information in ways that are understandable to the evaluation's stakeholders. The second principle, *competence*, refers to an evaluator's competence to perform an evaluation in ways that will address the information needs of its stakeholders. Competent evaluators possess the knowledge, skills, and abilities to conduct an evaluation and refrain from conducting them (or recruit additional experts) when their professional limits are exceeded. Competent evaluators are also sensitive to and respect differences reflected by cultural backgrounds, racial and ethnic heritage, sexual orientation, gender, and religious and other cultural beliefs and values. Culturally responsive "evaluators should also display *honesty and integrity*, [the third principle], in their own behavior, and attempt to ensure the honesty and integrity of the entire evaluation process." (American Evaluation Association, 2011). The fourth principle, *respect for people*, emphasizes an evaluator's "respect [for] the security, dignity and self-worth of respondents, program participants, clients, and other evaluation stakeholders." This means that during the conduct and reporting of an evaluation, an evaluator avoids physical or emotional harm to a person or the organizations and groups which they represent. Consistent with this principle is the final principle, *responsibilities for general and public welfare*, for which "evaluators articulate and take into account the diversity of general and public interests and values that may be related to the evaluation." As you may have observed, the American Evaluation Association's five Guiding Principles are very consistent with the *Program Evaluation Standards* developed by the Joint Commission.

If you work globally, you also should be aware of evaluation standards applied in other countries. Similar to the *Program Evaluation Standards* (Yarbrough, Shulha, Hopson, & Caruthers, 2011), the *African Evaluation Guidelines—Standards and Norms* (African Evaluation Association, 2006) more strongly emphasize community participation and ownership. The Canadians also have adopted a set of standards and evaluator competencies, which are described in *Competencies for Canadian Evaluation Practice* (Canadian Evaluation Society, 2010).

Why are these standards important to you? From an outsider's perspective (outside the evaluation profession), these professional standards are important for many reasons. First, they help you to understand the lens that guides an evaluator's work and thinking. Second, the standards also provide a set of guidelines for hiring an evaluator who possesses the appropriate knowledge, skills, and experiences to conduct an evaluation for you. From an insider's perspective, these standards provide guidance as you increasingly acquire knowledge, skills, and experience for conducting your own evaluations or contributing to an evaluation in a substantial way. For a leader of an evaluation, the standards are useful for managing conflict and upholding standards of professional and ethical practice.

ETHICS AND HUMAN SUBJECTS PROTECTIONS

In years past, some educators and other professionals presumed that evaluations were "exempt" from federal guidelines for ethical practice and the protection of human subjects that were commonly known among researchers. As a result, some institutions, researchers, and program evaluators experienced adverse consequences for not adhering to these practice standards (DuBois, 2002; Tomkowiak & Gunderson, 2004). Evaluators always should uphold standards for ethical practice and human subject protections and, when possible, gain an institutional review board's (IRB) approval or exemption for any evaluation study that is planned (James Bell Associates, 2008; Morris, 2008; Rice, 2008). Evaluators and researchers are responsible for protecting humans involved, or potentially involved, in research, including evaluation studies. The role of an IRB in the United States is to oversee research and implement the federal regulations for the protection of research subjects (i.e., 45 CFR 46 or the "Common Rule"). These regulations are guided by three ethical principles: beneficence, respect for persons, and justice (National Commission for the Protection of Human Subjects of Biomedical and Behavioral Research, 1979). These principles provide guidance for assuring that the benefits of research exceed the risks associated with participation, participants consent to participate in the research and can withdraw at any time, and the burdens of research are not experienced by any specific class or group of people.

Human Subjects Protections (HSP) programs expand beyond IRBs and include additional institutional oversight committees that serve nine primary functions: (1) minimize risks to research participants, (2) determine if a study's benefit-risk ratio is reasonable, (3) make sure that subject selection is fair, (4) there is adequate monitoring of the research, (5) informed consent has been obtained from research participants, (6) participants' privacy and confidentiality are maintained, (7) a researcher's conflicts of interest are made explicit, (8) peoples' vulnerabilities as research participants are addressed, and (9) researchers have participated in and are current in HSP training (Ross, Loup, Nelson, Botkin, Kost, Smith, & Gehlert, 2010). This means that, as an evaluator, you will need to provide the appropriate documentation for an IRB and other ethical oversight committees to make these determinations. Some studies are deemed "exempt" from ongoing IRB oversight, so once your study is deemed exempt, further oversight is not necessary, unless your study plan changes in a way that may increase risks to participants, alter the purpose of the study or data collection process, or contribute to generalizable knowledge. If your evaluation study does require IRB oversight, however, you will be expected to communicate any changes in your study plan (including personnel changes and changes to any forms or documentation used in the research), to maintain meticulous and accurate study records, and to provide annual reports. You are also responsible for reporting any adverse events involving study participants and keeping records in secure locations (electronic and physical spaces).

You may be thinking, "What if my organization does not have an IRB or I want to do independent consulting?" Your first step would be to determine whether a proposed evaluation is "non-research" or involves "non-human subjects." If you do not generalize the evaluation's findings nor publish the findings from the evaluation study, your work likely qualifies as "non-research," and you do not need to have your evaluation plan reviewed by an IRB. Quality-assurance and quality-improvement projects, for example, typically do not contribute to generalizable knowledge. If the evaluation study does not involve humans, then it likely can be deemed "non-human." There are, however, exceptions to these qualifiers, so an evaluator cannot make a determination of "non-research" or "non-human." You, therefore, have three options: (1) start an IRB at your institution (requires federal approval); (2) use an external, commercial IRB (which will likely charge a fee); or (3) partner with an institution that has an IRB and is willing to serve as the IRB of record for an evaluation study (Rice, 2008).

In participatory and community-based evaluation, the potential burdens and harm to people expand beyond individual research participants. Ross, Loup, Nelson, Botkin, Kost, Smith, & Gehlert (2010) describe potential risks to well-being and agency associated with individuals, groups, and communities when research involves participation to the extent that partners and participants are engaged in the research process (Figure 2.1).

At each level, participants are subject to risks associated with the research process (e.g., physical and psychosocial risks of interactions), outcomes (e.g., influence of findings on group structure or function), and individual, group, or community agency (e.g., undermining personal autonomy or the group's moral and sociopolitical authority). Therefore, the authors have recommended

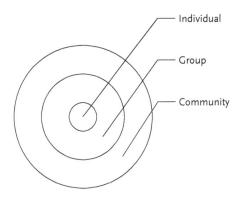

Figure 2.1. Three levels of risk in participatory evaluation.

several points to consider when reviewing this type of research or evaluation study. Among them are questions such as, "If there are plans to collaborate with community partners, have the community risks been identified and has a management plan been developed?" (p. 39); "What are the expected benefits to the individual, to the individual by association with the group or to the group as a whole?" (p. 40); and "Who will collect data, where will it be stored, and who will have access to stored data, including individual contact information?" (p. 42). These are helpful questions to use as guides when designing evaluation studies that use participatory approaches, so that all levels of human subject protections are considered in the inquiry process.

EVALUATION COMPETENCIES

As stated in evaluation standards and guiding principles, evaluators should possess the appropriate competencies to perform and manage an evaluation. What are those competencies? An original set of essential competencies for program evaluators was developed by Jean King and colleagues (King, Stevahn, Ghere, & Minnema, 2001), revised (Stevahn, King, Ghere, Minnema, 2005) and subsequently validated by Wilcox (2012). The revised set of 61 competencies includes the knowledge, skills, and dispositions that program evaluators need for effective professional practice. These competencies are organized into six categories that represent the major activities of an evaluator: (1) professional practice, (2) systematic inquiry, (3) situational analysis, (4) project management, (5) reflective practice, and (6) interpersonal competence (pp. 48–52). Three of these general categories or domains (i.e., situational analysis, systematic inquiry, and project management) have been deemed especially important for assessment of evaluation competence among Cooperative Extension academic professionals (Rodgers, Hillake, Haas, & Peters, 2012) who typically work closely with their local communities. The improvement of an organization's evaluation competency is critical to capacity building; therefore, Preskill and Boyle (2008) articulated the knowledge, skills, and attitudes needed to support capacity-building efforts. Many of these objectives for evaluation capacity building reflect the competencies described by Stevahn and colleagues (2005). Subsequently, Taylor-Ritzler and colleagues (Taylor-Ritzler, Suarez-Balcazar, Garcia-Iriarte, Henry, & Balcazar, 2013), developed a model and corresponding instrument for assessing evaluation capacity building among staff of nonprofit organizations. The Evaluation Capacity Assessment Instrument includes 14 general items (knowledge and skills) for assessing evaluation competence. Again, these items parallel those described by Stevahn and colleagues (Stevahn, King, Ghere, Minnema, 2005), but they are limited and lack the specificity of the full set of competencies described in other sources (Canadian Evaluation Society, 2010; ibstpi, 2006; Stevahn, King, Ghere, & Minnema, 2005). More recently, King and Stevahn (2015) cited the necessity for and challenges to updating evaluator competencies to include those that have evolved throughout the last decade and are relevant to: cultural competence, international settings, systems thinking and complexity, and developing technologies. What does it take to acquire this skill set?

Dillman (2012) studied the relationship between evaluation competencies and educational experiences and found that both coursework <u>and</u> field experience were necessary to support competency development. Traditionally, evaluators have acquired their education and training within other disciplines, such as education, sociology, public health, or international development. More recently, certificate and graduate programs have been developed, in addition to multiple specialized workshops, for evaluation training and education. The *American Evaluation Association*, a professional organization currently boasting over 7000 members, is a good place to start when looking for evaluation training. Other sources for evaluation training and resources include the Kellogg Foundation, United Way, The Evaluators' Institute (Claremont Graduate University; http://tei.cgu.edu/about/about-tei/), the Minnesota Evaluation Studies Institute (http://www.cehd.umn.edu/OLPD/MESI/), the Innovation Network, the National Science Foundation, among other state and national organizations. Why is it important to be a competent evaluator and how do competencies get used?

Evaluation competencies are useful in five major ways (Perrin, 2005). Most importantly, they can be used for self-assessment and monitoring and improving your own knowledge, skills, and attitudes about evaluation. Second, they are useful for assessing gaps in knowledge, skills, and attitudes and for designing or participating in education and training programs to fill those gaps. Third, they foster the development of the profession; and fourth, they provide information and support advocacy about the skills required for competent evaluations and professional practice. They also provide a useful set of standards for selecting, monitoring, and managing evaluators who are hired as consultants and coaches. From my experience, one of the most useful sets of competencies one can possess as an evaluator are skills for effective communication and negotiation. Many of the other important skills you will need for evaluation will be taught in forthcoming chapters. Unfortunately, effective communication skills are not given adequate attention in many training or education programs, and they can make or break a successful evaluation effort. In the next section, I will give special attention to the communication and negotiation competencies needed for evaluation.

COMMUNICATION AND NEGOTIATION

With the evolution of systems approaches, such as developmental evaluation and collective impact, which involve people representing multiple and diverse sectors and cultural groups that are more prominent in the field, it has become increasingly important for evaluators to be competent communicators and negotiators. So much so that in 2013, Jean King and Laurie Stevahn wrote a book titled, *Interactive Evaluation Practice*, which emphasized this topic. What are these skill sets?

To begin, clear and direct communication among all stakeholders involved in an evaluation are imperative for fostering good relationships and positive experiences in evaluation. Evaluators must be attentive and open listeners, able to convey a clear understanding and interpretation of information, be aware of cultural norms and values, be open to learning, and have a clear understanding of one's own biases when communicating with others. Furthermore, evaluators should strive to promote positive relations, shared understandings, and a trustful environment (King & Stevahn, 2013). To do this, evaluators must work with great integrity and be able to manage conflict in a timely manner. Some level of conflict will be likely in almost any evaluation but will be reduced if effective communication skills and strategies are routinely used and reinforced.

Several strategies can be used to promote and facilitate effective communications among those involved in an evaluation. It is often helpful to establish communication "ground rules" early in an evaluation partnership. The skills and strategies listed in Box 2.1 are those that I have found most helpful in my work.

Most often, these strategies will help to maintain a smooth and productive evaluation process; however, disagreements and conflicts are not uncommon, and they should be anticipated and expected. How can you manage conflict?

King and Stevahn (2013) provide an excellent chapter on *Managing Conflict Constructively in Evaluation Settings* (pp. 166–194), which I encourage you to read. In the next few paragraphs, I will highlight some of the major points from that chapter. The first thing to do is recognize that there is a conflict and manage it with intention and poise. Conflicts are recognized as "incompatible activities that block, delay or prevent the accomplishment of goals" (p. 167). If left unattended, they can lead to many hard feelings, possibly damaged reputations, and failure to make progress or complete the work. People respond to conflict in multiple ways, including attempts at forcing opinions or ideas on others, withdrawing all together, smoothing over the conflict, reaching a compromise, and working together to solve a problem (King & Stevahn, 2013). The most effective means of resolving conflict is through *mutual* problem solving in which everyone gains from the solution. King and Stevahn (2013) recommend 13 different strategies to foster positive interdependence and provide a list of skills and steps needed for successful cooperative negotiations (pp. 173–180) as summarized in Box 2.2.

Recently, I was facilitating a meeting of a new partnership, which had the goal of designing and evaluating a novel new program. During our first and daylong meeting, we decided to implement this program within a year's time. When I left the meeting that day, I felt some reservations about proceeding too quickly and I also sensed some partnering members to be a little disappointed in where we ended our conversation that day. At our next meeting, I decided I would facilitate a check-in session following an overview from our last meeting. To do so, I designed a graphic-friendly questionnaire that asked three questions: (1) What are your overall feelings about our partnership

> *Box 2.2.* SKILLS AND STEPS FOR SUCCESSFUL
> COOPERATIVE NEGOTIATIONS IN EVALUATION PRACTICE
> (KING & STEVAHN, 2013)
>
> - Express cooperative intentions
> - Mutually define the conflict
> - State wants
> - Express feelings
> - Explain underlying reasons/interests
> - Reverse perspective to communicate understanding
> - Generate multiple integrative solutions that attend to all interests
> - Reach agreement on a mutual solution
> - Process the effectiveness of the problem solving

today? (very apprehensive, cautiously optimistic, optimistic, very excited); (2) Does our plan for [action] seem realistic given what you know so far? (not sure, no, maybe, yes); and (3) What three things need to happen today to overcome any apprehensive feelings or move forward with our plans? Much to my surprise, most members of the partnership felt cautiously optimistic about moving forward. When explored further, the sense was that the group was moving a bit too fast, given a variety of circumstances. One partnering organization was in the midst of a reorganization that involved a budget cut. Another partner was looking to retirement with great uncertainty about her position's future—a position that was key to our program's success. What surprised me was how open our dialogue became and how well it provided a reality check that clarified next steps. This conversation went a long way toward moving forward with integrity and establishing open communication among partners. In essence, we collectively engaged in a process of exploring each person's experience of our collaboration by expressing our feelings, thoughts, wants, and observations in an open forum (Bushe, 2009). This exercise was effective because it acknowledged everyone's (as opposed to specific individuals') experiences in real time.

BUILDING PARTNERSHIPS AND CAPACITY
FOR EVALUATION

Partnerships and capacity building efforts are necessary to keep up with the growing demands for skilled evaluators in this age of accountability. By building evaluation capacity, organizations are better equipped to improve their programming efforts. For evaluation capacity building (ECB) efforts to be successful, however, organizations and key stakeholders must be empowered to use evaluation for learning and program or process improvement.

Evaluation capacity building efforts can be challenging, however. Labin and colleagues (2012) reported a research synthesis of the evaluation capacity building literature and found that formal training and hands-on experiences are necessary to change knowledge and behaviors in evaluation. Furthermore, the majority of capacity building efforts involve collaborating partners and participatory evaluation approaches, which are necessary to be adaptive and attend to cultural needs. Many organizations are not accustomed to being involved in evaluation processes, such as data collection, that are an integral part of participatory approaches to evaluation. So, evaluators are challenged by the difficulties of engaging partners throughout the evaluation process (Preskill, 2014). Resources, especially those related to technical assistance, are necessary to support ongoing data collection and analysis that are critical for process monitoring and ongoing feedback. It is imperative that these efforts be supported by an organization that has supportive leadership and a culture of learning and improvement. This means that an organization supports a culture in which it learns from its failures as well as its successes. It also means that blame is shared and not pointed and that efforts are in place to foster a culture of openness, integrity, and trust. This type of culture is not easy to build or maintain, but it can be done with effective leadership and a consistent emphasis on values and teamwork. As Hoole and Patterson (2008) point out,

> The commitment of organizational leadership is critical in transforming the role of evaluation from one of basic reporting and accountability to a true process of continuous organizational learning. This transformation requires leadership commitment to development of an evaluative learning culture and development of an infrastructure to support it. (p. 111)

However, the critical role of a supportive and knowledgeable leader in capacity building efforts remains one of the least understood and studied (Preskill, 2014).

Preskill (2014) highlights two additional challenges for those who desire to build evaluation capacity in organizations or communities. We need to acquire a better understanding of how knowledge, skills, and attitudes are transferred to sustained evaluation practice. This can be accomplished with expanded efforts to evaluate the effects and impacts of our capacity building work (Preskill, 2014). An example for some ways to evaluate ECB efforts can be found in Bakken, Núñez and Couture, 2014, as well as in King and Stevahn, 2013. From my experiences as an evaluator, there is nothing more enjoyable than partnering with a learning organization to do an evaluation.

These organizations typically are primed for ongoing assessment and evaluation because their learning is typically data driven. This tradition typically is grounded in disciplines other than program evaluation, such as quality improvement, human resources, or human factors engineering, so it is imperative that you align your program evaluation efforts with these ongoing activities. When entering a community consisting of multiple organizations, however, your role in building evaluation capacity can be more challenging because many organizations do not view themselves as continuing learning organizations. In these circumstances, knowledge of and skills for inclusive practice that builds and maintains effective partnerships for collaborative inquiry are useful and necessary.

EFFECTIVE PARTNERSHIPS AND COLLABORATIONS

An evaluator's ability to initiate and maintain effective partnerships and collaborations is crucial to evaluation practice. Today's complex evaluations typically require an array of expert skills that go beyond those of any single evaluator. Furthermore, relationships with stakeholders who are viewed as partners or collaborators in a participatory evaluation are essential to its success. Therefore, I would like to begin this section by citing one of my favorite sources for defining and clarifying the differences among terms such as partnership, cooperation, and collaboration, to name a few. Drawing from collaborative theory, Gadja (2004, pp. 67–70) described five principles that define effective collaborations (Box 2.3).

These principles are important because they help to define the differences among cooperation, coordination, collaboration, and coadunation—each reflecting a different level of integration along a continuum (Gadja, 2004). For those of you who typically become involved with collaboratives (e.g., coalitions) at various stages in their development, these distinctions are helpful for understanding and facilitating interrelationships among stakeholders as they work toward collaboration and effective participatory evaluation practice (Cousins, Whitmore, & Shulha, 2012). To collaborate effectively, "each person [should] feel equally responsible for the success of their joint project or process . . . ; [therefore], attempts to define who has the 'right experience' reduce collaboration" (Bushe, 2009, p. 19). So, it is important that open communication and dialogue be facilitated and advocated in participatory evaluation practice.

INCLUSIVE PRACTICE IN EVALUATION

Evaluators continually work with people who have a variety of cultural backgrounds. By culture, I mean cultural experiences derived through gender,

Box 2.3. FIVE PRINCIPLES THAT DEFINE EFFECTIVE
COLLABORATIONS (GADJA, 2004)

1. Collaboration is an imperative when dealing with complex social issues and community needs;
2. Collaboration is known by many names including, but not limited to, joint ventures, partnerships, coalitions, collaboratives, alliances, consortiums, task forces, and so on (p. 68);
3. Collaboration is a journey not a destination of efforts that "fall across a continuum of low to high integration. The level of integration is determined by the intensity of the alliance's process, structure, and purpose" (p. 68);
4. With collaboration, the personal is as important as the procedure or process of evaluation because unhealthy interpersonal connections and lack of trust can thwart the group's efforts.
5. Collaboration develops in stages as group members get to know one another and determine their collaborative vision, mission, and agenda.

race, ethnicity, age, sexual orientation, socioeconomic status, different work environments, family backgrounds, and so on. We are all different and sometimes those differences create tensions among us. It is, therefore, important to have a skill set that helps to both acknowledge difference and reduce tension when it occurs. Where do you begin? First, it is imperative that you understand your own cultural norms, biases, and values and realize that they are different from everyone else's. Moreover, you must work "inside-out" to "cultivate empathetic perspective taking [that] acknowledges and regularly polishes the lenses and filters that frame your perceptions and meaning-making reflections and interpretations—discover what they illuminate and, even more important, what they obscure or ignore" (Symonette, 2004, p. 97). Through understanding our own cultural identity and bias, we are better able to recognize the differences among us and open our minds and hearts to other perspectives. Second, you must learn what values, experiences, and ways of knowing the world are held by those with whom you work. When you are open to learning and knowing other cultures, you can begin to engage effectively with others and value their unique contributions. Third, you must look at strengths in others that can benefit your partnerships and evaluations. Doing so acknowledges everyone and can contribute something special to your work together.

Methods of Appreciate Inquiry can be particularly helpful (Coghlan, Preskill, & Catsambas, 2003; Preskill & Catsambas, 2006). For example, years ago I supervised a woman who was extremely detail oriented—an orientation that I do not have and must force myself into when needed. Our conversations initially drove me nuts as I had to hear every little detail about her work when I just wanted to "cut to the chase" and get the simplified version. I came to learn that her detail orientation was a great asset and complement to my big picture thinking. I grew to rely on her to keep track of details that seemed overwhelming to me but absolutely necessary for the function of our programming efforts. I bring this up because almost everyone has a quality like my detail-oriented colleague that can be an asset to an evaluation partnership. Capitalize on their talents, whether it be someone who likes rigid structure, someone who speaks another language (broadly defined), someone who likes to keep detailed notes, someone who likes to track progress, someone who shares experiences with program participants, someone who likes to work with numbers, or someone who likes to socialize—you can find a role for them that will make a valuable contribution to an evaluation.

When you are entering culturally unfamiliar settings, it is imperative that you develop relationships and do a thorough cultural analysis with a learning mindset (Dweck, 2006) before you begin any evaluation. This process can take from just a few weeks to one or two years depending on the evaluation and the culture in which you find yourself. Learn who has power, how things get done, how fast work gets done, who might have to give approval, what stakeholders should be involved, how contacts are made, how people communicate, who communicates most effectively, what different forms of communication mean and so on. BE A LEARNER—just as a toddler would explore his new world. Keep your eyes and ears open and learn.

In the context of understanding a community's needs, I recommend that you begin with a set of five questions described by Wambeam (Wambeam, 2015, pp. 11–12) to define your community (Box 2.4).

These questions provide a foundation for gaining a collective understanding of a community, which defines the context, or in some cases the "unit of analysis," for your evaluation. As you can see by the questions, they help to inform your understanding of the cultural context for your evaluation; however, this step is only the beginning. As evaluators we must be inclusive and perform our practice with cultural competence.

What does it mean to be a culturally competent and inclusive evaluator? In 2005, AEA's membership convened a task force of evaluation and cultural competence experts to tackle this question and issue a statement, which was approved in 2011. The statement's summary reads in part,

> Culture is the shared experiences of people, including their languages, values, customs, beliefs, and mores. It also includes worldviews, ways of knowing, and ways of communicating. Culturally significant factors encompass, but are not

1. Is your community geographic, organizational, or cultural? If your community is geographic, define the boundaries of your community's location and describe its size.
2. Describe your community. What is its culture like? Is it rural or urban? What kind of climate does it experience? What values, attitudes, and beliefs are most important? What kinds of jobs do people have? Are there dominant religions?
3. Document your community demographics, including the total population, median age, percentage of the population in various ethnic groups, percentage of the population with specific levels of education, and the median household income. Other demographics you may wish to include are gender, spoken languages, marital status, and other culturally relevant demographics.
4. In sum, what makes your community unique?
5. Where did you find the information to answer the above questions?

limited to, race/ethnicity, religion, spirituality, social class, caste, language, lineage, disability, sexual orientation, age, gender, geographic region, and socioeconomic circumstances. It is important to note that while these factors include culture they are not fixed and can change over time. (American Evaluation Association, 2011)

This statement's summary also provides three main reasons why cultural competence is important in evaluation.

First, the evaluation team is ethically responsible to be culturally competent in order to produce work that is honest, accurate, respectful of stakeholders, and considerate of the general public welfare. Second, cultural competence supports validity by insuring that diverse voices and perspectives are honestly and fairly represented, which in turn, helps to make valid inferences and interpretations. Third, evaluation is steeped in theories that are, themselves shaped by cultural values and perspectives; therefore, it is important to scrutinize theories in order to understand how they describe societal issues, and how to address them.

In Box 2.5, I summarize five essential practices for cultural competence in evaluation as they are listed in AEA's summary statement (2011). Detailed descriptions of each practice can be found at AEA's web site, www.eval.org.

By adhering to these practice guidelines, we reap the rewards of learning from and building and sustaining relationships across multiple cultural groups. By knowing ourselves and others in this way, our lives and careers become enriched with meaning and joy.

SUMMARY

This chapter described the essential competencies and interpersonal skills needed for evaluators and the standards of professional evaluation practice. It also highlighted the necessity and importance of protecting human subjects as subjects of and participants in evaluations. I emphasized the need to understand culture and be a self-reflective and culturally competent evaluator. These competencies and skills help to foster and facilitate positive relationships with stakeholders and clients that support successful evaluation practice. In the next chapter, you will learn about the major approaches to evaluation and how stakeholders may influence the approach you choose to evaluate a program.

REFERENCES

American Evaluation Association. (2004). *Guiding Principles for Evaluators*. Retrieved from http://www.eval.org/p/cm/ld/fid=51

American Evaluation Association. (2011). *American Evaluation Association Public Statement on Cultural Competence in Evaluation, Summary*. Fairhaven, MA: Author. Retrieved from http://www.eval.org/d/do/155.

African Evaluation Association. (2006). *African Evaluation Guidelines—Standards and Norms*. Retrieved from http://www.ader-evaluare.ro/docs/African%20 Evaluation%20Association.pdf

Bakken, L. L., Núñez, J., & Couture, C. (2014). A course model for building evaluation capacity through a university-community partnership. *American Journal of Evaluation, 35(4)*, 579–593.

James Bell Associates. (2008). *Evaluation Brief: Understanding the IRB.* Arlington, VA. January 2008. Retrieved from https://www.betterevaluation.org/sites/default/files/understanding%20the%20irb.pdf

Bushe, G. R. (2009). Learning from collective experience: A different view of organizational learning. *Organizational Development Practitioner, 41(3),* 19–23.

Canadian Evaluation Society. (2010). *Competencies for Canadian Evaluation Practice.* Retrieved from https://evaluationcanada.ca/txt/2_competencies_cdn_evaluation_practice.pdf

Catsambas, T. T. (2016). Facilitating evaluation to lead meaningful change. In R. S. Fierro, A. Schwartz, & D. H. Smart (Eds.), *Evaluation and Facilitation, New Direction for Evaluation, 149,* 19–29.

Coghlan, A. T., Preskill, H., Catsambas, T. T. (2003). An overview of appreciative inquiry in evaluation. In H. Preskill & A. T. Coghlan (Eds.), *New Directions for Evaluation, 100,* 5–22.

Cousins, J. B., & Whitmore, E. (1998). Framing participatory evaluation. In E. Whitmore (Ed.), *New Directions for Evaluation, 80,* 5–23.

Cousins, J. B., Whitmore, E., & Shulha, L. (2012). Arguments for a common set of principles for collaborative inquiry in evaluation. *American Journal of Evaluation, 34(1),* 7–22.

Dillman, L. M. (2012). Evaluator skill acquisition: Linking educational experiences to competencies. *American Journal of Evaluation, 34(2),* 270–285.

DuBois, J. M. (2002). When is informed consent appropriate in educational research? *IRB: Ethics & Human Research, 24(1),* 1–8.

Dweck, C. (2006). *Mindset: The new psychology of success.* New York: Random House, Inc.

Gadja R. (2004). Utilizing collaboration theory to evaluate strategic alliances. *American Journal of Evaluation, 25(1),* 65–77.

Hoole, E., & Patterson, T. E. (2008). Voices from the field: Evaluation as part of a learning culture. In J. G. Carman & K. A. Fredericks (Eds.), *Nonprofits and evaluation. New Directions for Evaluation, 119,* 93–113.

International Board of Standards for Training, Performance and Instruction (ibstpi). (2006). *Evaluator Competencies.* Retrieved from http://ibstpi.org/evaluator-competencies/

King, J. A., & Stevahn, L. (2013). *Interactive evaluation practice: Mastering the interpersonal dynamics of program evaluation.* Thousand Oaks, CA: Sage Publications.

King, J. A., & Stevahn, L. (2015). Competencies for program evaluators in light of adaptive action: What? So what? Now what? In J. W. Altschuld & M. Engle (Eds.), *Accreditation, certification, and credentialing: Relevant convers for U.S. evaluators. New Directions for Evaluation, 145,* 21–37.

King, J. A., Stevahn, L., Ghere, G., & Minnema, J. (2001). Toward a taxonomy of essential evaluator competencies. *American Journal of Evaluation, 22(2),* 229–247.

Labin, S. N., Duffy, J. L., Meyers, D. C., Wandersman, A., & Lesesne, C. A. (2012). A research synthesis of evaluation capacity building literature. *American Journal of Evaluation, 33(3),* 307–338. doi: 10.1177/1098214011434608.

Mertens, D. (2009). *Transformative research and evaluation.* New York, NY: Guilford Press.

Morris, M. (2008). *Evaluation ethics for best practice: Cases and commentaries.* New York, NY: The Guilford Press.

National Commission for the Protection of Human Subjects of Biomedical and Behavioral Research. (1979). *The Belmont Report.* Retrieved from the U.S. Department of Health and Human Services, Office for Human Research Protections website: https://www.hhs.gov/ohrp/regulations-and-policy/belmont-report/index.html

Perrin, B. (2005). How can information about the competencies required for evaluation be useful? *The Canadian Journal of Program Evaluation, 20(2)*, 169–188.

Preskill, H. (2014). Now for the hard stuff: Next steps in ECB research and practice. *American Journal of Evaluation, 35(1)*, 116–119. doi:10.1177/1098214013499439/

Preskill, H., & Boyle, S. (2008). A multidisciplinary model of evaluation capacity building. *American Journal of Evaluation, 29(4)*, 443–459. doi:10.1177/1098214008324182.

Preskill, H., & Catsambas, T. T. (2006). *Reframing Evaluation through Appreciative Inquiry*. Thousand Oaks, CA: Sage Publications, Inc.

Rice, T. W. (2008). How to do human-subjects research if you do not have an Institutional Review Board. *Respiratory Care, 53(10)*, 1362–1367.

Rodgers, M. S., Hillake, B. D., Haas, B. E., & Peters, C. (2012). Taxonomy for assessing evaluation competencies in extension. *Journal of Extension, 50(4)*. Retrieved from https://joe.org/joe/2012august/a2.php

Ross, L. F., Loup, A., Nelson, R. M., Botkin, J. R., Kost, R., Smith, G. R., & Gehlert, S. (2010). Nine key functions for a human subjects protection program for community-engaged research: Points to consider. *Journal of Empirical Research on Human Research Ethics, 5(1)*, 33–47.

Stevahn, L., King, J. A., Ghere, G., & Minnema, J. (2005). Establishing essential competencies for program evaluators. *American Journal of Evaluation, 26*, 43–59.

Symonette, H. (2004). Walking pathways toward becoming a culturally competent evaluator: Boundaries, borderlands, and border crossings. In M. Thompson-Robinson, R. Hopson, & S. SenGupta (Eds.), *In Search of Cultural Competence in Evaluation: Toward Principles and Practices. New Directions for Evaluation, Summer 2004(102)*, 95–109. doi: 10.1002/ev.118

Taylor-Ritzler, T., Suarez-Balcazar, Y., Garcia-Iriarte, E., Henry, D. B., & Balcazar, F. E. (2013). Understanding and measuring evaluation capacity: A model and instrument validation study. *American Journal of Evaluation, 34(2)*, 190–206.

Tomkowiak, J. M., & Gunderson, A. J. (2004). To IRB or Not to IRB? *Academic Medicine, 79(7)*, 628–632.

Wambeam, R. A. (2015). *The community needs assessment workbook*. Chicago, IL: Lyceum Books, Inc.

Wilcox, Y. (2012). An initial study to develop instruments and validate the Essential Competencies for Program Evaluators (ECPE) [doctoral dissertation]. Retrieved from the University of Minnesota. (http://conservancy.umn.edu/handle/11299/132042)

Yarbrough, D. B., Shulha, L. M., Hopson, R. K., & Caruthers, F. A. (2011). *The Program Evaluation Standards: A guide for evaluators and evaluation users* (3rd ed.). Thousand Oaks, CA: Sage Publications, Inc.

CHAPTER 3

Choosing an Evaluation Approach

Program evaluation designs are rooted in an array of philosophical perspectives and approaches. These approaches have evolved over time and are grouped in various ways depending on the source that describes them. For any given evaluation, it is common for an evaluator to use more than one approach. What are common approaches to evaluation in today's world of accountability? This chapter will begin with a discussion of the philosophical perspectives that ground each set of approaches, provide an historical overview of the evolution of evaluation approaches, and describe five groups of approaches commonly used today.

PHILOSOPHICAL PERSPECTIVES THAT INFLUENCE EVALUATION

Four fundamental philosophical perspectives (i.e., world views or lenses) influence the evaluation approaches described in this chapter. These perspectives orient the role of the evaluator in conducting an evaluation, the degree to which stakeholders are involved, the methodologies selected, and the level of objectivity or subjectivity of the evaluation's approach and findings. Authors who write about evaluation perspectives organize them in various ways. For the purpose of this section, I will use the philosophical distinctions defined and described by Fitzpatrick, Sanders, and Worthen (2011) in *Program Evaluation: Alternative Approaches and Practical Guidelines* and incorporate concepts from the ways other authors have described or organized them as a way to tie them together.

The aim of *positivist* and *postpositivist* approaches is to be as objective as possible in the conduct of an evaluation; therefore, the desirable role for an evaluator is to be positioned "outside" the evaluation so that the evaluation is less subject to personal bias. For this reason, too, stakeholder involvement in the evaluation's plan, conduct, or interpretation is typically limited in order to seek objective truth. Quantitative analytical methods typically are used because this perspective values the "more credible" evidence provided by these methodologies (see Chapter 5 for further discussions of credible evidence). In contrast, *humanist* perspectives highly value the ideas and opinions of stakeholders; therefore, any evidence provided by stakeholders is considered credible and useful when planning, conducting, or reporting an evaluation. Furthermore, the role of an evaluator is to engage with stakeholders to the extent that the stakeholders "own" the evaluation and its findings. Although positivists would consider this perspective and its accompanying approaches to be highly subjective, the humanist would argue that truth is best known through those who experience it. *Constructivists* acknowledge the important role of context in evaluation and the influence it has on knowledge construction. Context influences stakeholders and evaluators and the power relationships among them. Therefore, an evaluator might engage with stakeholders to varying degrees depending on power dynamics and their corresponding influences. *Transformative* approaches to evaluation emphasize political, social, and economic factors that shape reality. Therefore, stakeholder empowerment and social justice are emphasized (Mertens, 2009; Mertens & Wilson, 2012). Stakeholders' knowledge and experiences are highly valued along with the contextual influences that may have marginalized specific persons or groups.

These various perspectives are important because they have shaped evaluation approaches both historically and practically. As you read through the various approaches to evaluation, be mindful of the philosophical perspectives that form their foundations. Can you think of specific contexts in which certain approaches may be more acceptable or useful than others? Which approaches might be most useful with oppressed cultural groups? Which approaches might be most useful when working with government agencies or policymakers? How do your own values and beliefs align with these approaches?

EXPERTISE-ORIENTED APPROACHES

As their name implies, expertise-oriented approaches rely on experts to set the standards or criteria for which a program or individuals are to be judged. The goal of these approaches is to provide professional judgments of quality. Can you think of any examples that meet this definition within your own professional groups? Examples from practice include but are not limited to blue ribbon panels, accrediting organizations, and groups such as search and screen committees, dissertation committees, or judges at county fairs. Accreditation groups are numerous and highly respected in various professional fields. Some common examples that may be familiar to you are:

The Joint Commission that provides accreditation and certification to more than 19,000 healthcare organizations and programs in the United States (http://www.jointcommission.org);

The Leadership in Energy and Environmental Design (LEED) Certification and Accreditation for organizations and individuals that comply with a set of standards to protect human health and our environment (http://www.usgbc.org/leed);

The Council on Social Work Education's (CSWE) Commission on Accreditation (COA) "develops accreditation standards that define competent preparation [for social work] and ensures that social work programs meet them" (http://www.cswe.org/accreditation.aspx);

The Council for the Accreditation of Educator Preparation (CAEP) that creates standards for educators and accredits programs throughout the country (http://caepnet.org/); and

The Council for Higher Education Accreditation (CHEA).

CONSUMER-ORIENTED APPROACHES

When I think of consumer-oriented approaches, I think of the few times I have walked into a local dairy center and been invited to taste-test a new product. I am directed to a private booth where I find a scoring sheet and one to three food samples. Other, more common, examples include the occasional marketing surveys I am asked to complete when I make a store or online purchase. The defining feature of these evaluation approaches is their emphasis on judging the quality of products or services to aid purchasing decisions. In this case, evaluation criteria are established by the producer and used as a way to market products. Common data-collection tools are checklists or rating forms.

PROGRAM-ORIENTED APPROACHES

For educators, social workers, healthcare professionals, community developers, and other service providers, program-oriented approaches to evaluation are the most common approaches practiced in today's accountability-oriented society. These approaches are driven by program theory primarily derived through stakeholders' ideas and experiences and knowledge reported in academic literature. The goal of these approaches is to determine the extent to which program goals (i.e., desired outcomes) and objectives are achieved. Over the years, there has been an increasing emphasis on programs' *impacts* on communities or organizations as decisions are made by governing bodies to determine a program's public worth or value. Evaluation criteria, therefore, may be established collectively by involving representatives of various stakeholder groups. Program-oriented approaches are highly endorsed among local, state, and federal funding agencies and nonprofit foundations that require evaluations of their grantees, so they tend to dominate many evaluations done today.

There are three major types of program-oriented evaluation approaches: (1) objectives-based, (2) discrepancy-based, and (3) theoretical. *Objectives-based program evaluation* (Tyler, 1942) is common among educators who typically want to understand the extent to which learners have achieved a program's or curriculum's desired learning objectives or outcomes. The nursing and nutrition education fields use this approach extensively to evaluate learning and assess professional performance. The major steps in an objectives-based program evaluation (Fitzpatrick, Sanders, & Worthen, 2011, p. 155) are listed in Box 3.1. In many fields (e.g., nursing, medicine, and K–18 education), it is common practice to embed an objectives-based approach into an evaluation of an educational program.

A more recent emergence related to objectives-based evaluation is the assessment and evaluation of competence. King and Stevahn (2015) make an important distinction between competence and competencies.

Competence is the 'habitual and judicious use of communication, knowledge, technical skills, clinical reasoning, emotions, values and reflection in daily practice for the benefit of the individual and community being served' (Epstein & Hundert, 2002, p. 226). By contrast, the requirements for *competencies* are knowledge, skills, and attitudes that are applied and observable (Schoonover Associates, 2003), specific practices related to particular knowledge, skills or dispositions (p. 23).

Therefore, competency-based assessment and evaluation take objectives-based evaluation one step further by focusing the assessment on the *application* and *use* of knowledge, skills, and attitudes. Competency-based assessment in program evaluation is the cornerstone of medical education (Carraccio et al., 2016; ten Cate & Billett, 2014), and it is becoming increasingly popular in higher education (Lacey & Murray, 2015). Objectives- and competency-based approaches to assessment and program evaluation provide a means to maintain professional standards and monitor performance. Used as an assessment approach, however, competencies can create a mindset to learn and teach "to the test," so facts and memorization tend to be emphasized versus the higher-order thinking and learning required of application (Dweck, 2007).

Discrepancy-based program evaluation (Provus, 1971) is an extension of objectives-based program approaches that rely on a set of standards by which to judge a program's performance. This type of evaluation takes the form of a continuous information management process from which performance data is used to improve, maintain, or terminate all or part of a program. Steps for conducting this type of evaluation are to determine the inputs, processes, and outcomes that define a program; identify discrepancies between program design and implementation; collect data on participants' abilities to achieve "enabling" objectives; and determine whether program objectives have been achieved (Fitzpatrick, Sanders, & Worthen, 2011). A cost-benefit analysis may be added to determine whether a program's benefits to learners or a community exceed the costs associated with implementing or maintaining a program. Although not as common as in years past, it remains a useful approach for program evaluations.

Theory-based evaluations (Chen, 1990; 2005; Weiss, 1997) are the most common form of program-oriented approaches used today. They are extremely popular among funders who typically require them in grant applications. This requirement often can create anxiety for a program planner or coordinator with limited experience in designing or conducting an evaluation and is one of the reasons why program evaluators are frequently consulted. So, what is a *theory-based* or rather, *theory-driven* evaluation? Theory-driven evaluations capitalize on the features of objectives-based and discrepancy-based evaluations by combining program goals, objectives, and desired outcomes to create a theory about how a program is perceived to work. Dating back to Carol Weiss's work in 1997, program theory helps to focus an evaluation and its associated questions, and guides the evaluation's overall design.

Figure 3.1. Five elements of a basic logic model.

A *logic model* is a technique and tool for visually conceptualizing a theory about how a program affects desired changes. In simple terms, a logic model illustrates the relationship between *action* (what you do) and *change* (what you get) (Knowlton & Phillips, 2009). The basic elements of a logic model, as illustrated in Figure 3.1, include *inputs* (e.g., people, funding, or space) for a program, the program's *activities* (e.g., participant recruitment, a workshop, or informational brochure), immediate *outputs* (e.g., immediate knowledge or skills) from the program's activities, and the *outcomes* or changes (e.g., knowledge application or use) expected as a result of the program's activities. Program *impacts*, or the broad effects of a program on organizations and communities, have become an increasingly important component of program theory.

By incorporating impacts into logic models, program stakeholders can account for ways they expect a program and its associated outcomes to contribute or provide value to communities. For example, if I teach someone how to search, apply, and interview for a job (activities and outputs), then they apply those skills by applying and interviewing for jobs more often (short-term outcomes), and then they become employed (medium-term outcome). This effort will eventually lead to higher employment in a community (impact).

When developing program theory, it is important to identify the *assumptions* that influence the theory. Explicit assumptions can help to identify biases, limitations, overlooked components, or excluded stakeholders.

As you view the basic components of the logic model depicted in Figure 3.2, you will notice the arrows that connect each of its components. These arrows signify the relationships between the theory's components. All too often, insufficient attention is given to the various relationships between or among the program's activities and anticipated changes. The result is that critical components are omitted, components are identified that have no logical

Figure 3.2. Example of logic model for employment.

connection, or the model is oversimplified because the program has more than one "unit" of change.

As you read the extant literature on program theory, you may notice that "impact" is conceptualized in two main ways. Scholars such as Knowlton and Phillips (2009) and Preskill and Russ-Eft (2005) view impacts as the end point of a logical process; whereas, others (e.g., Bjurulf, Vedung, & Larsson, 2012) define impact as a type of evaluation design in which outcomes are assessed in relation to a comparison or counterfactual group. In my opinion, the latter definition is really only a direct assessment of a program's outcomes that is based on causal static models and does not provide evidence of the relationship of outcomes to impacts as previously defined. To truly demonstrate an impact, one must be able to provide evidence that a relationship exists between a program's outcomes and broader organizational or community change. This point is echoed in my forthcoming discussions of impact and will become clearer in Chapter 6, when I discuss the various study designs commonly used for program evaluations.

As typically illustrated, program theories are conveyed to summarize the results of a program's implementation. In other words, logic models are used to plan a *summative evaluation*. Indeed, many of you may be interested in assessing only the summative outcomes of a program. Outcomes can also be used, however, as information to improve a program and its associated outcomes by considering them as input in an ongoing process of change (Chen, 1996). Figure 3.3 provides a simple illustration of a program viewed as part of a program improvement cycle, or *formative evaluation* process. My point in illustrating this form of a logic model is twofold: (1) Program theories can take on multiple forms and (2) evaluations can be conceptualized as part of a program improvement process, or formative evaluation.

Why is it important to create a program's theory of change? Often, you may have a desire or be expected to determine the effectiveness of a program to create specific outcomes or an impact on individuals, organizations, or communities. Without having some idea or vision of how that happens,

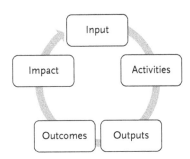

Figure 3.3. Logic model illustrated as a theory for formative evaluation.

programming efforts become a "hit or miss" game. In other words, the assessed outcomes may not have any association with the activities that are part of the program being evaluated. Moreover, in the absence of critical thought or dialogue with stakeholders about the broad effects of a program, evaluations often are limited to participants' *immediate* gains in specific knowledge and skills (as in objectives-based evaluations). As a result, longer-term changes (e.g., participants' actions or behavioral changes) that stem from programming efforts can be overlooked.

Another point to keep in mind is that in order to evaluate a program's effectiveness to achieve a desired change, an evaluator must rule out other factors that might contribute to that change. To do this, *theory-driven* approaches that consider potential mediators and moderators of change are needed (Chen, 2005). To truly understand whether a program has *caused* a desired change or *effect* (i.e., *efficacy* evaluation), very controlled conditions are necessary. However, as practitioners in social science fields, we know that highly controlled conditions are typically impossible to achieve because we work with humans who aren't very controllable. Chen (2005), therefore, advocates *effectiveness evaluations,* which encourage us to account for factors outside the program that could be influencing the desired change(s) (outcomes or impacts). By doing so, we can evaluate with greater certainty a program's contributions to those desired changes.

Program theory and its associated logic models have been criticized for their linear reasoning and oversimplification because programs don't operate in vacuums (Weiss, 1997). Group dynamics influence learning experiences, environmental factors influence program implementation, and social conditions influence program effects. When used in practice, components of logic models also may be misidentified or the relationships among them may not be clear and well-defined, or they may be missing. Consequently, data collected for evaluation becomes disassociated buckets of information that may have limited utility in making inferences about a program's effectiveness or need for improvement. More recently, logic models have been expanded to include action theory in order to reduce program planners' and directors' inclinations to "box" each element void of their relationships or restrict theories and corresponding assessments to program outputs and short-term outcomes that have no actionable effect (Funnell & Rogers, 2011, pp. 199–240). "In simple terms, the theory of action is about what the program does or expects to do in order to activate the change theory" (p. 199). The action elements of a robust program theory include the:

> Desired attributes of intended outcomes; attention to unintended outcomes;
> Program features and external factors that affect outcomes; and
> What the program does to address key program and external factors. (p. 200)

As a result, program theories often become less linear and more robust as they attempt to include more action-oriented components. These robust program theories are typically more complex and may require sophisticated study designs and analytical methods to evaluate them. Nonetheless, logic models can be useful tools for defining and establishing clear relationships among program elements and can provide useful frameworks for designing an evaluation plan when constructed and used appropriately.

It is important to understand that theory-based evaluation approaches and their accompanying conceptual models (e.g., logic models) do not by themselves constitute an evaluation plan. They simply help to visualize and focus program-related factors that are critical for designing an evaluation. Program theories also may include some different elements depending on their intended purposes and underlying theoretical perspectives of change (e.g., empowerment, diffusion, socioecological, or network theories). Variations of them exist with names such a "logframes" or "outcome maps" (Funnell & Rogers, 2011). Regardless of the approach or specific model, the steps listed in Table 3.1 are recommended by Donaldson (2007) when one works with stakeholders to develop program theory (Fitzpatrick, Sanders, & Worthen, 2011, p. 163). I have adapted these steps by adding an additional and optional step to conduct a logic analysis as a reminder to consider best practices, research, and expert knowledge (including stakeholders') when developing or analyzing a program theory.

A *logic analysis* (Brousselle & Champagne, 2011) offers a process for determining the accuracy of a program's theory of change. It is guided by three steps that evaluate the plausibility or reasonableness of a program's theory based on criteria established through a literature review and expert knowledge. In the first step of a logic analysis, a logic model is created or obtained through a situational analysis to understand a program's *current* or *active* theory of change. In the second step of the logic analysis, knowledge of best practices and approaches for achieving the desired outcomes and impacts are obtained through field experts and a targeted literature review. I would like to

---

Table 3.1. STEPS FOR DEVELOPING A PROGRAM THEORY

STEP 1. Engage relevant stakeholders

STEP 2. Develop a first draft of a program theory

STEP 3. Present the draft to stakeholders for further discussion, reaction, and input

STEP 4. Communicate these findings to key stakeholders and revise the program theory as needed

STEP 5. Probe arrows for model specificity

STEP 6. Finalize program impact theory

STEP 7. Conduct logic analysis (optional)

---

note that in participatory evaluation, key stakeholders are considered experts. When experts' information is compared with the logic model developed in Step One, new information is obtained that can be used to improve programming and evaluation efforts.

As an example, I and colleagues at an academic medical center used logic analysis to expand an educational series' program theory to a systems' theory for improved patient care. When our team began to learn about how the program's key stakeholders envisioned a theory for how the program impacted patient care, we quickly learned that many of the desired short- and long-term changes they expected were not reflected in an existing logic model or being assessed. Moreover, the stakeholders identified key people and relationships to other units within the academic medical center that highlighted the organization's emphasis on continual learning, quality improvement, and improved patient care within a complex medical system. By using logic analysis to incorporate local expertise about the healthcare center and literature on organizational learning, systems change, and similar programming efforts, we were able to illustrate a more robust systems theory for how the educational series contributed to patient care (Bakken, Olson, Ross, Turco, Jackson, & Murphy, 2015). This effort provided a foundation for designing a three-phase evaluation study and targeting our data collection efforts, so we could determine how and, ultimately, the extent to which, the educational series influenced healthcare providers' practices toward improving patient outcomes.

DECISION-ORIENTED APPROACHES

Decision-oriented approaches build on program-oriented approaches by using information about outcomes, impacts, or costs to inform or make decisions about a program. Evaluators tend to work closely with managers or other administrators in decision-making roles when planning and conducting these types of evaluations. A common example includes a funder who may use evaluation findings to discontinue or provide continued funding for a program. It is also not uncommon for an administrator to ask, "What is my return on investment for that program?" Consequently, an evaluator's knowledge of the analyses used to determine a program's cost to benefit ratio, cost-effectiveness, or return on investment are particularly useful. The decision-making criteria in this case often are determined by directors, administrators, governing boards, or others who have a financial stake in the program, but who often don't design or implement a program.

Two models have been described to guide evaluations directed at making decisions. The Context, Input, Process, Product (CIPP) Model (Stufflebeam, 1983, 2013) was developed to support programming decisions for accountability, dissemination, and understanding. It has been described by some evaluators as "four evaluations in one," because each component is meant to address a question or questions typically raised at various points in the evaluation process. To understand the *context* of a program, evaluators typically ask, "*What are the needs and problems of those being served?*" The answer to this question guides planning decisions and leads to the next question related to program *input: "In what ways should their needs be addressed?"* Once these questions are answered and the program is designed and implemented, a *process* evaluation is needed to answer the question, "*Was the program implemented as planned?*" When the program's *products* or outputs are determined, the final questions can be evaluated. "*Should the program be revised, expanded, or discontinued?*" As you carefully critique each step in the CIPP Model and think about my earlier descriptions of other approaches, can you identify some of the major assumptions and limitations of this model?

The UCLA Model (Alkin, 1991) expands the CIPP Model by accounting for not only the program planning and implementation process, but by considering the purpose(s) of an evaluation aimed at decision-making. For example, a program's purpose might be to determine whether or not to implement a program. Another purpose might be to improve or terminate a program. Yet another purpose of an evaluation might be to determine whether a program meets accreditation criteria.

Decision-oriented approaches can create tension among staff and administrators. To ease this tension, it is helpful to combine these and other program-oriented approaches with approaches advocating participation. In the sections that follow, an evaluator's role begins to shift when he or she utilizes approaches that emphasize stakeholders as important and valued experts and contributors to an evaluation.

PARTICIPANT-ORIENTED APPROACHES

As their categorization implies, these approaches advocate stakeholder inclusion and empowerment throughout the program planning, implementation, and evaluation process. Today, the goal of these approaches centers on social justice by incorporating multiple realities of key stakeholder groups. "The term participatory, however, is used quite differently by different people. For some it implies a practical approach to broadening decision making and problem solving through systematic inquiry; for others, reallocating power in the production of knowledge and promoting social change are the root issues" (Cousins & Whitmore, 1998, p. 5). Participatory approaches tend to have greater emphasis on the formative process of a program's evolution and typically strive to build an organization's or community members' capacity for evaluation through participation and learning. Using participatory approaches, the evaluator serves the roles of coach, teacher, and facilitator and works collaboratively with a variety of stakeholders to determine the questions and criteria for an evaluation.

Participatory evaluation is divided into two general approaches based on goals, purposes, and historical and ideological roots—namely, Practical Participatory Evaluation and Transformative Participatory Evaluation (Cousins & Whitmore, 1998). Practical approaches emphasize utilization; whereas, transformative approaches emphasize "principles and actions in order to democratize social change" (p. 7). Practical approaches include responsive (Stake, 1973), utilization-focused (Patton, 1997, 2004), developmental (Patton, 1994, 2012), and naturalistic (Guba & Lincoln, 1985, 1989) evaluation. Transformative approaches include empowerment (Fetterman, 1994; Fetterman & Wandersman, 2005), deliberative democratic (House & Howe, 1999, 2000), and transformative evaluation (Mertens, 2009).

Responsive evaluation carved the pathway for participatory approaches by emphasizing flexible and changing methods and approaches; recognizing multiple realities and the value of pluralism; and valuing local knowledge, theories, and program "particulars" (Fitzpatrick, Sanders, & Worthen, 2011, p. 193). An evaluator's goal in a responsive evaluation is to be responsive to the needs and desires of the clients requesting an evaluation. Similarly, *Utilization-focused evaluation* (Patton, 1997, 2004, 2012) expands this approach by focusing on the people (i.e., users) who care about the results of an evaluation. The intent of these approaches is to involve key users of the evaluation in the conduct of the evaluation study, interpretation of its results, and decisions about a program. *Naturalistic evaluation* (Guba & Lincoln, 1985, 1989) focuses on the evolution of an evaluation through its primary stakeholders. This type of participatory approach may or may not directly involve stakeholders in the conduct of an evaluation, but an evaluator does seek the input and ideas of key stakeholders throughout the evaluation process. When an evaluator actively involves key stakeholders as designers, data collectors, and results interpreters throughout the evaluation process, an evaluation becomes fully participatory. In practice, full stakeholder participation is not always possible for reasons often related to their availability or relationships of power or privilege within or across organizations. Participation also may be limited by lack of perceived skills to conduct evaluation, restricted timelines, or available staffing. Therefore, participatory evaluations vary by the amount of evaluator control over the process, breadth of stakeholders involved in the evaluation, and the stages of an evaluation in which stakeholders are involved (Chouinard, 2013; Cousins, Whitmore, & Shulha, 2012).

Four key principles guide *transformative evaluation* approaches: (1) cultural respect, (2) promotion of social justice, (3) furtherance of human rights, and (4) addressing inequalities (Mertens, 2009; Mertens & Wilson, 2012).

When executing these principles, an evaluator's goal is to engage and involve marginalized groups; therefore, an evaluator's cultural competence is absolutely necessary for recognizing "multiple social identities and group memberships (e.g., gender, income or educational level, race/ethnicity, disability); and [engaging in] transparent discussions of relevant issues of power and privilege" (Mertens & Wilson, 2012, p. 165). Transformative approaches to evaluation include, but are not limited to, deliberative democratic evaluation (House & Howe, 1999, 2000), empowerment evaluation (Fetterman, 1994; Fetterman & Wandersman, 2005), those grounded in critical race theory (Mertens & Wilson, 2012), indigenous evaluation (LaFrance & Nichols, 2010), culturally responsive evaluation (Hood, 2000), transformative participatory evaluation (Mertens, 2009), and those approaches targeting specific circumstances and cultures (e.g., disability, feminism, race, or ethnicity). All of these approaches seek to engage stakeholders in activities or action steps that improve their lives and create a more just society. In doing so, these approaches utilize collaborative forms of inquiry and "grass roots" participation that require time, patience, and resources to build and maintain strong relationships and efforts that lead to social change. An important distinction among these approaches is the level of evaluator control over the evaluation and stakeholder participation. In empowerment evaluation, for example, evaluators relinquish their control to stakeholders. In contrast, in other approaches to transformative evaluation (e.g., transformative participatory), evaluators retain some control of the evaluation in order to exercise their professional responsibilities and avoid "chaos" (Cousins, Whitmore, & Shulha, 2012, pp. 14–15). Because these approaches differ in practice but are built from a set of core values and goals, Cousins, Whitmore, and Shulha (2012) argue that forms of collaborative inquiry be driven by principles (shown in Box 3.2) rather than be described

---

Box 3.2. PRINCIPLES TO GUIDE COLLABORATIVE APPROACHES TO EVALUATION (SHULHA, WHITMORE, COUSINS, GILBERT, & HUDIB, 2016)

Clarify motivation for collaboration
Foster meaningful relationships
Develop a shared understanding of the program
Promote appropriate participatory processes
Monitor and respond to resource availability
Monitor evaluation progress and quality
Promote evaluation thinking
Follow through to realize use

as "compartmentalized," "discrete genres," or approaches to evaluation. These principles emphasize collaboration, shared understanding, evaluative thinking and capacity building, and use of findings.

SYSTEMS APPROACHES

Because evaluators increasingly are asked to evaluate "wicked" social problems involving programs within interdependent systems of people, organizations, and communities, systems thinking and approaches to evaluation are gaining popularity in the evaluation field. This topic will be discussed in greater detail in the final chapter of this book, so this section is limited to a brief introduction of systems approaches in the evaluation field. Grounded in systems theories, such as systems dynamics, complexity theory, soft and critical systems, network theory, and learning systems, among others, these approaches to evaluation require an understanding of concepts unfamiliar to many social scientists (Hargreaves & Podems, 2012). Fundamentally, these approaches embrace three interactive concepts: boundaries (or distinctions among them), interrelationships, and perspectives (Cabrara & Cabrara, 2015; Eoyang & Holladay, 2013; Williams & Hummelbrunner, 2011). To date, these approaches have been described as an evolution of program theory (Funnell & Rogers, 2011), as a way to re-frame outcomes evaluation through realism (Pawson & Tilley, 1997), and as a utilization-focused developmental evaluation process (Patton, 2012). The dialogue among most scholars has thus far been limited to theoretical or conceptual descriptions, so information is limited about how to effectively engage in the practice of systems evaluation. As the field rapidly grows in this direction, however, more complex and practical approaches to evaluation are likely to emerge.

APPROACHES AND THE EVALUATION TREE

Alkin and Christie (2004) summarized evaluation approaches in what they called the evaluation theory tree (Figure 3.4). This metaphorical tree aligns the philosophical paradigms with the different foci of each set of approaches (i.e., methods, use, values, social justice). The Pragmatist branch aligns best with humanism philosophy and the importance of stakeholder involvement in the evaluation process.

In 2004, Michael Patton questioned the tree metaphor and suggested that a river and its associated branches might be a better metaphor for evaluation paradigms and approaches (Patton, 2004). A river metaphor not only would

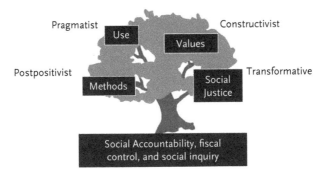

Figure 3.4. The Evaluation Tree. Adapted from Mertens and Wilson (2012). Reprinted with permission from Guildford Press © 2012.

capture the various "branches" of evaluation, but it would illustrate flows between branches and their potential blending as well as the complexity of problems that are common in evaluation practice (Mertens, 2012). These metaphorical illustrations provide helpful ways to organize and distinguish the various approaches to evaluation that guide our selection of an appropriate approach or approaches for an evaluation design. You should be aware, however, that these metaphorical descriptions, or any of the approaches described in this chapter, do not necessarily account for approaches that are field specific. Examples include the RE-AIM model in public health (Glasgow, Vogt, & Boles, 1999), The Roberta Straessle Abruzzese (RSA) model in nursing (Abruzzese, 1996; DeSilets, 2010), and the Snyder model in agriculture (Dart, Petheram, & Straw, 1998, p. 81). I mention them because, if you work with multiple disciplines or across disciplines, it is important to know and understand the philosophical foundations, methods, assumptions, and approaches of these discipline-specific models.

MATCHING APPROACHES WITH EVALUATION QUESTIONS

As mentioned earlier, a single approach to an evaluation is typically not adequate for addressing the variety of questions posed by stakeholders at any given time. Common evaluation questions include, but are not limited to, those listed in Table 3.2. Table 3.2 also indicates the approach or approaches that an evaluator likely would use to answer commonly posed evaluation questions. It should be recognized, however, that this table provides only a guideline. The selection of an evaluation approach or approaches will depend not only on the evaluation questions, but on the context, power dynamics, and political dynamics of those involved.

Table 3.2. EVALUATION APPROACHES THAT CAN BE USED TO ANSWER COMMON EVALUATION QUESTIONS

	Expertise	Program	Decision	Participatory	Systems
Did that professional meet the accreditation standards?	X				
Is my program effective or successful?		X	X	X	X
Is the program achieving its intended goals or outcomes?		X		X	
Are participants learning as a result of the program?	X	X		X	
Why don't participants apply what we teach them/what they learn?		X		X	X
Does *variable x* improve or decline following the program?		X			
What outcomes result from my program?		X			
What are the impacts of my program on organization *x* or community *y*?		X	X	X	X
What programs should we create to tackle issue *x*?			X	X	
Should we continue program *x*?			X		
What does program *x* cost and is it worth the expense?			X		
How or to what extent is my program being implemented?		X			
Which programs should we continue, and which should we eliminate?			X		
What contributions is my program making to outcome *x* in my organization?					X
How and to what extent does my program impact *x* in my local community?		X		X	X

EXAMPLES OF INTEGRATED APPROACHES
TO EVALUATION

As mentioned at the beginning of this chapter, evaluators often draw from multiple approaches when evaluating programs in practice (Bledscoe & Graham, 2005). This section offers an example of how multiple approaches become embedded in an evaluation design.

A few years ago, and on short notice, I was asked to evaluate a leadership training program for emerging leaders in agricultural business. The program participants were selected by their superiors to attend this leadership training program. Over the course of a year, the participants met approximately once per month for two days. Summers were used to practice and apply skills acquired through the leadership program. For each two-day session, a specific content area was defined, and learning objectives were articulated. Additionally, the program's goals were to develop organizational leadership capacity so there was an interest in building the skills of new employees. The program's directors were accountable to a state-level funder, so the evaluation had to demonstrate its value and effectiveness in training new leaders in agriculture.

Because I was under a short timeline to plan and begin this evaluation, I drew from the leadership literature to derive a theoretical foundation for the program that articulated some of the outcomes desired by the program's directors and by participants' superiors. This theory provided a set of variables that could be assessed to determine whether participants' knowledge and skills were being effectively applied. Interestingly (or maybe not, given the short timeline), a logic model was never prepared for this evaluation; however, this evaluation was clearly informed by theory so that links could be made between the immediate program outputs (in the form of achieved learning objectives) and outcomes identified by both the theory and those desired by the program directors. In this evaluation, I drew from *objectives-based* approaches to evaluate each session's immediate learning outcomes; I drew from *theoretical* approaches to connect learning outcomes to behavioral changes that could be observed and recorded by the participants' supervisors and colleagues, and I used the supervisors and colleagues to collect data about the program's participants, thus, drawing from *participatory* approaches.

This is just one example of how various approaches to evaluation may be used to respond to a program director's goals and need for information. More often than not, in practice you will rely upon multiple approaches to evaluation, especially as your evaluations become more complicated or complex (e.g., systems-level evaluations). I, therefore, encourage you to think about the various approaches to evaluation as part of your toolbox and to use them as appropriate to the context, purpose, and questions for the evaluation.

SUMMARY

In summary, an evaluator has a large and varied toolbox of approaches to guide an evaluation's design. A single approach is seldom used in evaluation practice. Instead, an evaluator draws from more than one of these approaches to customize and adapt the evaluation to each context and set of questions posed by a client. In other words, one size does not fit all, and a skillful and knowledgeable evaluator will draw from these multiple approaches to focus and guide an evaluation. In the next chapter, I will discuss how you select and refine your approach based on the purpose of the evaluation and stakeholders' values and needs for information.

REFERENCES

Abruzzese, R. S. (1996). *Nursing staff development: Strategies for success* (2nd ed.). St. Louis: Mosby Year Book.

Alkin, M. C. (1991). Evaluation theory development II. In M. McLaughlin & D. Phillips (Eds.), *Evaluation and education at quarter century* (pp. 91–112). Chicago, IL: University of Chicago Press.

Alkin, M. C., & Christie, C. A. (2004). An evaluation theory tree. In M. Alkin (Ed.), *Evaluation roots* (pp. 12–66). Thousand Oaks, CA: Sage Publications

Bakken, L.L., Olson, C. A., Ross, J. M., Turco, M. G., Jackson, L. M., Murphy, W. (2015). *MM&I Phase I Evaluation Report.* Hanover, NH: Department of Medicine, Dartmouth-Hitchcock Medical Center.

Bjurulf, S., Vedung, E., & Larsson, C. G. (2012). A triangulation approach to impact evaluation. *Evaluation, 19(1),* 56–73.

Bledscoe, K. L., & Graham, J. A. (2005). The use of multiple evaluation approaches in program evaluation. *American Journal of Evaluation, 26(3),* 302–319.

Brousselle, A., & Champagne, F. (2011). Program theory evaluation: Logic analysis. *Evaluation and Program Planning, 34,* 69–78.

Cabrara, D., & Cabrara, L. (2015). *Systems thinking made simple: New hope for solving wicked problems.* New York, NY: Odyssean Press.

Carraccio, C., Englander, R., Van Melle, E., ten Cate, O., Lockyer, J., Chan, M-K., Frank, J. R., & Snell, L. S. (2016). Advancing Competency-Based Medical Education: A Charter for Clinician-Educators. *Academic Medicine, 91(5),* 645–649.

ten Cate, O., & Billett, S. (2014). Competency-based medical education: Origins, perspectives and potentialities. *Medical Education, 48,* 325–332.

Chen, H-T. (1990). *Theory-driven evaluations.* Newbury Park, CA: Sage Publications, Inc.

Chen, H-T. (1996). A comprehensive typology for program evaluation. *Evaluation Practice, 17(2),* 121–130.

Chen, H-T. (2005). *Practical program evaluation: Assessing and improving planning, imple-mentation, and effectiveness.* Thousand Oaks, CA: Sage Publications.

Chouinard, J. A. (2013). The case for participatory evaluation in an era of accounta-bility. *American Journal of Evaluation, 34(2),* 237–253.

Cousins, J. B., & Whitmore, E. (1998). Framing participatory evaluation. In E. Whitmore (Ed.), *Understanding and practicing participatory evaluation. New Directions in Evaluation, 80,* 3–23.

Cousins, J. B., Whitmore, E., & Shulha, L. (2012). Arguments for a common set of principles for collaborative inquiry in evaluation. *American Journal of Evaluation, 34(1)*, 7–22.

Dart, J., Petheram, R. J., & Straw W. (1998). *Review of evaluation in agricultural extension* (Publication No. 98/136). Barton, Australia: Rural Industries Research and Development Corporation.

DeSilets, L. D. (2010). Another look at evaluation models. *Journal of Continuing Education in Nursing, 41(1)*, 12–13.

Donaldson, S. I. (2007). *Program theory-driven evaluation science. Strategies and applications.* New York, NY: Lawrence Erlbaum Associates.

Dweck, C. S. (2007). *Mindset: The new psychology of success.* New York, NY: Ballantine Books.

Epstein, R. M., & Hundert, E. M. (2002). Defining and assessing professional competence, *JAMA, 287(2)*, 226–235.

Eoyang, G. H., & Holladay, R. J. (2013). *Adaptive action: Leveraging uncertainty in your organization.* Stanford, CA: Stanford Business Books.

Fetterman, D. M. (1994). Empowerment evaluation. *Evaluation Practice, 15(1)*, 1–15.

Fetterman, D. M., & Wandersman, A. (Eds.). (2005). *Empowerment evaluation principles in practice.* New York, NY: The Guilford Press.

Fitzpatrick, J. L., Sanders, J. R., & Worthen, B. R. (2011). *Program evaluation: Alternative approaches and practical guidelines* (4th ed.). Upper Saddle River, NJ: Pearson Education.

Funnell, S. C., & Rogers, P. J. (2011). *Purposeful program theory: Effective use of theories of change and logic models.* San Francisco, CA: Jossey-Bass Publishers.

Glasgow, R. E., Vogt, T. M., & Boles, S. M. (1999). Evaluating the public health impact of health promotion interventions: The RE-AIM framework. *American Journal of Public Health, 89(9)*, 1322–1327.

Guba, E., & Lincoln, Y. S. (1985). *Naturalistic inquiry.* Beverly Hills, CA: Sage Publications.

Guba, E. G., & Lincoln, Y. S. (1989). *Fourth generation evaluation.* Newbury Park, CA: Sage Publications.

Hargreaves, M. B., & Podems, D. (2012). Advancing systems thinking in evaluation: A review of four publications. *American Journal of Evaluation, 33(3)*, 462–470.

Hood, S. (2000). Commentary on deliberative democratic evaluation. In K. E. Ryan & L. DeStefano (Eds.), *Evaluation as a Democratic Process: Promoting Inclusion, Dialogue, and Deliberation. New Directions for Evaluation, 85*, 77–83.

House, E. R., & Howe, K. R. (1999). *Values in evaluation and social research.* Thousand Oaks, CA: Sage Publications.

House, E. R., & Howe, K. R. (2000). Deliberative democratic evaluation. In K. E. Ryan & L. DeStefano (Eds.). *Evaluation as a democratic process: Promoting inclusion, dialogue, and deliberation. New Directions in Evaluation, 85*, 3–12.

Lacey, A., & Murray, C. (2015). *Rethinking the regulatory environment of competency-based education.* Washington, DC: American Enterprise Institute. Retrieved from the American Enterprise Institute website: http://www.aei.org/publication/rethinking-the-regulatory-environment-of-competency-based-education/.

LaFrance, J., & Nichols, R. (2010). Reframing evaluation: Defining an indigenous evaluation framework. *The Canadian Journal of Program Evaluation, 23(2)*, 13–31.

King, J., & Stevahn, L. (2015). Competencies for program evaluators in light of adaptive action: What? So what? Now what? In J. W. Altschuld & M. Engle (Eds.),

Accreditation, certification, and credentialing: Relevant concerns for U.S. evaluators. New Directions for Evaluation, 145, 21–37.

Knowlton, L. W., & Phillips, C. C. (2009). *The logic model guidebook: Better strategies for great results.* Thousand Oaks, CA: Sage Publications.

Mertens, D. M. (2009). *Transformative research and evaluation.* New York, NY: The Guilford Press.

Mertens, D. M., & Wilson, A. T. (2012). *Program evaluation theory and practice: A comprehensive guide.* New York, NY: The Guilford Press.

Patton, M. Q. (1997). *Utilization-focused evaluation: The new century text* (3rd ed.). Thousand Oaks, CA: Sage Publications.

Patton, M. Q. (1994). Developmental evaluation. *Evaluation Practice, 15(3),* 311–319.

Patton, M. Q. (2004). The roots of utilization-focused evaluation. In M. Alkin (Ed.), *Evaluation roots* (pp. 276–292). Thousand Oaks, CA: Sage Publications.

Patton, M. Q. (2012). *Developmental evaluation: Applying complexity concepts to enhance innovation and use.* New York, NY: The Guilford Press.

Pawson, R., & Tilley, N. (1997). *Realistic evaluation.* Thousand Oaks, CA: Sage Publications.

Preskill, H., & Russ-Eft, D. (2005). *Building evaluation capacity: 72 activities for teaching and training.* Thousand Oaks, CA: Sage Publications.

Provus, M. M. (1971). *Discrepancy evaluation.* Berkeley, CA: McCutchan.

Schoonover Associates. (2003). *FAQ: Competency model building.* Retrieved from http://www.schoonover.com/schoonover-faqs.asp.

Shulha, L. M., Whitmore, E., Cousins, J. B., Gilbert, N., & Hudib, H. (2016). Introducing evidence-based principles to guide collaborative approaches to evaluation: Results of an empirical process. *American Journal of Evaluation, 37(2),* 193–215.

Stake, R. E. (1973). Program evaluation, particularly responsive evaluation. Keynote address at the conference "New Trends in Evaluation." Institute of Education, University of Goteborg, Sweden, October 1973. In G. F. Madaus, M. S. Scriven, & D. L. Stufflebeam (Eds.), *Evaluation models: Viewpoints on educational and human services evaluation.* (1983, pp. 287–288). Boston, MA: Kluwer-Nijhoff Publishing.

Stufflebeam, D. L. (1983). The CIPP model for program evaluation. In G. F. Madaus, M. S. Scriven, & D. L. Stufflebeam (Eds.), *Evaluation modes: Viewpoints on educational and human services evaluation* (pp. 117–141). Boston, MA: Kluwer-Nijhoff Publishing.

Stufflebeam, D. L. (2013). The CIPP evaluation model: Status, origin, development, use and theory. In M. C. Alkin (Ed.), *Evaluation roots: A wider perspective of theorists' views and influences* (2nd ed., pp. 243–260). Thousand Oaks, CA: Sage Publications.

Tyler, R. W. (1942). General statement on evaluation. *Journal of Educational Research, 35,* 492–501.

Weiss, C. H. (1997). How can theory-based evaluation make greater headway? *Evaluation Review, 21(4),* 501–524.

Williams, B., & Hummelbrunner, R. (2011). *Systems concepts in action; A practitioner's toolkit.* Stanford, CA: Stanford University Press.

CHAPTER 4

Planning a Program Evaluation

In this chapter, I describe an evaluation plan as a major component of a program plan and discuss why it is important that it be linked to program elements. To begin, it is important to understand the broad *context* of a program. This understanding is important for determining what is valued by the organization(s) or communities that are planning or conducting the program, for whom the evaluation is important, whom the program influences, why it is being planned or implemented the way it is, what traditions ground the program, and who will be supportive and involved (or not) in the program planning or evaluation process (i.e., stakeholders).

Common to both program and evaluation planning and implementation is the involvement of *stakeholders*. Stakeholder involvement is important for increasing the relevance of a program for its participants, gaining administrative buy-in for successful implementation and financial support, executing a program in a manner that aligns with staff roles and responsibilities, and communicating with and engaging personnel who are critical to the design, implementation, and evaluation of a program.

Stakeholders are key to providing various perspectives that are knowledgeable of or can inform a program's *purpose, goals,* and *activities*. Moreover, knowledge of these program components (i.e., purpose, goals, and activities) is necessary for helping to focus and align an evaluation plan with a program plan. A *theory* about how a program affects changes in learners, organizations, or communities helps to situate the program within a defined context, establish relationships among program components, and give clarity to a program's elements for evaluation and assessment.

Evaluation questions are the primary anchor for an evaluation plan and reflect the various program elements and processes described in a theory. These questions are best determined by engaging stakeholders in a dialogue that draws from their various perspectives and addresses questions and needs of importance to them. By engaging stakeholders in discussions about the program and any questions associated with it, you can begin to *focus the evaluation* and *establish its purpose, goals, scope,* and *use.* Once these main elements are clearly established, you can design an evaluation and draft a *proposal* or *contract* to describe a plan that will clarify and guide your work.

UNDERSTANDING THE EVALUATION'S CONTEXT

Before you begin any program evaluation, it is necessary to have a thorough understanding of the evaluation's context. I suggest that you begin by having conversations with one or two of the program's key stakeholders. These stakeholders are typically program directors, program coordinators, administrators, or individuals requesting the evaluation. A context analysis probes for information about the program and its context to help you make choices and decisions about the approaches and methods for a program evaluation. In essence, it helps evaluators answer the question, "What evaluation approach provides the highest quality and most actionable evidence in which contexts?" (Rog, 2012, p. 26). A context analysis also helps you to understand the culture in which the evaluation will be conducted, so that it is sensitive to issues such as political, organizational, racial, ethnic, and community dynamics, among others (Fitzpatrick, 2012). Rog (2012) recommends that five "contexts" be considered when performing a context analysis: problem, program/intervention, decision-making, evaluation, and the broader context of the environment. Within these five areas, she suggests that seven dimensions be probed: physical, organizational, social, cultural, traditional, historical, and political. Within each of these dimensions and contexts, a series of questions could be asked to gain an in-depth understanding of the context surrounding a program evaluation. The questions would vary according to whether the context analysis is being done during the planning, implementation, or decision-making/use phase of an evaluation (Conner, Fitzpatrick, & Rog, 2012). Table 4.1 includes some examples of questions from my own experiences that I might pose within the contexts and dimensions suggested by Rog (2012) and at various phases of an evaluation.

A context analysis, therefore, requires careful and attentive listening skills to understand various factors that will influence the evaluation. Because I advocate participatory approaches to evaluation, I typically involve multiple stakeholders when I perform an informal or formal context analysis. This process can typically take a few days to two to three months or more and often continues as an evaluation is planned, implemented, and used. Consequently,

Table 4.1. QUESTION MATRIX FOR A CONTEXT ANALYSIS

	Problem	Program	Decision-making	Evaluation	Broader Environment
Physical	Is the physical location influencing the problem or reason for the evaluation?	Where is the program being held? Why is it held at that location?	Who made the decision to hold the program at its location and why?	Are there sufficient resources (space, personnel) to support the evaluation?	Is this the ideal location for the program for the targeted participants?
Organizational	What stakeholders determined the problem or need for the program?	What organizations are involved in designing, planning, and implementing the program? What resources does each organization bring to the program?	Who are the organization's key decision-makers?	Are staff training in evaluation? What staff might be helpful in performing the evaluation, and to what extent can or would they be willing to engage?	How are the organizations situated in the community? Are they viewed favorably? To which organizations are they linked?
Social	What social issue or problem is necessitating the program/intervention? What are the cultural considerations surrounding the issue?	Is the program conceptualized in a way that is sensitive to cultural backgrounds and needs?	Who are the decision-makers? How will their decisions influence the social issue? What assumptions are they making about the issue?	Who benefits from the program and how? How will the information be used by key stakeholders?	To what extent does the community support efforts to resolve this social issue? Who are advocates and champions from the community?
Culture	Does the problem or issue involve marginalized groups?	Does program planning involve stakeholders representing a variety of cultural groups, especially those targeted for the program?	Are stakeholders from various cultural groups involved in the decision-making?	Is the evaluation inclusive of stakeholders from important cultural groups?	Who holds power within the broader community and how does this influence various cultural groups?
Traditional	In what ways might cultural traditions be influencing the way the problem is perceived?	Are cultural traditions creating barriers or facilitators to program-related change?	How or in what ways do traditions influence program decision-making?	How will cultural or community traditions influence the evaluation approach or ways of data collection?	To what extent are community traditions shaping the program or effecting attitudes about intended changes?
Historical	How long has the organization or community been trying to tackle the issue?	How as the program evolved over time? What factors influenced program development?	Over time, how have decisions been made in the organization or community?	Has the program been evaluated before? What was learned and how was the information used?	To what extent have different programs been implemented to tackle the issue? What's been successful?
Political	In what ways have political agendas helped to shape the problem?	Who or what group determined the program was needed and how was it determined?	Who holds decision-making power for the program or organization?	To what extent will political agendas try to influence the evaluation or its findings?	Whose needs are being served in the community and who decides?

I typically begin these conversations by asking two to three key stakeholders the following questions:

> Why do you want this program evaluation?
> What do you hope to learn from the program evaluation?
> How do you intend to use the results of this program evaluation?
> Who cares about the evaluation's findings?
> Who supports or does not support this evaluation?
> What is the budget and time frame for the evaluation?
> Tell me about the program being evaluated.
>> Who is involved?
>> Where, when, and how frequently does it occur?
>> Who benefits from the program?
>> Who is excluded from the program and why?
>> Why is the program being implemented? Whose needs does it serve?
>> Is the program evaluated or was any evaluation done to inform program planning?
>> What are the intended outcomes for the program?
>> Who values this program and why?
>> Who has power and control over programming decisions?

After gaining this information, I reach out to some of the people mentioned in my discussions with these few key stakeholders and pose the same questions. In other words, through these key stakeholders, I identify some additional stakeholders and ask them the same questions in an iterative process. By doing so, I gain a variety of perspectives and identify the best approaches for the program evaluation. I am also careful to note my observations related to political influences, people who are referred to as champions, the interactions of coworkers, the physical space and location of the program, and other contextual factors. In the next section, I will talk about additional ways to identify key stakeholders and how to engage them in the evaluation's design and planning.

IDENTIFYING AND ENGAGING STAKEHOLDERS

Stakeholders are the individuals or groups of people who have a vested interest or "stake" in a program and its evaluation. Common examples include participants, program planners and coordinators, instructional designers, program administrators or directors, funders, board members, members of the community, and other program beneficiaries. In early phases of a program and evaluation design, it is important to determine a program's key stakeholders and explicitly identify their "stake" in the program. Williams and

Hummelbrunner (2011, p. 110) recommend that four key questions be asked to guide a stakeholder analysis:

Who is affected by the strategy, that is, the program?
Who has an interest in it?
Who can affect its adoption, execution, or implementation?
Who cares about it?

By clearly articulating the stakeholders' interests and stake in the program, you begin to understand the program's context and can narrow the focus and scope of an evaluation. Shown in Figure 4.1 is a checklist adopted from Fitzpatrick, Sanders, and Worthen (2011, p. 289) that is useful for determining key stakeholders in program planning and evaluation. As you consider the list of entities along the left-hand column, you may wish to swap out the word "evaluation" for "program," and vice versa, in order to gain a comprehensive list of the program evaluation's stakeholders. Once identified, stakeholders' perspectives during the planning process are critical for engaging their buy-in and facilitating or providing resources for the programming and evaluation efforts.

Often, you must begin your conversations with known stakeholders, such as program directors, to determine the full scope of individuals or groups who have a stake in the program. While doing so, you can gain their impressions of the program, what they expect from it, what questions they may have about the program, and how they perceive it working to impact change. As you speak to them, you also will learn about the political, economic, and physical context of the program. This information is helpful in understanding how these contextual dynamics may influence your programming efforts.

Stakeholders can be engaged in several ways. One-on-one interviews or discussions with them can reveal personal biases that may be critical for negotiating some of the more political challenges of program delivery or evaluation and for determining where, with whom, or when obstacles might be confronted in the planning process. When conducted with those who are in positions to provide resources for the program, interviews provide opportunities to discuss the specific resources that will be needed for the evaluation. Small group meetings or focus groups with specific groups of stakeholders can provide an efficient means of collecting the perspectives of those most affected by the program, such as potential program participants or community groups. You also will want to explore stakeholders' opinions about evaluation and how they may or may not support efforts or provide resources to evaluate the program. Surveys of various stakeholder groups also may help to gain their perspectives and provide insights into the planning process. Knowing these contextual elements of a program is important for understanding the stakeholders' values and beliefs about evaluation

Evaluation Audience Checklist					
Entity to be Evaluated	(Check all appropriate boxes)				
Individuals, Groups, or Agencies Needing the Evaluation's Findings	To Make Policy	To Make Operational Decisions	To Provide Input to Evaluation	To React	For Interests Only
Developer of the program					
Funder of the program					
Person/agency who identified the local need					
Boards/agencies who approved delivery of the program at local level					
Local funder					
Other providers of resources (facilities, supplies, in-kind contributions)					
Top managers of agencies delivering the program					
Program managers					
Program deliverers					
Sponsor of the evaluation					
Direct clients of the program					
Agencies who manage other programs for this client group					
Groups excluded from the evaluation					
Groups losing power as a result of use of the program					
Groups suffering from lost opportunities as a result of the program					
Public/community members					
Others:					

Figure 4.1. Checklist of Potential Stakeholders and Audiences. Reproduced by permission from Jody L. Fitzpatrick, James R. Sanders, and Blaine R. Worthen. *Program evaluation: Alternative approaches and practical guidelines* (4th ed.) (Upper Saddle River, NJ: Pearson Education, Inc., 2011).

and for selecting an evaluation approach that will likely gain their support. Stakeholders also can be helpful in the implementation of a program and its evaluation. They can serve as advocates, group facilitators, instructors, data collectors, reporters, and disseminators. I encourage you to think about ways to involve stakeholders and engage them in a program's planning, implementation, and evaluation as much as possible.

A PROGRAM'S PURPOSE, GOALS, AND ACTIVITIES

As you analyze context, you will want to gain an understanding of the program's purpose, goals, and activities. A program's *purpose* establishes the reason(s) for developing and implementing it. Purpose statements often reflect a community problem, organizational need, or gap in learners' knowledge, skills, or attitudes that the program is trying to address. For example, if a program's *goal* or aim is to reduce a high teen pregnancy rate in a community (i.e., an *impact*), it might be designed to target middle-school youth with a *purpose* to empower youth to make wise decisions about contraceptive use. A program's objectives "provide clear statements of the anticipated results to be achieved" through the program (Caffarella, 2002, p. 156). Therefore, program objectives can be reframed as the *intended* outcomes (i.e., resulting changes) desired by its stakeholders. Extending the previous example, the objectives of the program might be to (1) engage youth as peer-educators to encourage and practice open communication among participants, (2) create a climate that is sensitive to and respectful toward cultural values about contraception, and (3) increase the number/proportion of youth who use contraceptive devices and/or practices by 20% in the year following the program. Notice how the first two objectives reflect the educational *process* in contrast to the third objective, which represents an expected *outcome*. Embedded in these statements are clues about the type of evaluation design that is needed. Program objectives also become a guide for defining a set of learning or behavioral objectives and designing activities that will help to achieve them.

By definition, programs are a set of *activities* that promote or facilitate learning and behavioral change among participants. For example, "engaging youth as peer-educators" and "creating a sensitive and respectful climate" as reflected in the program's objectives, are examples of program strategies or activities that are intended to facilitate the intended process outcomes of "youth who openly communicate about contraception" and "youth who acknowledge and respect their peers' cultural values toward contraception."

When designing educational programs, *learning objectives* are used to guide the selection and design of learning activities and the specific content that each activity will contain. Learning objectives are defined as the knowledge, skills, and attitudes that participants develop as the result of engaging in a program's learning activities. In evaluation terms, learning objectives can be defined as a set of *intended* short-term outcomes. *Outcomes* are *changes* that occur as the result of a set of activities (Knowlton & Phillips, 2009). Personally, I prefer to think of learning objectives as evidence that the program's activities have been conducted (i.e., *outputs*), rather than as outcomes of program activities, because participants must apply and use what they learn in order for change to occur. Defined this way, *learning outcomes* are the higher order changes (e.g., transfer of knowledge and behavioral changes) that are expected as the result of participating in a program's activities. If successfully achieved, most of a program's objectives should be accomplished.

To illustrate this point, I will elaborate on the aforementioned hypothetical program by using the second program objective, "create a climate that is sensitive to and respectful toward cultural values about contraception," as a specific example. From a program designer's perspective, I would want to achieve this objective by acknowledging different views toward contraception and procreation among different racial, ethnic, gender, and religious cultural groups. I also might want to acknowledge various perspectives about the co-existence of procreation and contraception and engage youth participants in discussions about how this could occur. To achieve this program objective, then, *instructors* or *facilitators* will . . .

> Describe various cultural views toward procreation and conception,
> Engage youth in discussions about how their backgrounds influence their views on contraception and procreation, and
> Challenge youth to think about how they would handle cultural differences when confronted with contraceptive choices.

These *sub objectives* or *instructional objectives* help to define learning activities (e.g., discussion) and content (contraceptive values and beliefs among various cultural groups) for this program. From a learner's perspective, I would expect that learners would come away with *knowledge* of how their own cultural backgrounds influence their and others' beliefs about contraception, respectful *attitudes* toward others' desires for contraception, and the *skills* to communicate openly and respectfully with sexual partners about their desire and preferences for contraception. So, learning objectives for this program would be articulated as follows:

> *At the end of this program, learners will . . .*
> Explain how contraception and procreation differ among racial, ethnic, gender, and religious groups,
> Describe how cultural differences might influence contraceptive preferences or choices, and

From a scenario, explain how they would handle cultural differences when confronted with contraceptive choices.

Notice how these and the previous lists of objectives (i.e., instructor and learner) were derived through different perspectives or orientations. These orientations represent two perspectives toward achieving a *program's* objectives. Both perspectives are important and both of them align with the program objective to "create a climate that is sensitive to and respectful toward cultural values about contraception." In evaluation terms, all three perspectives can be associated with the primary *unit of analysis*—the program. The instructor and learners are *sources* of information for evaluating the program. Typically, the instructor's objectives are not tracked in a program evaluation. One exception might be a study of a program's fidelity or implementation. In this case, an evaluator would assess the extent to which the instructor is achieving his or her own objectives in addition to those of the learner and overall program. Notice, too, that I have defined sets of outcomes (program and learning) that can be assessed in an evaluation of a program's effectiveness. However, the evaluation questions posed by stakeholders may not suggest an evaluation of this type; therefore, it is necessary to determine the stakeholders' questions and needs for information before designing an evaluation plan. Before doing so, it can be helpful to engage key stakeholders in a process of describing a theory for how they think the program will work to produce the desired changes or effects. The next session revisits and describes the utility of program theory, how it is developed, and how it has been expanded to a systems level in recent years.

USING THEORY TO FOCUS AN EVALUATION

As described in Chapter 3, program theories provide conceptual models or frameworks that describe how the elements of a program relate to one another to produce desired changes in learners, organizations, or communities. Program theory has dominated evaluation practice in recent years; however, collective impact models and systems theory is beginning to permeate the evaluation field as demands for information become broader, more sophisticated, and highly complex. I will begin this section with a description of program theory and how it is used in practice; then, I will introduce and describe collective impact, briefly describe systems theory, and provide examples of situations that suggest how they can be applied and used.

Program Theory and Logic Models. Program theory is a useful tool for defining and establishing factors and processes that may be assessed in your efforts to evaluate a program. Simply put, a program theory describes the associations between what we *do* as part of a program and what we *get* as the result of doing it (Knowlton & Phillips, 2009). Theories described in the academic literature may be used as a basis for developing a program's theory or incorporated into a theory that is created in collaboration with stakeholders. For example, when I and my colleagues studied clinical research self-efficacy, we used social cognitive career theory (Lent, Brown, & Hackett, 1994) to inform our work and the development and evaluation of an educational intervention (Bakken, Byars-Winston, Gundermann, Ward, Slattery, King, Scott, & Taylor, 2010). Program theories also can be developed inductively through qualitative studies of existing programs in order to determine a theory about what is actually occurring versus what was planned or intended.

Multiple models can be used as tools to develop a program's theory (Funnell & Rogers, 2011). Common to program evaluation and used across many disciplines are logic models (discussed in Chapter 3). Because logic models are commonly used across disciplines as a tool for developing program theory, their application and use are elaborated upon in this chapter.

To specify some of the long-term changes expected from a program, it is helpful to ask the question, "If you achieve the program's goals and program participants learn, what do you expect will happen to individuals, within organizations, or in communities?" This question is one that is typically referred to by evaluators and researchers as the "So what?" question. This question is very important because it forces us to think beyond the immediate or short-term outcomes of a program to the longer-term and broader outcomes and impacts on those whom a program serves. This is why efforts to develop a program theory are useful and important.

When working with stakeholders to develop logic models, it is often helpful to begin with "the end in mind" and work backward to establish a rationale for how a program will work to produce the anticipated or desired changes. This backward process often calls into question the original activities specified for the program because it initiates a discussion about what a program's stakeholders should be doing to achieve the desired change (i.e., "get"). Logic models are also helpful for reflecting on *intended* program outcomes and the *actual* or possible *unintended* outcomes that may occur as part of the program's implementation.

To critique a program's theory, whether developed using a logic model or other model, it is also helpful and important to examine some of the assumptions that underlie that theory. By examining the underlying assumptions of a program theory, potential roadblocks (e.g., a targeted participant's ability to travel to the program's location or planned activities that misalign with cultural norms) to the program's success at achieving the desired outcomes are revealed. Once established, a program's logic model provides a useful tool for aiding discussions with stakeholders about the purpose of an evaluation, what questions come to mind about the program, and how findings of an evaluation will be used. These discussions lay the groundwork for developing an evaluation plan.

Collective Impact. Frequently, a program is one of several programs aimed at achieving an impact within an organization or community. Often, these impacts are defined by an organization's strategic plan. For example, a group of graduate programs aimed at preparing innovative practitioners and researchers who will improve the efficiency and cost-effectiveness of healthcare delivery and management. So, the goal or expected outcome of a graduate program preparing practitioners to work in public health settings (Program A1) might be that practitioners are able to analyze the effectiveness of existing community programs to provide cost-effective health care. On the other hand, researchers educated in this graduate program (Program A2) might be prepared to develop and study more efficient and cost-effective models for providing basic health care services (e.g., prenatal care or immunizations). Notice that each program prepares students toward different outcomes, but both outcomes support the impact that graduate education is trying to achieve for this organization. More broadly, this organization might also have a quality improvement office that is working independently to change the way physicians practice so that they provide more cost-effective health care (Program B). Again, the desired impact is the same, but the programs, strategies, or mechanisms to create this impact are different and have different goals or intended outcomes. In a community setting, programs to inform the general public about ways to manage their own health in order to reduce healthcare spending as an outcome toward cost-effective health care may be in existence (Program C). All these programs have the desired impact of reducing the costs of health care in the community—some more directly than others, but each program uses different strategies for creating outcomes that will contribute to the overall desired impact. If this is the case in your settings, I encourage you to consider using systems-oriented approaches or a collective theory of change for the organization's or community's set of programs.

To successfully achieve a *collective impact,* five key conditions are necessary: (1) a shared vison for change (i.e., common agenda), (2) shared measurement systems, (3) mutually reinforcing activities, (4) continuous communication, and (5) a backbone support organization (Kania & Kramer, 2011). Two of these conditions (shared vision/agenda and mutually reinforcing activities) resemble those common to the "do → get" logic of program theory and one of them (shared measurement systems) can be directly tied to evaluation. By applying modeling approaches commonly used to develop program theory, one could envision a theory of collective impact (a desired "get") to consist of multiple programs or mutually reinforcing activities (the "do") designed to achieve a shared vision (presumably synonymous with a desired collective impact) in several ways. In this section, I offer three linear ways to theorize collective impact as a baseline.

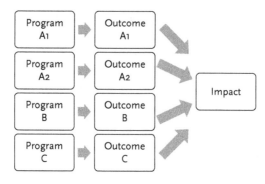

Figure 4.2. Independent Model of Collective Impact.

One way to conceptualize a theory of collective impact is to think about how the goals/outcomes achieved by each autonomously functioning program contribute to the desired collective impact (Figure 4.2). Viewed this way, the activities used by each program are independent, and they lead to independently determined outcomes toward achieving the collective impact and shared vision of change.

In an alternative model, each program contributes separately to achieving a common or shared set of goals aimed at making an impact, as illustrated in Figure 4.3. Viewed in this way, each program's individual set of activities would need to be mutually reinforcing and produce outcomes that serve as benchmarks toward achieving a collective impact. Funders typically use this type of model when evaluating the efforts of multiple grantees toward a collective change.

A third way to conceptualize a collective impact model is to envision each program as an activity among a set of activities aimed at achieving a collective

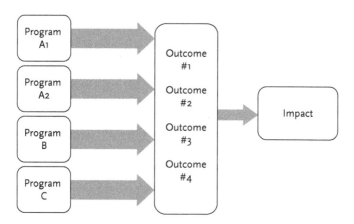

Figure 4.3. Shared Outcomes Model of Collective Impact.

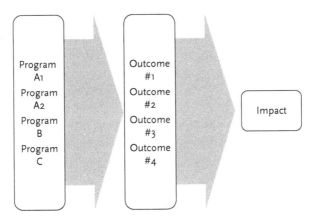

Figure 4.4. Integrated Model of Collective Impact.

set of outcomes toward a specific impact (Figure 4.4). This model views programs and outcomes with the least amount of independence and requires the most amount of collaborative effort and collective visioning among stakeholders to create the desired impact.

In all three models, a shared measurement system, supportive backbone organization, and continuous communication are key to effectively producing a collective change. As an example of a collective model of change, Woodhouse and colleagues (Woodhouse et al., 2013) illustrate a model for a Comprehensive Asthma Management Program and describe the utility of interfacing this model with the Plan-Do-Study-Act cycle for improving the quality of this program. These efforts require a significant amount of commitment to ongoing communication and collaboration. In practice, the more integrated and collaborative the group's efforts, the more likely they are to achieve a collective impact successfully (Kramer, Parkhurst, & Vaidyanathan, 2009). In my experience, however, problems occur when groups within a collective model have different visions of achieving collective impact, or their programs are at different stages of the development or implementation process.

The three hypothetical frameworks for collective impact illustrated in this chapter reflect highly structured and linear models for a system of activities or programs oriented toward changes in society. Systems theorists would argue that these models are oversimplified because programs and their associated outcomes and impacts rarely occur in ways they are conceptualized (Friedman, 2001; McDonald, 2015). In other words, programs often are not implemented as planned. Unanticipated outcomes occur. Program outcomes are produced at different times and in different ways depending on the organization that implements them. Program theories omit critical elements that influence programs' effects and so on. In other words, programs often don't happen in the way we theorize them. Traditionally, evaluators have managed this level of uncertainty and complexity in programming efforts by carefully monitoring a program's development and implementation through mixed methods approaches and procedures such as that provided through logic analysis (Brousselle & Champagne, 2011).

Pawson and Tilley (1997) proposed that evaluators abandon causal linear models for evaluating outcomes and impact in favor of models and evaluation approaches based on scientific realism. "To be realistic is to acknowledge that there is no universal 'logic of evaluation', no absolute 'science of valuing', no general 'warranty for decision-making' applicable to all judgements" (p. xiii). This approach requires a shift of thinking from outcomes that can be *attributed* to programs to outcomes for which programs have *contributed*. Therefore, outcomes are evaluated by understanding the mechanisms and context from which they are derived. These evaluations typically require both qualitative and quantitative forms of data collection and their associated analytical methods. In the final chapter of this book, I will describe realistic evaluation in greater detail and discuss how it can provide one way of evaluating systems-level change.

EVALUABILITY ASSESSMENT

Assuming that a theory or conceptual framework has been determined with key stakeholders, it is time to take a step back and ask yourself whether or not the program is *ready to* be evaluated. Not all programs are ready for evaluation nor is it necessary to evaluate all programs all the time. Fitzpatrick, Sanders, and Worthen (2011, p. 269) describe four conditions necessary for meaningful evaluation:

> Program goals and priority information needs are well defined (including agreement on performance criteria),
> Program objectives are plausible,
> Relevant performance data can be obtained at reasonable cost, and
> Intended users of the evaluation have agreed on how they will use the information. (Wholey, 2004, p. 34)

These criteria can be summarized with four short words: necessity, plausibility, feasibility, and utility. To determine a program's readiness for evaluation, an *evaluability assessment* (Wholey, 1987, 2004) can be performed using the following major steps listed in Box 4.1 (Fitzpatrick, Sanders, & Worthen, 2011, p. 269):

Figure 4.5 provides a useful 10-step checklist for guiding this process and a determining a program's evaluation readiness.

Box 4.1. STEPS IN DETERMINING A PROGRAM'S READINESS FOR EVALUATION

STEP 1. Clarify the intended program model or theory.
STEP 2. Examine the program in implementation to determine whether it matches the program model and could, conceivably, achieve the program goals and objectives.
STEP 3. Explore various evaluation approaches to determine the degree to which they meet stakeholders' information needs and are feasible to implement.
STEP 4. Agree on evaluation priorities and intended uses of the study.

Once you determine that a program is ready to be evaluated, you can begin to develop an evaluation plan. This plan begins by determining the purpose and use for the program evaluation.

AN EVALUATION'S PURPOSE AND USE

It is essential that you gain clarity about the purpose for evaluating a program or set of programs. Is it to learn about ways to improve a program? Do stakeholders want to know if a program was implemented as planned? Do they want to know how effective a program was at facilitating learning and behavioral change? Do they want to know what impact a program has in an organization or community? Do stakeholders want to know if a program is effective at facilitating a change in learners, organizations, or communities before making a decision about whether the program should continue? An evaluation's purpose is different from the purpose of a program and should be clearly understood before an evaluation is planned or implemented. Using my earlier example of the youth contraception program, the program's purpose was to *empower youth to make wise decisions about contraceptive use*, but the purpose of an evaluation would likely be to determine whether the program is effectively contributing to the impact of *reducing a high teen pregnancy rate* in the community. A purpose statement for an evaluation communicates the reason why the evaluation is being conducted, and it should be stated in a clearly articulated manner. If an evaluation does not have a clear purpose, it should not be conducted.

At the same time, you should be clear about how stakeholders will *use* the findings of an evaluation study once it is completed. Do they wish to use the findings to make decisions about a program's continuance? Do they wish to

		Check One for Each Item	
		Yes	No
Step 1	Is there a contractual requirement to evaluate? (If yes, initiate the evaluation; if no, go to step 2.)		___
Step 2	Does the object of the evaluation have enough impact or importance to warrant formal evaluation? (If yes, go to step 3; if no, formal evaluation is unnecessary and you should discontinue further use of this checklist.)		___
Step 3	Is there sufficient consensus among stakeholders on the model for the program? Its goals and objectives? (If yes, go to step 4; if no, consider a needs assessment study.)		___
Step 4	If the program has begun, are its actions consistent with the program model? Is achievement of goal(s) feasible? (If yes, go to step 5; if not, consider a needs assessment or monitoring evaluation to study program modifications.)		___
Step 5	Is the proposed evaluation feasible given existing human and fiscal resources and data availability? (If yes, go to step 6; if no, find more resources before proceeding or revise the scope of the plan.)		___
Step 6	Do the major stakeholders agree on the intended use of the evaluation? (If yes, go to step 7; if no, discontinue or focus on those stakeholders who can use the information effectively.)		___
Step 7	Are the stakeholders in a position to use the information productively? (If yes, go to step 8; if no, discontinue or focus on other stakeholders who can use the information to make decisions or take action.)		___
Step 8	Will the decisions of your primary stakeholders be made exclusively on other bases and be uninfluenced by the evaluation data? (If yes, evaluation is superfluous – discontinue; if no, go to step 9.)		___
Step 9	Is it likely that the evaluation will provide dependable information? (If yes, go to step 10; if no, discontinue.)		___
Step 10	Is the evaluation likely to meet acceptable standards of propriety? (If yes, go to summary. If not, consider other means of data collection or discontinue.)		___
Summary:	Based on steps 1–10 above, should an evaluation be conducted?		

Figure 4.5. Checklist for determining a program's readiness for evaluation. Reproduced by permission of Jody L. Fitzpatrick, James R. Sanders, and Blaine R. Worthen, *Program evaluation: Alternative approaches and practical guidelines* (Upper Saddle River, NJ: Pearson Education, 2011).

use the findings to support additional or future funding? Would stakeholders like to use the evaluation's findings to make judgments about the best way to implement a program? Do they want to use the evaluation's findings to demonstrate a program's success to a governing board or other administrative group? These and other reasons for doing evaluation and using its findings are important and should be explicit among a program's stakeholders. Therefore, I encourage you to always write a statement that clearly conveys an evaluation's purpose and how its findings will be used. Here's an example:

> *The purpose of this evaluation is to determine whether the teen contraception program is effective at reducing the community's teen pregnancy rate over the next five years. The results will be used to inform future program funding and continuance.*

An evaluation can serve more than one purpose, so you may have more than one intended use for the evaluation's findings. Multiple purposes tend to expand the scope of an evaluation, so be sure that adequate resources and time are provided to meet those expanded demands. Stakeholders who are insistent on broadening the scope of a program evaluation are great targets for invitations to be involved in participant recruitment, data collection, and reporting and disseminating the evaluation's findings. Some stakeholders may volunteer their time to be involved in later phases of the evaluation simply because they are interested in them. Others may volunteer because they wish to influence the findings or the ways findings are reported. Again, be cautious and rely on the *Program Evaluation Standards* (Yarbrough et al., 2011) and AEA's *Guiding Principles for Evaluators* (American Evaluation Association, 2004) to support ethical and fair practices. I don't wish to paint a negative image of stakeholders. Most of them are very helpful, supportive, and cooperative. When you least expect it, however, you may be confronted with at least one of these situations, and these tips are my effort to prepare you for these instances should they occur.

Another critical component of an evaluation plan is the *evaluation questions*. The next section will discuss why they are so important and why they are necessary to maintain a focus and scope for the evaluation. The purpose, use, and questions for an evaluation provide an anchor for other components of an evaluation plan (Figure 4.6). These elements are crucial for establishing the focus and direction for an evaluation.

EVALUATION QUESTIONS

After the evaluation's purpose, goals, and use are clearly defined and articulated, it is time to refine your list of stakeholders' evaluation questions and work with them to prioritize them so that a limited number of questions can be answered through your program evaluation. When working with stakeholders and clients, their evaluation questions are typically vague and often posed in a manner that cannot be immediately operationalized for analysis. For example, a program director or administrator might wish to ask, "Is

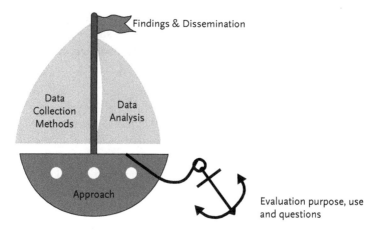

Figure 4.6. Figure illustrating how the evaluation purpose, use, and questions anchor an evaluation's approach, data collection methods, data analysis, findings, and dissemination.

the program successful?" To determine whether a program is successful, it is important to engage them in a conversation about what it means for the program to be successful. What does a successful program look like? By doing so, you establish a set of *criteria* from which to evaluate the program's success. Another question commonly asked in these days of accountability is, "How can I measure the outcomes of my program?" Your next question is, "What outcomes do you anticipate for your program?" This type of question typically stimulates a series of conversations as you attempt to determine the logical process by which the program produces desired outcomes. Some stakeholders may confuse outcomes with other program elements, such as activities or outputs. Often, this is evidenced through program evaluation forms in which the items referred to as learning outcomes are expressed as activities. My point in describing these various scenarios is that evaluation questions almost always come in a way that needs to be clarified and operationalized for an evaluation.

Once clarified, the evaluation questions can be prioritized with stakeholders. Fitzpatrick, Sanders, & Worthen (2011) provide an excellent matrix for prioritizing evaluation questions when working with stakeholders (Figure 4.7). Briefly, the parameters or criteria used to prioritize evaluation questions include the feasibility of time and resources needed to answer the question, the extent to which information gleaned by answering the question will be of major interest to stakeholders and help to influence decisions or events, and whether the question's answers will provide information that has sustainable value. Again, evaluation questions are the primary anchor for an evaluation. Once established and prioritized, they determine the focus, scope, and information collected for the evaluation.

	Evaluation Question
Would the evaluation question...	*1 2 3 4 5 ... n*
1. Be of interest to key audiences?	_____
2. Reduce present uncertainty?	_____
3. Yield important information?	_____
4. Be of continuing (not fleeting) interest?	_____
5. Be critical to the study's scope and comprehensiveness?	_____
6. Have an impact on the course of events?	_____
7. Be answerable in terms of	_____
1. Financial and human resources?	_____
2. Time?	_____
3. Available methods and technology?	

Figure 4.7. Matrix for Ranking or Selecting Evaluation Questions. Reproduced by permission from Jody L. Fitzpatrick, James R. Sanders, and Blaine R. Worthen, *Program evaluation: Alternative approaches and practical guidelines* (Upper Saddle River, NJ: Pearson Education, 2011).

Often, stakeholders will be tempted by interesting and emergent information that threatens the focus or scope of the evaluation during its implementation. If this information is unrelated or unhelpful for answering an evaluation question, remind the stakeholder(s) of the evaluation questions and discourage them from changing course. An evaluation gone off-course will expend valuable time, resources, and energy. One of the best ways to avoid or manage such an occurrence, is to develop a formal or informal written evaluation plan that is shared with all key stakeholders before an evaluation begins. Written evaluation plans are not only helpful for maintaining the scope and focus of the evaluation, but help to clarify and codify roles, responsibilities, expectations, processes, and procedures prior to the evaluation's commencement.

EVALUATION PROPOSALS AND CONTRACTS

Another helpful step in planning for an evaluation is to prepare a written proposal, memo of understanding, or contract that describes as many of its components as possible. Early drafts of this document help to clarify each component of an evaluation plan and facilitate clear communication and understanding among the evaluation's key stakeholders, which is the reason I discuss proposals and contracts in this chapter. Their details vary depending on the complexity, scope, and context of the evaluation. Stufflebeam (1999) provides a comprehensive list of items to include in an evaluation contract or plan, which I use as a guide or checklist when preparing formal contracts. I also use it to select the most helpful and relevant items for a less formal evaluation plan. Minimally, I recommend that all evaluation plans contain the eight elements listed in Box 4.2. Although I have discussed only three of those elements, I present them here as a way of emphasizing your goals in creating a clear evaluation plan that both you and the program's stakeholders are comfortable with implementing.

O'Sullivan (2004) recommends that an evaluation proposal or plan also include a statement describing the qualifications of personnel who will conduct the study and the organizational resources that will be available to them. Often, I will refer to the *Program Evaluation Standards* in my plan, so it is clear that I am upholding professional standards of practice. If you do this, I recommend including a brief copy of the standards in the appendices of your plan.

When incorporating evaluation plans within program grant proposals, it is important that an evaluation plan be aligned with the goals and purpose of the grant in addition to that of the program you are evaluating (which should also align with them). It is also important that the evaluation plan include all components required in the request for application or proposal and include

---

Box 4.2. EIGHT ELEMENTS TO INCLUDE IN AN EVALUATION PLAN

1. A description of the *object* (i.e., the program) of the evaluation and its *context*
2. Statements specifying the evaluation's *purpose, goals,* and *use*
3. A brief list of *evaluation questions* in prioritized order
4. *Evidence* and *indicators* for data collection
5. Data collection *methods* and *tools*
6. An analytical plan
7. Processes and procedures for *reporting* and *disseminating* findings
8. A management plan
   a. Roles and responsibilities of the evaluation team (which may include key stakeholders)
   b. Protection of participants as humans involved in an evaluation study
   c. A section on data ownership and who holds primary decision-making power over the evaluation
   d. A timeline with anticipated dates for deliverables (e.g., data summaries or interim reports)
   e. A budget

linkages between program outcomes and the goals or impact a funder is trying to achieve. Typically, I include the funder's desired goals, outcomes, or impacts as a component of a program theory or logic model in the proposed plan. These days, funders are very familiar with the language of an evaluator, but it is helpful to use language from the Request for Application (RFA) or Proposal (RFP) and clarify these terms in the plan's narrative by using parentheses, italics, or other ways of denoting their connections. For example, if a desired goal is to increase access to food for those in need and an outcome is defined as increased access to or placement of grocery or thrift stores in specific community locations, you might write the following in a grant's narrative:

> *"Increase the proportion of grocery or thrift stores located in impoverished neighborhoods of Clark City from 20% to 80% in five years (outcome)"*

You might also follow it with a statement such as the following in order to link it to the funder's (a state agency) goals:

> *"This program will contribute to the state's goal to reduce food insecurity by 10% in five years by increasing nearby food sources in impoverished neighborhoods."*

The logic model, then, would look similar to the one shown in Figure 4.8 (in very simplified form). With a visual representation of the program's activities and outcomes in relation to the funder's goals and objectives, the funder is better able to understand the potential contribution of the proposed program to the intended use of and benefits from the funding.

Funders also typically look for a clear connection between program outcomes and their indicators and measures. These connections can be clearly identified by using matrices, such as the one shown in Table 4.2.

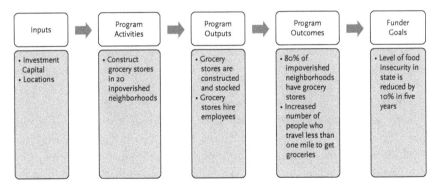

Figure 4.8. Example of a logic model for a program targeting an impact to reduce food insecurity by 10% in five years.

Table 4.2. MATRIX SHOWING THE RELATIONSHIPS OF INDICATORS, DATA
SOURCES/METHODS TO PROGRAM OUTCOMES

Program Outcome	Evidence/Indicator of Change	Data Source and Methods
80% of impoverished neighborhoods have grocery stores	• Pre/post mapping shows an increase in the number of dots that represent grocery stores • Dots appear in impoverished neighbors where previous "dots" did not exist.	Neighborhood maps of grocery stores
Increased number of people who travel less than one mile to get groceries	• Pre/post survey of the number of miles people travel to get groceries and the locations of those facilities relative to a person's residence	Survey of residents

In this example, you will notice that the program's outcomes also serve as indicators toward meeting the funder's goal to *reduce food insecurity by 10% in five years.*

Often, program planners do not incorporate sufficient funds in a grant's budget to adequately cover the evaluation that they desire. As a rule of thumb, an adequate program evaluation typically requires about 10% of the total budget for a program. Some funders will even request that a specific proportion of the budget include funds to support an evaluation. When planning and preparing a grant application to support a program, I strongly urge you to develop an evaluation plan (with or without an external evaluator) early in the process so that a reasonable budget for an evaluation can be incorporated into the proposal.

SUMMARY

In this chapter, I described the basic elements of a program design and plan that contains the elements of an evaluation plan. This chapter marks the major preparation and planning activities that lay the ground work for an evaluation's design. By now, you should have a clear idea about the program's context and its stakeholders, the stakeholder's questions and vision or theory about how the program works to bring about change, and an idea of what approach(es) you will use for the evaluation. The next five chapters will walk you through some of the choices you will make in designing the evaluation, including the methods you will use to collect and analyze information. As you may have gleaned by now, an evaluation plan generally comprises at least half of a thorough program plan. Therefore, it takes time and resources to develop it. Typically, an evaluation plan's data collection and analysis methods are somewhat vague when I share early drafts of an evaluation plan with key stakeholders. As discussions about the plan ensue with stakeholders, the plan is further refined to include specific elements of the evaluation's design. The next two chapters (Part II) cover key elements of an evaluation's design. Chapter 5 will cover several design options and guide you through their selection based on the evaluation's purpose and questions. Chapter 6 will provide guidance for choosing a sample, sampling methods, and data sources.

REFERENCES

American Evaluation Association. (2004). *Guiding principles for evaluators*. Retrieved from http://www.eval.org/p/cm/ld/fid=51

Bakken, L. L, Byars-Winston, A., Gundermann, D. M., Ward, E. C., Slattery, A., King, A., . . . Taylor, R. E. (2010). Effects of an educational intervention on female biomedical scientists' research self-efficacy. *Advances in Health Sciences Education, 15,* 167–183.

Brousselle, A., & Champagne, F. (2011). Program theory evaluation: Logic analysis. *Evaluation and Program Planning, 34,* 69–78.

Caffarella, R. S. (2002). *Planning Programs for Adult Learners* (2nd ed.). San Francisco: Jossey-Bass.

Conner, R. F., Fitzpatrick, J. L., & Rog, D. J. (2012). A first step forward: Context assessment. In D. J. Rog, J. L. Fitzpatrick, & R. F. Conner (Eds.), *Context: A framework for its influence on evaluation practice. New Directions for Evaluation, 135,* 89–105.

Funnell, S. C., & Rogers, P. J. (2011). *Purposeful program theory: Effective use of theories of change and logic models.* San-Francisco: Jossey-Bass Publishers.

Fitzpatrick, J. L. (2012). An introduction to context and its role in evaluation practice. In D. J. Rog, J. L. Fitzpatrick, & R. F. Conner (Eds.), *Context: A framework for its influence on evaluation practice. New Directions for Evaluation, 135,* 7–24.

Fitzpatrick, J. L., Sanders J. R., & Worthen, B. R. (2011). *Program evaluation: Alternative approaches and practical guidelines* (4th ed.). Upper Saddle River, NJ: Pearson Education.

Friedman, V. J. (2001). Designed blindness: An action science perspective on program theory evaluation. *America Journal of Evaluation, 22(2),* 161–181.

Funnell, S. C., & Rogers, P. J. (2011). *Purposeful program theory: Effective use of theories of change and logic models.* San Francisco: Jossey-Bass.

Kania, J., & Kramer, M. (2011). Collective impact. *Stanford Social Innovation Review, Winter,* 35–41. Retrieved from www.ssireview.org.

Knowlton, L. W., & Phillips, C. C. (2009). *The logic model guidebook: Better strategies for great results.* Thousand Oaks, CA: Sage Publications, Inc.

Kramer, M., Parkhurst, M., & Vaidyanathan, L. (2009). *Breakthroughs in shared measurement and social impact,* 1–52. Retrieved from www.fsg-impact.org/ideas/item/breakthroughs_in_measurement.html.

Lent, R., Brown, S., & Hackett, G. (1994). Toward a unifying social cognitive theory of career and academic interest, choice and performance. *Journal of Vocational Behavior, 45,* 79–122.

McDonald, N. (2015). The evaluation of change. *Cognition, Technology and Work, 17,* 193–206. doi: 10.1007/s10111-014-0296-9.

O'Sullivan, R. G. (2004). Designing collaborative evaluations. In R. G. O'Sullivan (Ed.), *Practicing evaluation: A collaborative approach* (pp. 53–74). Thousand Oaks, CA: Sage Publications.

Pawson, R., & Tilley, N. (1997). *Realistic evaluation.* Thousand Oaks, CA: Sage.

Rog, D. J. (2012). When background becomes foreground: Toward context-sensitive evaluation practice. In D. J. Rog, J. L. Fitzpatrick, & R. F. Conner (Eds.), *Context: A framework for its influence on evaluation practice. New Directions for Evaluation, 135,* 25–40.

Stufflebeam, D. L. (1999). Evaluation contracts checklist. Available online at: http://www.wmich.edu/sites/default/files/attachments/u350/2014/contracts.pdf.

Wholey, J. S. (1987). Evaluability assessment: Developing program theory. In L. Bickman (Ed.), *Using program theory in evaluation. New Directions for Evaluation, 33,* 77–92.

Wholey, J. S. (2004). Evaluability assessment. In J. S. Wholey, H. P. Hatry, & K. E. Newcomer (Eds.), *Handbook of practical program evaluation* (2nd ed.). San Francisco: Jossey Bass Publishers.

Williams, B., & Hummelbrunner, R. (2011). *Systems concepts in action: A practitioner's toolkit.* Stanford, CA: Stanford University Press.

Woodhouse, L. D., Toal, R., Nguyen, T., Keene, D., Gunn, L., Kellum, A., . . . Livingood, W. C. (2013). A merged model of quality improvement and evaluation: Maximizing Return on Investment. *Health Promotion Practice, 14(6),* 885–892.

Yarbrough, D. B., Shulha, L. M., Hopson, R. K., & Caruthers, F. A. (2011). *The Program Evaluation Standards: A guide for evaluators and evaluation users* (3rd ed.). Thousand Oaks, CA: Sage Publications.

PART TWO

Design

By now you should be prepared with the fundamental knowledge and skills to begin the design phase of a program evaluation process. Part Two will walk you through a variety of evaluation study designs and provide guidance on how to choose them. You will learn about various qualitative, quantitative, and mixed study designs along with additional designs that do not easily fit into one of those categories. You also will learn how to control for threats to internal and external validity in an evaluation design, so that you and a program's stakeholders can be more confident in the evaluation's findings.

Part Two also will discuss sampling, samples, and data sources. Often, we take the evaluation's sample for granted when we think of it only as those who participate in a program. Rigorous evaluation designs, however, challenge us to think beyond the program's participants to include other programs and people who provide comparisons from which we can make attributional claims about program outcomes and improve the credibility of the evaluation's findings. You also will learn how to manage biases imposed by a sample so that the findings can be attributed to the program and not necessarily the specific individuals who participated in it. Strategies for participant recruitment and selection are discussed, so that your efforts result in the size and composition of a sample that is needed to make inferences about a program. Tips and tools for data collection plans and protocols are provided as a way to accurately track the participants and account for the information they provide in an evaluation.

CHAPTER 5

Designing a Program Evaluation

The first four chapters of this book focused on the fundamental knowledge necessary to focus and prepare for a program evaluation. In this chapter, I describe the qualitative, quantitative, and mixed methods study designs commonly used in program evaluation. The selection of a design is driven by the questions posed for an evaluation study. Allow me to repeat myself. *A study design is driven by the questions posed for an evaluation.* One of the biggest mistakes I observe in practice is that program staff often will design data collection tools, such as survey questionnaires, without considering the evaluation's purpose, broad questions, or the type of design most appropriate for answering those questions. They also may neglect to consider whether the questions can be appropriately answered with a written survey. Data collection tools should be selected based on the type of study design used to answer the evaluation questions and on the methods and approaches appropriate for answering those questions.

Questions that explore a program's implementation or processes leading to anticipated or unanticipated outcomes, generally suggest *qualitative study designs*. These questions typically begin with the terms *how* or *why*. For example, "How is the program being implemented?" "Why doesn't the program achieve its desired outcomes?" "How does the program impact the community it serves?" In contrast, quantitative study designs generally answer questions that attempt to understand whether a program's anticipated outcomes have been achieved, if one program is better than another or none at all, or whether one or more programs are having a quantifiable impact in an organization or community. These questions typically begin with the terms *did* or *what*. "Did the program achieve its desired outcomes?" "What program is most effective at producing the desired outcomes?" "Did the program improve the services it provides to community members?" Notice that these questions typically include terms, such as *most effective* or *improve* that indicate a desire to assess a change. When you have a question such as, "Which program activities are associated with the knowledge gained by Hispanic participants?" you will use a correlation design. If your question is, "Can the knowledge gained by Hispanic participants be explained by the program (compared to a nonparticipant group)?" you would likely use a causal-comparative design. Correlation and causal-comparative designs assess relationships among one or more variables and are used to determine factors that predict or explain a single outcome.

In practice, qualitative and quantitative methods often are combined to answer the various types of questions posed in an evaluation study. Questions, such as "Was the program effective at increasing teens' knowledge about healthy food choices?" coupled with questions such as "How are teens motivated to make healthy food choices?" are those that suggest a *mixed methods design*. These methods can be used *sequentially* or *simultaneously*. The first question suggests a quantitative design to determine the program's effectiveness, whereas the second question suggests a qualitative design (e.g., interview) to determine what teens are doing with the information they learned in the program. This design would be sequential because the teens must *learn* about healthy foods before they can make healthy food choices. When using mixed methods designs, one method can be emphasized more than another, too. For example, when conducting a survey that contains some open-ended responses. The quantitative nature of surveys suggests an emphasis on quantitative methods, but the open-ended responses would require qualitative methods and analysis. Mixed methods designs are thoroughly explained by Teddlie and Tashakkori (2009) and will be described with more detail in a later section of this chapter.

QUALITATIVE DESIGNS

Qualitative study designs and their associated data collection and analysis methods are best for answering questions about process or a phenomenon (e.g., why people do or don't take advantage of community resources when needed). These designs provide an in-depth understanding of a phenomenon, help to develop a theory for how something works or happens, convey stories that mark significant events or historical trends, and allow you to access and intimately experience cultures and the daily lives of those from whom you wish to learn. My personal bias reflects a strong epistemological conviction toward humanism when applying these approaches. What that means is that I try to avoid the imposition of frameworks for data collection and analysis and allow the data to speak to me—I use an *inductive* approach to my inquiry. This approach is in contrast to a *deductive* approach, which makes specific assumptions about the processes or phenomenon of interest and imposes an analytical framework when studying them. Although frameworks are useful for focusing data collection and organizing data analysis, I prefer to use them loosely and with flexibility in order for ideas to emerge from my data and findings. With that said, I will describe five major types of qualitative study designs and how they are used in evaluation.

Ethnographic designs are those in which the evaluator becomes immersed in the culture of a program, policy effort, or intervention. This approach is very common among anthropologists who readily study different contexts and cultures. For example, an evaluator who becomes accepted by tribal elders and gains membership to a native tribe in the process of acquiring an in-depth understanding of the tribe and its associated cultural beliefs, norms, values, and ways of everyday life. In program evaluation, an ethnographic approach is useful when you are trying to gain a rich understanding of the context in which a program is embedded. This approach begins with relationships that are developed and nurtured over time in order to gain understanding of the culture or context you are evaluating. Careful observations and journaling are commonly used as data collection methods in these types of studies.

Phenomenological designs are used to acquire a rich description of a phenomenon by thoroughly examining multiple sources of information associated with that phenomenon. In contrast to ethnography, an evaluator typically doesn't share the experiences of those who are closest to the phenomenon or process being studied. Instead, an evaluator will build relationships with participants and use rigorous data collection methods to gain a thorough understanding of participants' lived experiences. An excellent example of a phenomenological study of adults who experienced mild traumatic brain injuries was conducted by Dr. Ellyn Kroupa several years ago (Kroupa, 1996). Using a combination of in-depth interviews and participant observations, Dr. Kroupa came to understand what it was like to live with a mild traumatic brain injury and how those injuries impacted the daily lives and relationships of those she studied.

Narrative inquiry seeks a rich description of an event or series of events through story. This may be a particularly useful and effective form of inquiry with Native American Tribes who typically learn and communicate through story as part of their cultural traditions (Hodge, Pasqua, Marquez, & Geishirt-Cantrell, 2002). Typical examples of narrative inquiries can be found in studies of veterans who provide detailed accounts of their experiences of specific historical events (e.g., the attack on Pearl Harbor). Interviews are typically used to collect richly detailed stories, which often are analyzed and disseminated through documentaries or lengthy written accounts, such as books.

Grounded Theory , as its name implies, is a method used to develop a theory about how or why a process or phenomenon occurs. It is useful for understanding processes and relationships among multiple constructs or ideas. Therefore, the evaluator enters a study with no or extremely few predisposed notions about the process or phenomenon to be studied. In other words, a conceptual framework for a grounded theory study is deliberately vague and somewhat tentative in order not to influence the developed theory. For example, a grounded theory approach could be especially helpful for empirically developing a program's theory of change when none exists or is ambiguous.

As an example, I will describe my doctoral dissertation, which used the grounded theory method to develop a theory about how physicians learn to diagnose Lyme disease (Bakken, 1998). Lyme disease is difficult to diagnose because its symptoms resemble other illnesses. I wanted to learn why some physicians were able to diagnose it easily, while other physicians found it difficult. To conduct the study, I interviewed physicians who were general practitioners, as well as those who were specialists. I was also certain to interview physicians who practiced in "hotbeds" of Lyme disease and those who did not. As I analyzed the interview transcripts, a theory emerged that suggested the importance of encountering a variety of patients who presented with similar and different symptoms and diseases. For novice physicians who relied on information learned from textbooks in early stages of their careers, these rich experiences were lacking. More experienced physicians had a mental "repository" of patient cases that could be drawn from and compared with the patient before them. They also had richer networks of colleagues and other resources that could be relied upon for assistance. I concluded my study with a theory about how physicians learn to diagnose Lyme disease, which had implications for developing educational programs that prepared them to diagnose this disease with greater accuracy.

CASE STUDY DESIGNS

Case studies are a rather unique set of designs that can be qualitative or quantitative (Yin, 2009). In program evaluation, they are typically qualitative or employ mixed methods, because you are trying to gain a rich understanding of a "case." In Yin's words, "a case study is an empirical inquiry that investigates a contemporary phenomenon in depth and within its real-life context, especially when the boundaries between phenomenon and context are not clearly evident" (p. 18). What makes these designs unique is that the units of analysis are not a program or groups of participants, but groups of people or a program(s) within certain types of situations, organizations, or communities, in other words "cases."

As an example, one of my former graduate students wanted to study how for-profit organizations were contributing to civil society beyond philanthropic efforts. Her units of analysis were for-profit organizations that represented three very different types of business or *cases*. She used a *multiple* case study design (Yin, 2009) in which multiple units of analysis (i.e., administrators, staff, websites, and other documents) were *embedded* within each case (i.e., type of organization). To perform her study, she conducted interviews with stakeholders in each organization who represented different perspectives and roles within their respective organizations to gain their views of how the organization was contributing to civil society. She then compared stakeholders' perspectives within and across stakeholder groups and within and across each type of organization to acquire an overall picture of how for-profit organizations contribute to civil society. She also used documents, such as websites and strategic plans, as data sources in her analysis. If she had wanted to expand this study, she could have designed a survey to quantify the extent to which for-profit organizations across a larger geographic area or for-profit sector were contributing to civil society more broadly.

Case studies can be designed in multiple ways. In *single-case designs*, a case within a single context is the unit of analysis, but you also can embed multiple units of analysis (e.g., people or documents) in a single case. *Multiple-case designs* are case designs in which multiple cases and their corresponding contexts are studied. As in single-case designs, one can embed multiple units of analysis within each case of a multiple-case design. In my previous example, the student used a multiple case design with multiple units of analysis embedded within each case. According to Yin (2009), a single-case design is appropriate when you wish to study a critical, unique, typical (i.e., representative), revelatory, or longitudinal case (pp. 47–49). Multiple-case designs tend to be more robust and detailed than single-case designs. They typically are used to study how a phenomenon does or does not vary across contexts. For more information about multiple case study designs, see Stake (2006).

QUANTITATIVE DESIGNS

Before I describe the quantitative study designs typically used for program evaluations, it is important to understand the definitions of and difference between the terms, *dependent* and *independent* variable. A *dependent* variable is a variable of interest to you and the one that is commonly "measured" in a quantitative study. It is also typically an output (evidence of implementation) or outcome (evidence of change) of interest. The *independent* variable is the program, intervention, or policy you are implementing to influence a desired outcome (dependent variable). Other independent variables include demographic variables (e.g., age, geographic location, race, or ethnicity) or conditions (e.g., comparison groups or external factors) that may affect the dependent variable of interest. *Indicators* are simply the evidence or measures of either independent or dependent variables.

Table 5.1 summarizes basic designs for quantitative studies commonly used in program evaluations. The first row begins with the least rigorous and

Table 5.1. SUMMARY OF QUANTITATIVE STUDY DESIGNS USED TO DETERMINE THE EFFICACY OR EFFECTIVENESS OF PROGRAMS

Design	**Pretest (T0)**	Intervention or Test Condition	**Posttest (T1)**	**Posttest (T2)**	Type
One-shot/ cross-sectional	None	P	MDV_p @ T1	none	Descriptive
Posttest only	None	P, C or P2	MDV_p @ T1 $MDV_{C \text{ or } P2}$ @ T1	none	
Pretest/Posttest	MDV @ T0	P	MDV @ T1	none	
Interrupted time series	MDV @ T0	P	MDV @ T1	MDV @ T2	Effectiveness
Pretest/Posttest with Control or Comparison	MDV @ $T0_p$ MDV @ $T0_C$	P C	MDV @ $T1_p$ MDV @ $T1_C$	Optional	
Pretest/ Posttest with randomization	MDV @ $T0_p$ MDV @ $T0_C$	RP RC	MDV @ $T1_p$ MDV @ $T1_C$	Optional	Efficacy

MDV = Measure of Dependent Variable, T = Time, R = Random, P = Program, C = Control or Comparison Group

simplest of these designs, known as a one-shot or cross-sectional design. These *nonexperimental* quantitative studies are used to obtain rich descriptions of the opinions, demographics, and/or activities of a population at a particular "slice" in time. These designs will not allow you to make causal claims about a program or other activity, but they will allow you to examine associations between a program and its outcomes or claims relative to a broad population. Surveys (oral or written) typically are used to collect information in quantitative nonexperimental designs, because they provide a means to obtain information from large samples relatively quickly and cost-effectively. Surveys common to daily life include the census survey, marketing surveys (such as those used by grocery stores or fast-food chains), and satisfaction surveys, such as those you might be asked to complete at a doctor's office or restaurant. Ten steps for designing a survey are listed in Box 5.1.

How you design a survey is critical to the quality of information you will gain from it. Surveys must be designed and delivered with the respondent in mind, so that your completion rate is maximized. *Cognitive interviews* (Shafer & Lohse [year unknown]; Willis, 1999) can be conducted during a pilot phase to determine how respondents are interpreting questions, identify items that may be missing from a response, or question items that may be missing from the survey. Chapter Seven provides details about how to design a high-quality survey.

Working our way down the rows in Table 5.1, the rigor of these designs increases with the addition of pretests, control groups, and finally, sample randomization. *Experimental* and *quasiexperimental* study designs allow you to determine a program's efficacy and effectiveness. By that I mean, they provide the means for making simple inferences (i.e., claims) about outcomes related to a program, policy, or intervention. The bottom row summarizes the elements of a tightly controlled design, referred to as a randomized controlled trial, which often is characterized as the "gold standard" or ideal study design to determine a program's *efficacy*. With these designs, study conditions, including but not limited to the numbers of participants and precise way a program is implemented, must be highly controlled. Given the realities of program evaluation, however, one can rarely control these conditions to a degree that is necessary, so *effectiveness* designs provide the next best degree of rigor.

Effectiveness designs are very similar to efficacy designs, except that they lack randomized sampling from a population and allow for a natural sample selection process. As such, they are referred to as *quasiexperimental* designs. These designs, however, do contain a control or comparison group and are more rigorous than other effectiveness designs, because participants are randomized to either a control or intervention group after they decide to participate in an evaluation study. In the rest of this section, I will go through each of these designs and describe typical examples of the circumstances and evaluation questions that suggest their use.

The simplest form of a quantitative study design is one in which only outputs or outcomes are assessed following an intervention or program (Figure 5.1).

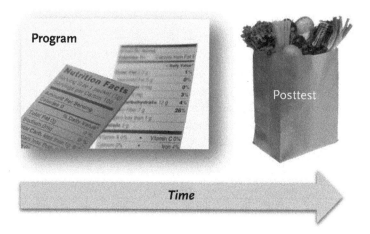

Figure 5.1. One-shot design to determine program outputs.

As an example, I will use a Healthy Eating program designed to increase fruit and vegetable purchases and presumably consumption—a relationship that I will return to later in this chapter. In its simplest form, the intervention would encourage participants to purchase more fruits and vegetables. So, I might use grocery store receipts to indicate the amount of fruits and vegetables purchased by program participants and calculate this as a proportion of total food purchases. Notice that with this design, my measure of fruit and vegetable purchases is not a measure of *change*, but a measure that captures information as a *one-shot* or slice in time. Consequently, I am not able to assess outcomes accurately (defined as changes resulting from a program) and can only assess program *outputs*. I also *assume* that this measure is affected by my Healthy Eating program, which may not necessarily be true. These designs are known to evaluators and researchers as *one-shot, nonexperimental,* or *cross-sectional* designs, because there is only one chance to assess outputs. A typical example of this design is when participant satisfaction or knowledge acquisition is assessed at the end of a workshop. An example of a question that could be answered using this type of evaluation design is, "Do participants purchase a high proportion of fruits and vegetables during the month following the workshop?" A major limitation of the one-shot design is that one cannot be certain that the desired output (i.e., high proportion of fruit and vegetable purchases) can be attributed to the workshop, because external factors outside one's control may influence the outcome of interest to stakeholders (e.g., a local farmers' market or television advertising campaign that was begun at about the same time). Your ability to assess a desired outcome (i.e., a change, such as increased fruit and vegetable purchases) is, therefore, extremely limited.

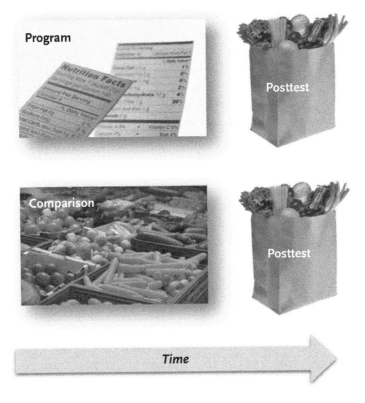

Figure 5.2. One-shot design with a comparison group.

You can gain some certainty about a workshop's contributions to the desired outcome by adding a comparison or control group to the design. Figure 5.2 illustrates an example of a *posttest-only* design that uses a comparison group. Building from my previous example, a comparison group might be a group of matched participants (e.g., individuals of the same age, family size, and income level living in the same neighborhood) who did not attend the Healthy Eating workshop but received a weekly flyer from a local grocery store. Notice that the outcome measure, high proportion of fruit and vegetable purchases, doesn't change—only the intervention, so you still cannot assess change. This design will only allow you to compare a dependent variable (proportion of fruits and vegetables) between two groups (i.e., Health Eating workshop or group receiving a flyer). So, by adding a comparison group, you can learn whether one intervention is more effective than a comparison or control group in producing an output.

A question that this type of design could answer is, for example, "Did participants in the Health Eating workshop (i.e., intervention) purchase a higher proportion of fruit and vegetables than those who received the flyer (i.e., comparison group)?" A limitation of this design is that you cannot assume that the effect is due to the intervention, because the intervention group's greater proportion of fruit and vegetable purchases may have been due to self-selection. In other words, the intervention group already may have been purchasing greater amounts of fruits and vegetables than their counterparts prior to the intervention. Or, perhaps, what was intended as a neutral flyer from the local grocery store actually stimulated the comparison group to purchase higher proportions of fruits and vegetables than the participants in the Health Eating workshop. Even more remarkable, what if the workshop participants taught their neighbors what they learned about healthy eating and influenced them to purchase high proportions of fruit and vegetables?

To reconcile the uncertainty inherent in designs with only a posttest (with or without a comparison group), you can gain some additional certainty about the intervention's effects by including a pretest or baseline assessment in the design, which will allow you to assess a change, or *outcome*, resulting from the workshop (Figure 5.3). *Pre-/posttest* designs with or without a control or comparison group help to answer questions such as, "Did the participants' fruit and vegetable purchases increase following their participation in the Healthy Eating workshop?" By adding a control or comparison group, you can ask the question, "Is the workshop effective at increasing the proportion of fruits and vegetables purchased by workshop participants when compared to a control group?" As you probably noticed, the fundamental evaluation question didn't really change all that much, but the level of certainty you have toward attributing the workshop to that change (increased fruit and vegetable purchases) has improved because a baseline measure was added that will allow you to assess change (i.e., increased food and vegetable consumption). A control group is added to reduce the likelihood that the increase in fruit and vegetable purchases was due to chance.

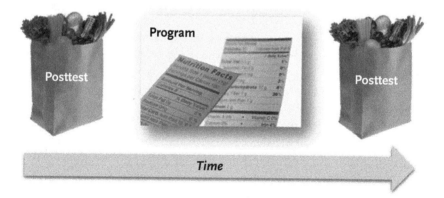

Figure 5.3. Pre-/Posttest study design.

This type of design is referred to as a *quasiexperimental design* because it lacks random selection from the population of interest.

Up until this point, I have assumed that participants have self-selected into the workshop and that the comparison group was selected through the local grocery store's marketing efforts. Let's assume now that I (1) randomly selected participants from the local neighborhood of interest and (2) randomly assigned them to either the Health Eating workshop or comparison group as illustrated in Figure 5.4.

Efficacy designs are the only type of *experimental design* that provide a means to attribute causation. In other words, they are the only quantitative designs for which we can determine whether an outcome of interest is actually caused by or can be attributed to a program. You may have heard these designs called by their common name, randomized controlled designs. They often are referred to as the "gold standard" for designing quantitative studies because they are conducted under tightly controlled conditions. Two primary conditions define these study designs: (1) randomization and (2) control or comparison groups. These designs are often very difficult to execute in a manner necessary to achieve the degree of certainty for which they are intended, because in the social sciences, we work with humans and humans are

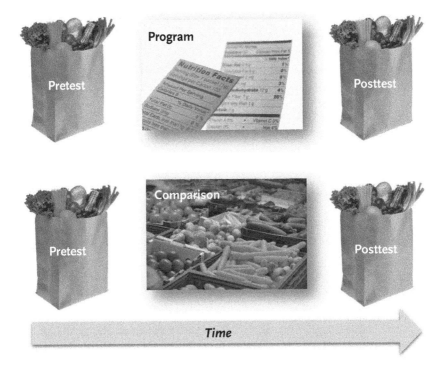

Figure 5.4. Randomized design with a comparison group.

difficult to control. They don't show up for workshops, they drop out, they talk to peers, they cross into other study groups, and generally do things that mess with our fine-tuned study designs. So, we do the best we can and track their movements, in an effort to account for these unanticipated behaviors. In a best-case scenario, you can randomize study participants to an intervention or comparison group; however, institutionalized norms may prohibit you from doing so. For example, children generally cannot be randomized to a classroom or teacher because they are grouped by grade level or subject. As often as possible, however, it is helpful to randomize to a study's condition or randomly select a sample from a population of interest in order to improve the rigor of evaluation studies. Even then, those who volunteer to participate in these studies can be biased toward a study in some way, so effectiveness designs tend to be most commonly used for quantitative evaluation studies involving humans or social issues.

The designs listed in Table 5.1, and described so far, are intended to answer questions for assessing characteristics of a sample, differences between groups, or changes resulting from a program. Sometimes, you may wish to understand factors that explain or predict an outcome. *Correlational* designs are quantitative nonexperimental designs that allow you to determine what factors or variables can be *associated* with an outcome. For example, high school grade point averages (GPA) can predict college GPA. Alternatively, you may have assessed an outcome of a program and want to determine what variables or factors associated with that program were strongest at *explaining* the outcome. *Causal-correlational* designs provide a means of *retrospectively* assessing factors that are associated with a measured outcome. Similarly, you could determine to what extent a program versus a comparison group can explain an outcome by using a *causal-comparative* design. A point to emphasize about causal-comparative and causal-correlational designs is that they are done ex post facto and cannot be used to attribute causation because the program's implementation was not carefully controlled. These designs can only tell you whether relationships between program variables and an outcome exist and how strongly those variables are associated with that outcome.

STUDY DESIGNS FOR EVALUATING CONTRIBUTION

An alternative way to examine a program's influence on an anticipated outcome is to perform a contribution analysis (Mayne, 2001, 2008).

> Contribution analysis explores attribution through assessing the contribution a programme is making to observed results. It sets out to verify the theory of change behind a programme and at the same time, takes into consideration other influencing factors. (Mayne, 2008, p.1)

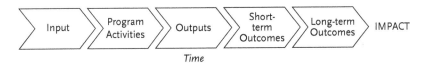

Figure 5.5. Program inputs, activities, outputs, and short- and long-term outcomes.

This analysis involves five steps, which include developing, documenting, and collecting evidence of a program's theory of change; seeking additional evidence to support or adjust the theory; adjusting the program's theory to account for additional evidence; and then repeating the cycle to strengthen the contribution story (Mayne, 2008). This analysis is like conducting a logic analysis (Brousselle & Champagne, 2011) as part of a program improvement cycle, because a program is continually refined to produce a desired outcome. This continuous cycle of learning helps to fine tune a program's activities in ways that can strengthen its relationship to a desired outcome and account for intervening or extraneous factors that may be influencing both programming efforts and a program's relationships to desired outcomes. The notion of contribution also can be helpful when assessing a program's outcomes as they relate to broader impacts in an organization or community.

Evaluators and program planners are increasingly being asked to assess a program's impact or track long-term outcomes resulting from their programs. Consequently, a level of complexity is added when we try to relate short-term program outcomes to long-term outcomes and impacts. This complexity is forcing us to extend our thinking about a program's *contributions* to longer term outcomes and impacts, rather than a set of outcomes that can be *attributed* to a specific program. So, program outcomes become situated among a chain of variables that lead to a social impact (Figure 5.5). Therefore, multivariate study designs are gaining more prominence in the evaluation field as ways to assess long-term and incremental change.

THREATS TO INTERNAL AND EXTERNAL VALIDITY IN QUANTITATIVE STUDIES

Internal and external factors can influence an evaluator's ability to draw generalizable conclusions from quantitative studies. These factors threaten the extent to which we can make inferences to a population based on a study's findings. Internal validity is acquired "internally" in the study design by controlling for factors that may influence the dependent variable other than the "test" condition. Often the "test" condition is a program or intervention that is believed to be responsible for a desired change (i.e., the dependent variable of interest). Typical internal threats to validity are variations in how a program is implemented, characteristics of participants (such as previous knowledge or experiences related to the dependent variable or selection bias), or shared knowledge between an intervention and control group. External factors that threaten the validity of a study's findings are those that are external to the study and influence the dependent variable of interest. Common examples are study participants who have been sensitized by pre- or posttest assessment tools or strategies, different types of measures used to assess the dependent variable of interest, time intervals between the intervention and assessment of the dependent variable, and similar programs or interventions in which study participants are simultaneously engaged during the course of a study. Evaluators must do their best to control for or limit these threats and report their potential influence on a study's findings as a limitation.

MIXED METHODS DESIGNS

In general, mixed methods designs are useful when you want to evaluate both process and outcomes. Mixed methods designs can be thought of in several ways that vary by sequence and emphasis. Teddlie and Tashakkori (2009) wrote extensively on mixed methods study designs in their book titled, *Foundations of Mixed Methods Research*. Briefly, qualitative studies can be used before, in tandem with, or following a quantitative study to help inform variables and their corresponding relationships for a quantitative study, obtain a thorough understanding of relationships or processes linking variables in a study, or be used to understand the nature of the quantitative information obtained from an inferential or descriptive study. These three major types of designs are illustrated in Table 5.2.

As an example of a complex study employing mixed methods, I will describe a study that I and some of my colleagues at Dartmouth-Hitchcock Medical Center designed a couple of years ago. The purpose of this study was to understand how an educational program was contributing to improvements in

Table 5.2. PURPOSE AND USE FOR VARIOUS TYPES OF MIXED METHODS STUDY DESIGNS

Design	Purpose and Use
QUAL > quant	Use qualitative methods to design a subsequent quantitative study
QUAL + QUANT or QUANT + QUAL	Perform qualitative and quantitative study simultaneously to acquire a detailed understanding of a phenomenon or process
QUANT > qual	Conduct a quantitative study and use qualitative methods to gain a deeper understanding of the data, participants, or program

patient care (an impact). The study was designed using a complex model that involved the outcomes of the educational program and four hypothesized pathways and relationships to changes in clinical practice (an intermediate outcome), which, in turn, were associated with changes in patient care. Before we could study the four hypothesized pathways of change, we needed to understand better what short-term outcomes were occurring because of the educational program, so we began a three-phase study by performing a qualitative study to determine outcomes of the educational program. The second phase of the study was designed as a simultaneous mixed methods study, in which we would use qualitative methods to track the various pathways between the program's outcomes and its impacts on patient care, and use quantitative methods to assess the outcomes identified through the first phase of the study. The third phase of the study was designed as a quantitative study to assess the contributions of the educational program to changes in patient care and determine whether and how those changes were mediated or moderated by changes in clinical practice or other activities identified through the second phase of the study. This example demonstrates a sequential mixed methods design, in which a qualitative study needed to be done in advance of a rigorous quantitative study.

COMPLEXITY IN STUDY DESIGNS

As mentioned earlier in this chapter, evaluation study designs are becoming more complex. This level of complexity in evaluation studies forces us to think more carefully about other factors that might be intervening in or contributing to the impacts a program is trying to have on organizations or communities. It's very likely that a single program is not the "only game in town" but rather only one of several efforts attempting to achieve a desired impact. Therefore, collaborative studies involving mixed methods, multivariate designs, and systems approaches to evaluation (the latter of which will be addressed in the final chapter) are needed to determine the extent to which a program(s) is contributing to a desired impact. These methods, designs, and approaches provide a way to create more robust program theories and quantify the contributions of programs to longer-term changes. Additionally, systems thinking and developmental approaches are used to evaluate the complexity associated with solving many of today's social issues and problems.

I bring this to your attention because many of you may be asked by funders or governing organizations to assess program outcomes as part of collaborative efforts to evaluate social change or assess a program's broader impacts in your local communities. In these circumstances, a program cannot be viewed in isolation, and evaluations based in experimental or quasiexperimental designs may not be sufficient for understanding the relationships between a program and broader changes in the community. Therefore, evaluation approaches that account for this complexity are needed. These approaches are described in the final chapter of this book to familiarize you with their associated ways of thinking and prepare you for some of the challenges you may encounter in your attempts to evaluate a program as part of a more expansive evaluation.

SUMMARY

Figure 5.6 illustrates a basic decision tree for selecting an evaluation study design. As indicated in this illustration, an evaluation's design is determined by the evaluation's purpose and types of questions guiding the inquiry. Qualitative designs are used to understand processes and phenomenon. These designs seek rich descriptions, stories, or theories that help to understand how or why a phenomenon occurs. In contrast, quantitative designs help to quantify outcomes and assess the impacts programs have on organizations or communities. Methodological rigor is achieved through highly controlled experimental conditions and comparisons within and across groups. Quantitative designs also help to assess the relationships among two or more variables, such as the relationships among several outcomes, across clusters, or between outcomes and impacts. Mixed methods designs are common and necessary when working with multiple programs, mixed data sources or types, or evaluation questions that require sequenced answers. Case study designs are a unique set of designs that often incorporate mixed methods to understand a phenomenon in-depth within and across one or more contexts

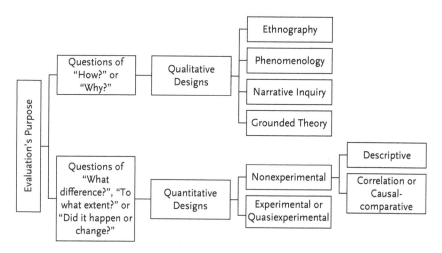

Figure 5.6. A basic decision tree for selecting an evaluation study design.

when boundaries between a phenomenon and context are difficult to discern. In total, evaluators have an array of design options that can be used and combined to answer a variety of questions and purposes that make each evaluation study unique. In the next chapter, I provide information that will help you make decisions about an evaluation's sample, sampling methods, and data sources.

REFERENCES

Bakken, L. L. S. (1998). *The interactions of experience, implicit knowledge and reflection in learning to diagnose Lyme disease* (Order No. 9839370). Available from ProQuest Dissertations & Theses Global. (304456750). Retrieved from http://search.proquest.com.ezproxy.library.wisc.edu/docview/304456750?accountid=465

Brousselle, A., & Champagne, F. (2011). Program theory evaluation: Logic analysis. *Evaluation and Program Planning, 34,* 69–78.

Hodge, F.S., Pasqua, A., Marquez, C. A., Geishirt-Cantrell, B. (2002). Utilizing traditional storytelling to promote wellness in American Indian communities. *Journal of Transcultural Nursing, 13(1),* 6–11.

Kroupa, E. L. (1996). *Forced to the edge: How adults learn to build meaningful lives after traumatic brain injury* (Order No. 9632905). Available from ProQuest Dissertations & Theses Global. (304289788). Retrieved from http://search.proquest.com.ezproxy.library.wisc.edu/docview/304289788?accountid=465

Mayne, J. (2001). Addressing attribution through contribution analysis: Using performance measures sensibly. *The Canadian Journal of Program Evaluation, 16(1),* 1–24.

Mayne, J. (2008, May). *Contribution analysis: An approach to exploring cause and effect* (ILAC Brief 16). United Kingdom: Institutional Learning and Change (ILAC). Retrieved from the Innovation Network website: http://www.innonet.org/resources/files/Contribution_Analysis.pdf.

Shafer, K., & Lohse, B. (n.d.). *How to conduct a cognitive interview: A nutrition education example.* Available at: www.au.af.mil/au/awc/awcgate/usda/cog-interview.pdf.

Stake, R. E. (2006). *Multiple case study analysis.* New York, NY: The Guildford Press.

Teddlie, C., & Tashakkori, A. (2009). Sampling strategies for mixed methods research. In *Foundation of mixed methods research: Integrating quantitative and qualitative approaches in the social and behavioral sciences* (pp. 168–196). Thousand Oaks, CA: Sage Publications.

Willis, G. B. (1999). *Cognitive interviewing: A "how to" guide.* Available at: http://www.hkr.se/pagefiles/35002/gordonwillis.pdf.

Yin, R. K. (2009). *Case study research: Design and methods* (4th ed.). Thousand Oaks, CA: Sage Publications.

CHAPTER 6

Choosing Samples, Sampling Methods, and Data Sources

To begin Chapter 6, I reflect on an evaluation in which I was involved several years ago. My role was to help develop a conceptual framework for a study conducted about a women's leadership program. The researchers carefully described their ideas for the program, how it would relate to and be supported by other efforts on campus, and what they would need to know to determine whether their program was a success. The lead evaluator (not me), took this information and constructed a single logic model using the format previously described in this textbook. As I later examined this logic model and thought about the conceptual framework for the study and evaluation questions posed by the researchers, it occurred to me that we were trying to evaluate two or more major groups: (1) the women involved in the new leadership program and (2) the people and programs supporting them. Subsequently, we split the original logic model into two distinct, but linked, logic models. This change to the overall program theory meant that our data collection efforts would be focused on two samples (i.e., female participants and those who support them), two primary units of analysis (i.e., the main program and its supporting set of activities), and multiple data sources including, but not limited to, program documents and interviews with participants. This evaluation example represents several terms and concepts that will be defined and explained in this chapter; namely, samples, units of analysis, and data sources. I also will discuss criteria for sample selection, sample bias, and sampling in relation to study designs. This chapter concludes with sections about tips for participant recruitment and retention, as well as important considerations for ethical practice.

DATA SOURCES AND UNITS OF ANALYSIS

Data Sources are the documents, individuals, groups of people (e.g., families), and communities that provide information for an evaluation study. Evaluators use tools, such as surveys, interviews or other *data collection methods*, to collect information from these sources. In program evaluation, data sources are typically program participants, but they also can be program coordinators, administrators, or other key stakeholders. You may want to use documents, such as evaluation reports or program planning materials, as sources for an evaluation. Beyond the program context, beneficiaries, such as employing organizations or community residents, may be sources of information in an evaluation. The extent to which these various sources are used will depend on the scope and purpose of an evaluation. How are data sources selected? Data sources are selected based on the stakeholders' primary population of interest, approach to the evaluation, and types of questions to be answered by the evaluation.

It is so easy to query data sources for all sorts of interesting information, but that could lead your efforts astray, waste countless hours of time, and not accomplish the evaluation's purpose. Instead, it is important to query data sources for information that is relevant only to the study and is focused on answering the evaluation questions. For example, a few years ago I was involved in designing an evaluation for a regularly scheduled educational series in an academic medical center. When we began our process of identifying key stakeholders, understanding the context for the evaluation, the program's goals, and questions for the evaluation, we not only identified several evaluation questions of interest, but also learned that key stakeholders were interested in understanding how the program contributed to quality practice and patient care. In other words, some key stakeholders wanted to know how the program contributed to outcomes that were associated with a system of patient care delivery. These stakeholder conversations led us to design a systems level evaluation involving three stages of data collection and analysis using mixed methods approaches. Each stage of the study had its own set of evaluation questions. One of my colleagues on our evaluation team was an educational researcher who was greatly interested in confirming the overall theory we had developed for the program's contribution to quality practice and patient care. This interest often pulled his focus away from the Phase I evaluation questions, which were oriented toward understanding actual learning outcomes of healthcare providers who participated in the weekly series—a step that needed to be undertaken before we could assess the effects of learning on clinical practice and patient care. Had it not been for my continuous reminders to stay focused on the evaluation's purpose and questions, the evaluation could have been led astray by my colleague's interests. Consequently, the team may not have answered the questions that were most important at the time.

It is also important to obtain information that will be used and to refrain from collecting information that is not useful. If you stay focused on collecting information that will help to answer the evaluation's questions and engage stakeholders in the evaluation to the extent possible, the findings more likely will be used. With that said, it is important to try to anticipate a variety of potential answers to the evaluation questions, so that you have collected information in sufficient detail to yield the quality and depth of answers you expect.

How are data sources influenced by *units of analysis*? A unit of analysis is the "who" or "what" you are analyzing for the study (Pell Institute, 2016). In program evaluation, a program is typically the unit of analysis, or object that is being evaluated, and it is evaluated by collecting data from multiple sources, such as program documents, previous surveys, coordinators, participants, and beneficiaries. Information collected directly from data sources is then analyzed to answer the evaluation questions. It is not uncommon to use multiple sources of data collection for a single unit of analysis. In case studies, for example, an organization or healthcare team might be a unit of analysis from which multiple sources of information are collected that may include, interviews, observations and documents generated by different organization or team members.

SAMPLE SIZE, SELECTION, AND STRATEGIES

How do you determine who, what, and how many people, organizations, communities, or documents need to be sampled to acquire valid and reliable answers to the evaluation questions? In evaluation, we typically do not generalize an evaluation's findings to broad populations as is done in research. Instead, we are usually interested in very specific and often narrowly focused populations. For example, we may be interested in studying the work of a specific coalition in a single community or region. Or we may be interested in evaluating a single program provided by a nonprofit organization whose scope is defined by a specific community or geographic region. In the case of a single program, the sample is typically limited to program participants who have intentionally enrolled (self-selected) in the program. This latter case is an example of what we call a *convenience sample,* because we make no deliberate attempt to sample from or generalize to a larger population (McMillan, 2008). Examples include groups of people within organizations, those with whom the program associates on a regular basis (e.g., immediate coworkers or friends), people in area neighborhoods, or folks who voluntarily participate in programs of interest to them. The limitations of convenience samples are that they rarely represent a broad population of interest, and their selection is typically biased. This may be OK if the evaluation's conclusions are limited to the sample studied and do not attempt to generalize the findings more broadly. Alternatively, *quota sampling* may be used to achieve a sample that is more representative of a population of interest. This is done by identifying different composite profiles of major groups in the population and selecting participants who represent each group based on specific criteria (McMillan, 2008, p. 119).

Suppose, however, that stakeholders are interested in how a coalition's programming efforts impact a community, and you need to determine which and how many community members to sample to evaluate impact. So, one of your first considerations is to think about who in the community might be impacted most by the coalition's efforts and how those impacts might trickle over to others less directly affected. In this case, you would target your sampling efforts to specific members of the community—sampling would be *deliberate* or *purposeful*. *Purposeful sampling*, therefore, means that an evaluator samples a population of interest in a deliberate and methodical manner in order to obtain specific information from specific individuals to answer an evaluation question. Purposeful sampling typically is selected and used to (1) achieve representativeness or comparability; (2) obtain information about special or unique cases; (3) sample sequentially with the aim of developing theory (i.e., theoretical sampling), confirming or disconfirming cases (i.e., confirming/disconfirming sampling), seeking opportunities (i.e., opportunistic sampling), or informing further sampling (i.e., snowball sampling), and (4) acquire information in combination with other methods (Teddlie & Tashakkori, 2009, p. 174).

Theoretical sampling is a specific form of purposeful sampling used to develop theory. When using this sampling approach, evaluators simultaneously collect and analyze information using qualitative methods. This sampling approach allows an evaluator to maximize the sample's variation and infer its characteristics to a broader population (Strauss & Corbin, 1990). This form of sampling can be useful when an evaluator wishes to develop program theory through an empirical process, rather than through personal experiences and assumptions. *Snowball samples* are a form of purposeful sampling for which each study participant is asked to provide the names of one or two associates who meet a specific criterion. These associates are then contacted and invited to participate in the study, thereby expanding the participant pool. This form of sampling is useful when it is necessary to study relationships among networked individuals or when recruitment efforts are challenged by sensitive topics or trust. Contacts with *key informants* are another strategy of purposeful sampling. This strategy is used to obtain information from people who have influential status, key roles in organizations or communities, or special access to samples or information of interest. These are some of the more common strategies for purposeful sampling. For a comprehensive list of these strategies, see Mertens & Wilson, 2012, pp. 421–428.

Teddlie and Tashakkori (2009, pp. 173–174) describe four characteristics of purposive sampling that distinguishes it from other strategies:

> A researcher/evaluator selects cases that are information rich in order to address specific purposes related to research/evaluation questions;
>
> Expert judgement of researchers/evaluators and informants often select the sample;
>
> Sampling procedures focus on obtaining in-depth information from individual cases; and
>
> Sample size is typically small, but its size depends on the type of research being conducted (qualitative or quantitative) and the research/evaluation questions.

These four characteristics describe strategies that can be collectively referred to as *nonprobabilistic sampling,* because they are limited in terms of their ability to allow us to generalize an evaluation's findings to a broad population.

In contrast, *probablistic sampling* is a more rigorous strategy that provides evaluators with the ability to generalize a study's findings to a broad population of interest. These strategies most commonly are used in large quantitative evaluation studies that are designed to allow inferences to broad populations; therefore, they typically require large sample sizes. The main goal of sample selection is to acquire a sample that best represents the *population* of interest. This starts by defining that population; for example, individuals and families who are vulnerable to food insecurity. You might further describe a population by its geographic location, such as a state, region, city, or neighborhood. Because the population of people who are food insecure is large and extends to all regions of the United States, you may wish to sample from a subgroup of states that have demographics and rates of food insecurity similar to those of the entire U.S. population. This subpopulation of states is termed a *sampling frame.* It helps to think about who or what programs or interventions you are targeting when determining a sampling frame. Once a population of interest is clearly defined, and you have established a sampling frame, you can then determine an optimal *sample* from which to collect data. A sample is a subset of a sampling frame that best represents the characteristics of the population in which you are interested (Figure 6.1).

The most popular type of probablistic sampling is simple random sampling. *Random samples* are collected by selecting study participants at random from a defined population. Sometimes, random samples are selected using *systematic sampling* strategies. Systematic strategies sample a population at numeric intervals, such as every sixth person listed in a roster. This strategy helps to

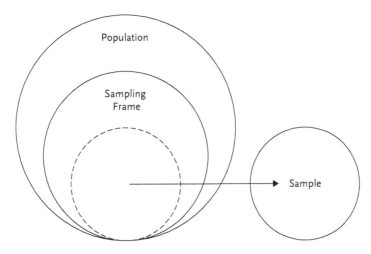

Figure 6.1. The relationships among samples, sampling frames, and populations. Samples are a subset of the sampling frame that best represents a population of interest.

reduce potential bias that might be introduced by the order in which people or items are listed. Randomization schemes, such as blocking, are used to assure a representative sample.

Stratified samples are samples that have been divided according to demographic, cultural, or other unique characteristics that may influence a study's findings. Typical sample stratifications include gender, race, socioeconomic status, age, or geographic location. Once a sample is stratified, study participants are randomly selected to assure representation across groups. Samples of groups, as opposed to individuals, for which members are naturally occurring and highly dependent on one another (e.g., a family), are called *cluster samples*. For example, if a parenting intervention is targeting families, we would want to use family "clusters" as the unit of analysis, as opposed to individuals, to avoid potentially misleading results due to highly dependent interactions among family members. Cluster sampling also can be employed to gather a representative sample of clusters in order to extrapolate findings to a broad population when the members of that population are not identifiable (Creswell, 2008, Ch. 6, p. 155).

Sampling strategies can be combined in multiple ways to enhance an evaluation's findings; however, these *mixed methods strategies* can be resource and time intensive, so choose them according to the type and nature of the evaluation questions and scope of the evaluation study. "Mixed methods sampling strategies employ all of the probability and purposeful techniques" (Teddlie & Tashakkori, 2009, p. 180) described in this chapter and combine both qualitative and quantitative methods to answer evaluation questions. What characterizes these strategies is that sampling techniques are selected to obtain both breadth and depth of information in a sequence that is determined by the study design. For example, a sequential mixed methods design that used a survey to collect quantitative data from a large randomly sampled population and is followed by a purposeful sample of participants who responded a specific way and were selected for phone interviews.

To provide a more practical example, we conducted a feasibility study to implement an outreach program in a new area of our state. For this study we purposefully sampled key informants and conducted informal interviews with them. We also conducted phone interviews and online surveys of random volunteers who represented primary beneficiaries of the program, so we could protect their identities. As a final stage of that study, we reached out to local community stakeholders representing multiple sectors and held listening sessions with them. These listening sessions, combined with our observations of resources in those communities, provided information to assess program "fit." Mixed samples also can be used in parallel to address different types of evaluation questions. An evaluator who randomly surveys community members on, for example, their knowledge of local food resources (To what extent do community members have knowledge of food resources in their area?) and simultaneously conducts in-depth interviews with local policymakers to answer the question, "How and why was a policy made to limit big chain grocers from the community?" For more detailed information about mixed methods sampling, I encourage you to read *Foundations of Mixed Methods Research* by Charles Teddlie and Abbas Tashakkori (2009).

Evaluators also use *multistage sampling* strategies in complex studies that require multiple strategies over the course of a study. For example, one of the study teams I led used purposeful sampling and qualitative methods (interviews and focus groups) to understand the learning outcomes of the weekly seminar series described earlier in this chapter. Once the learning outcomes were known, we could then design an effectiveness study and randomize a sample of participants to either the weekly seminar series or a comparison group using a different instructional approach. Notice that in this example we needed to select the sampling strategy and sample for the first stage of our study before we could select and randomize a sample for the second stage of the study. Regardless of your strategy, you will want to sample in a way that makes the most sense for collecting information in a timely, feasible, cost-effective, and useful manner.

DEFINING INCLUSION AND EXCLUSION CRITERIA FOR YOUR SAMPLE

The period of time I spent as an evaluator in the medical profession taught me the utility of explicitly defining inclusion and exclusion criteria for a sample.

Inclusion criteria are the criteria used to sample or include participants in an evaluation. For sampling purposes, it is equally, if not more, helpful to think about who you will *exclude* from a sample. Some people may wish to volunteer or be available as participants in a study, but not all of them will meet the criteria defined by the population of interest or sampling frame. For example, let us assume that you are trying to sample from a specific state and someone who lives near the border suggests to his friend in the adjacent state to contact you about participating in the evaluation. The fact that the friend lives in a state that is outside the sampling parameters (i.e., inclusion criteria) for the evaluation, would exclude him from participation.

The process of defining inclusion and exclusion criteria is particularly important for recognizing potentially marginalized groups and being inclusive in your sampling practices. Through establishing these criteria, you have an opportunity to think about people with cultural backgrounds or demographic characteristics that should not be excluded from an evaluation study, but who may be excluded based on limitations imposed by the inclusion criteria. It's important that an evaluation be as inclusive as possible (given its context and population of interest), and you uphold the ethical principles of respect of persons, beneficence and justice, as described in the Belmont report (National Commission for the Protection of Human Subjects of Biomedical and Behavioral Research, 1979) when selecting a sample for an evaluation study.

SAMPLING BIAS

As you may have gathered from my description of probability and nonprobability sampling strategies, sampling strategies alone can introduce bias into your sample. However, probability samples also can be biased when, after random sampling, a certain segment of a population no longer wishes to participate and drops out of the evaluation or when certain segments of the population volunteer. Some people are more willing to participate in studies than others; some hold negative images of evaluation and research that keep them from participating. In addition, some program topics may be more attractive to women than men or to younger adults than older adults, for example. Some people have more time to participate in evaluations, such as retirees who may have fewer family commitments, so their wisdom and experience as older adults may bias the results of an evaluation. Certain segments of populations may be restricted by access to travel and, therefore, not able to participate, even if willing. Randomization in probability sampling and heterogeneous sample selection in nonprobability sampling are ways to reduce sample bias. Can you think of other ways to reduce sample bias?

SAMPLE SIZE

Sample size is determined by the nature of a sample (convenience, purposeful, random, or other), types of evaluation questions, and the analytical methods used to answer those questions. For studies using qualitative methods, sampling is typically very purposeful and targets relatively small numbers of individuals or groups that are of most interest to stakeholders. Surveys typically involve large samples, but also can be used to collect information from small samples depending on the population of interest and how a survey is being used to inform the evaluation.

When quantitative methods are used, much larger samples are typically needed to make inferences about a population of interest. The specific size of those samples can be estimated using sample size calculators, such as GPower (Erdfelder, Faul, & Buchner, 1996), or appropriate functions in a statistical program. Mertens and Wilson (2012, pp. 434–436) provide some useful rules of thumb for samples sizes according to common evaluation designs. Their recommendations are summarized in Table 6.1. Don't forget to oversample to account for attrition; 10% is generally a good amount to account for with most

Table 6.1. SAMPLE SIZE RECOMMENDATIONS[a]

Evaluation Design	Recommended Sample Size
Quantitative Designs	
Bivariate Correlations among two or more variables	64 (one-tailed) to 82 (two-tailed) participants
Multiple regression	15 observations per variable
Survey research	100 for each major subgroup; 20–150 for each minor subgroup
Causal comparative designs	51 participants per group (one-tailed hypotheses); 64 for two-tailed hypotheses
Experimental or quasiexperimental designs (pre-/posttest)	21 participants per group (one-tailed)
Qualitative Designs	
Ethnography	Approximately 30–50 interviews
Phenomenology	Approximately 6 participants
Grounded Theory	Approximately 30–50 interviews
Participative Inquiry	Small working team; whole community for meetings; samples for surveys
Case Studies	1 or more cases
Focus Groups	6–9 people per group; 4 groups for each major audience

[a] Adapted from Mertens and Wilson (2012, pp. 434–436). Reprinted with permission from Guildford Press © 2012.

samples, unless you are working with a highly sensitive topic, low group representation, or a transient population. When conducting a qualitative study, a general rule of thumb is to sample until you reach "saturation." *Saturation* is the point at which you hear repetitive information and no new information is emerging as you conduct interviews, focus groups, video observations, or document reviews.

SAMPLING CONSIDERATIONS IN RELATION TO STUDY DESIGNS

All too often, I have observed program coordinators or directors who want to survey an entire sampling frame or population of interest. This practice has led to a concern among evaluators and researchers about survey fatigue (Porter, Whitcomb, & Weitzer, 2004). In other words, people have been surveyed with such frequency or duration that they will no longer provide the valuable information needed. Often, it is not necessary or desirable to survey an entire sampling frame to achieve credible results. In fact, it is unethical to oversample a population when it is not necessary. What do you do to determine the minimum number of people to sample for a survey? You estimate the sample size needed for your analysis based on known population statistics using a computer program (e.g., GPower).

When conducting *effectiveness* studies, sampling often depends on those who are willing to participate in a program; however, if you are going to infer effectiveness, a specific number of participants are needed to draw valid conclusions. If you decide to use a comparison group, you may wish to recruit a sample of participants who are willing to be randomized to either a comparison or intervention group. Either way, it is important to think about the characteristics and locations of the people a program is targeting, the inferences to be made from the evaluation study, and how best to recruit participants who will allow accurate inferences about the population of interest.

Sampling for an *efficacy* study requires that you clearly determine your sampling frame and randomly sample from a population of interest. This means that you will need to track and account for all participants and nonparticipants very carefully. Quite often, this is a huge challenge for social scientists because we typically work with populations that are transient, ill-defined, complex, or undependable. *Cross-over effects* also can occur when working with human participants, especially if they are located in close proximity to one another. Participants in an intervention or program may share what they learn with those in a comparison group, thereby potentially limiting the observed effect of the intervention.

Another important consideration about sampling in relation to study designs, is that the more factors or variables of interest, the greater the sample size needs to be to make credible inferences. Therefore, impact studies that involve multiple intermediate outcome variables that may serve as mediators or moderators in causal pathways require sample sizes that are typically greater than the number of participants in many programs. Therefore, quantitative impact studies require that a program be replicated over several years or across multiple sites.

On the other end of the spectrum are *one-shot* study designs and simple (no comparison group) *pre/posttest* designs. These designs, if kept simple, require small samples of the size typical of most programs' participation levels. This does not mean you should stick with these designs. I strongly encourage you to expand your use of study designs in order to answer the more challenging questions posed by key stakeholders and assess the impacts of programs in the communities they serve.

Qualitative studies typically require sample sizes ranging from a few cases to 15 to 50 participants. As mentioned earlier, the sample size will be determined by the purpose of the evaluation and the point at which "saturation" is reached. Other factors that affect sample size in qualitative studies are stakeholder representation, geographic scope, or other contextual or cultural elements that may influence an evaluation's findings.

STRATEGIES FOR PARTICIPANT RECRUITMENT AND RETENTION

Once you have determined the sample size and population(s), you will be faced with the challenge of recruiting participants for an evaluation study. Recruitment of study participants is often the hardest task when conducting an evaluation study. Some successful strategies based on my own experiences are listed in Box 6.1.

Some evaluation studies, such as impact or longitudinal studies, require that data be collected at several points over long periods of time. In these studies, it may be difficult to retain participants through the duration of the study. In (Box 6.2), I offer several suggestions for retaining participation, based on my own experiences and tips gleaned from colleagues.

ETHICAL PRACTICE

When recruiting for and engaging participants in an evaluation, it is critical that you maintain the highest standards of professional and ethical conduct. This means that we must perform our work with great integrity and personal respect. "Evaluations should [therefore] be designed and conducted to protect human and legal rights and maintain the dignity of participants and

Box 6.1. RECRUITMENT STRATEGIES FOR EVALUATION
STUDIES

- Utilize your and your stakeholders' networks. Stakeholders, in particular, have formed relationships with potential study participants and can be more successful in reaching out to them.
- Piggyback data collection on a standard processes or procedures.
- Make your expectations of participants clear to them.
- Stick to your protocols.
- Offer incentives when possible.
- Engage key stakeholders in data collection.
- Be mindful of how gender, race, ethnicity, and other cultural [aspects] may influence data collection. For example, cultures that embrace face-to-face communication or communal decision-making.
- Make participation easy.
- Avoid overburdening participants with forms that are unnecessarily long or difficult to read.

other stakeholders" (Yarbrough et al., 2011, p. 125). How are these standards realized in practice? Evaluation participants should be made aware of their rights as volunteers and their ability to withdraw or have their information withdrawn from an evaluation study at any time. They also should be given opportunities to confirm their information and be aware of how it will be reported. Performing an evaluation in a culturally competent manner is critical for respecting a community's values, norms, practices, and rules, as well as for being inclusive in our practice. Our goal is to prevent any physical or emotional

Box 6.2. RETENTION STRATEGIES FOR EVALUATION
STUDIES

- Scale up incentives over time
- Provide incentives in a timely manner
- Send frequent but not excessive reminders
- Schedule times for face-to-face or phone collection
- Maintain current contact information
- Acquire names of alternate contacts
- Keep participants engaged through frequent but not excessive communications, for example, through newsletters or websites.

harm that could come to individuals during an evaluation study and avoid any actions that may put participants at risk. It is also your responsibility to ensure that your work will benefit those involved and maintain individuals' rights by keeping their personal identities and information confidential. This we can do by limiting access to an evaluation participant's information, retaining information in secured files and locations, and avoiding evaluations that serve personal, rather than group interests.

When describing an evaluation's sample and reporting an evaluation's findings, individual identities can be avoided by using group summaries, pseudonyms, and only the most relevant information, and by removing any information that could potentially identify a small group or an individual. It is equally important to be mindful of the ways that not only individual reputations, but those of organizations and communities, can be harmed by evaluations. Information, such as geographic location or other descriptors that can reveal the identity of an organization or specific community or group should be stripped. Careful attention also must be given to how information is reported, to whom, and for what reasons. This doesn't mean we should "sugarcoat" or withhold an evaluation's findings, however. We have a professional duty to report accurate and reliable information. It is essential that we know how to present information in ways that are sensitive to the political and cultural context in which the evaluation is imbedded. This is most effectively accomplished when we develop positive relationships with study participants and other stakeholders and communicate openly and honestly with them. Use professional mediators or legal help when necessary to reduce harm or risk to anyone involved in an evaluation study.

SAMPLING AND DATA COLLECTION PLANS AND PROTOCOLS

When designing an evaluation study, it is extremely helpful to prepare a thorough sampling and data collection plan with detailed strategies for how you will sample the population of interest and collect information from that sample. This plan should be aligned with the evaluation questions and include data sources, data collection methods (e.g., interview or survey), and frequency of data collection (e.g., pre- and posttest). A simple matrix for a sampling and data collection plan is shown in Table 6.2.

When working with teams, it is also important to have a clear and detailed sampling, recruitment, and data collection protocol so that information is collected and managed in the same way across team members. This effort will help to avoid biases that may be introduced by the study team when collecting information from the evaluation's participants.

Table 6.2. MATRIX FOR DATA COLLECTION AND ANALYSIS

	Evaluation Question #1	Evaluation Question #2	Evaluation Question #3
Evaluation Questions			
Analyzable form of question (if applicable)			
Evidence Needed to Answer the Question			
Data Collection Methods (How evidence is collected)			
Data Collection Source (From whom or what evidence is collected)			
Data Collection Points (When evidence is collected)			
Analytical Methods (How you will analyze data)			

SUMMARY

Sampling and sample selection is one of the most important elements of an evaluation's design. Careful consideration must be given to a sample's composition, size, and potential biases. Human participation in evaluation studies necessitates attention to demographic, cultural, political, ethical, and geographic factors. Careful strategizing and planning can help to assure a consistent and accurate sampling process. At all times, evaluators must maintain the highest professional standards of practice and protect those involved in evaluation. Furthermore, as evaluators face challenges presented by an accountability-based mindset that emphasizes technocratic approaches to evaluation, they must remain firm advocates for the approaches and methods that are most suitable for addressing stakeholders' questions and needs for information. Chapter 7 begins the third part of this book, which teaches you how to collect, store, and track information as you conduct a program's evaluation. You can keep track of your decisions about data collection by completing the cells in Table 6.2 provided near the end of this chapter.

REFERENCES

Creswell, J. W. (2008). *Educational research. Planning, conducting, and evaluating quantitative and qualitative research.* Upper Saddle River, NJ: Pearson Education.

Erdfelder, E., Faul, F., & Buchner, A. (1996). GPOWER: A general power analysis program. *Behavior Research Methods, 28(1),* 1–11.

McMillan, J. H. (2008). *Educational research: Fundamentals for the consumer.* Boston, MA: Pearson Education.

Mertens, D. M., & Wilson, A. T. (2012). *Program evaluation theory and practice.* New York, NY: The Guilford Press.

National Commission for the Protection of Human Subjects of Biomedical and Behavioral Research. (1979). *The Belmont Report.* Retrieved from the U.S. Department of Health and Human Services, Office for Human Research Protections website: https://www.hhs.gov/ohrp/regulations-and-policy/belmont-report/index.html

Pell Institute. (2016). Define unit of analysis. Retrieved from http://toolkit.pellinstitute.org/evaluation-guide/analyze/define-unit-of-analysis/.

Porter, S. R., Whitcomb, M. E., & Weitzer, W. H. (2004). Multiple surveys of students and survey fatigue. In S. R. Porter (Ed.), *New Directions for Institutional Research, Overcoming Survey Research Problems, 121,* 63–73. doi: 10.1002/ir.101

Strauss, A., & Corbin, J. (1990). *Basics of qualitative research. Grounded theory procedures and techniques.* Newbury Park, CA: Sage Publications.

Teddlie, C., & Tashakkori, A. (2009). Sampling strategies for mixed methods research. In *Foundation of mixed methods research: Integrating quantitative and qualitative approaches in the social and behavioral sciences* (pp. 168–196). Thousand Oaks, CA: Sage Publications.

Yarbrough, D. B., Shulha, L. M., Hopson, R. K., & Caruthers, F. A. (2011). *The Program Evaluation Standards: A guide for evaluators and evaluation users* (3rd ed.). Thousand Oaks, CA: Sage Publications.

PART THREE
Conduct

Part Three provides the knowledge and skills you will use to enhance an evaluation's design and conduct an evaluation study. In chapters seven through nine, you will learn how to collect, store, and track information from a variety of data sources using multiple strategies and tools. You also will learn how to analyze qualitative and quantitative data with the aim of focusing your analysis to answer the evaluation's questions and achieve its purpose. In doing so, you will learn how to understand and interpret basic univariate statistical methods from a user's perspective, so that you are prepared to perform statistical analyses that will allow you to make substantiated claims about a program. You also will learn about various approaches to qualitative data analyses and how those approaches alter a basic analytical process. Furthermore, these chapters provide you with tips, strategies, and tools that will prepare you for managing quantitative and qualitative data. Examples from evaluations are incorporated throughout these chapters to facilitate your understanding and use of the concepts covered within them.

CHAPTER 7

Collecting, Storing, and Tracking Information

When determining optimal ways to collect information, it is extremely important to think about how you intend to collect, analyze, and use it. Do you have the appropriate knowledge and skills to collect and analyze the data? Do you have sufficient resources (e.g., software, time, or additional expertise) for data collection and analysis? What do stakeholders consider to be credible evidence? How will the data be used? What is the most useful information to collect so that collection of unnecessary information can be avoided? It is common for stakeholders to want to collect "interesting" information, but that information may or may not be necessary or useful in an evaluation, so it is important to keep a steady eye on achieving the evaluation's purpose and answering the evaluation's questions. It is also important to collect and track information in a way that is analyzable and efficient. For example, I was once involved in an evaluation that tracked community impacts in narrative form using loosely defined criteria. This form of data collection led to several hours of combing through narratives to identify any statement that resembled community change (i.e., impact). Had more specific criteria and instructions been provided to respondents, information could have been more precise and required less time to analyze. So, I recommend that you give careful thought to how information will be analyzed, as well as how long the analyses will take, as you make decisions about how best to collect it.

In Chapter 7, I describe common and emerging ways that information is collected in the evaluation field. I will review key elements of good instrument design and provide a somewhat detailed description of how to electronically record, store, and track data. Often, there is a tendency to jump to a data collection method without considering the best way to collect desired information. The first step in data collection is to determine what *indicators* or *evidence* are needed to achieve the evaluation's purpose and answer its questions. This step is important because it forces you to think about how you will operationalize each construct, concept, or variable of interest. For example, program planners may wish to know whether critical thinking is occurring during an educational intervention. Critical thinking can be operationalized by observing or listening to dialogue that contains open-ended questions, proposes new ideas or alternative viewpoints, and challenges one's own assumptions. Alternatively, an evaluator could provide a case scenario and ask respondents to demonstrate their critical thinking through written responses to a series of questions designed to elicit these types of responses. Regardless of the data collection method you choose to use, it is important to think about the information needed to answer the evaluation questions, how best to obtain it from data sources, and how feasible it is to obtain, given available resources. It is often helpful to create a matrix like the one shown in Table 7.1 to summarize your data collection plan and be certain that the information you collect will answer the evaluation questions.

After you determine what forms of evidence are needed, you can determine data collection strategies and design data collection tools (or obtain existing tools) that will be used to collect information that will answer the evaluation questions. Your decisions about what data to collect and how to collect it will undoubtedly be influenced by the type of evidence that stakeholders (including funders) consider to be credible. The following section highlights the influences of various philosophical paradigms and fields on the types of data or evidence deemed credible.

WHAT AND WHO DEFINES CREDIBLE EVIDENCE?

Across various contexts and disciplines you will discover differences of opinion regarding the type of information that is considered credible evidence. In disciplines that are grounded in the positivist or postpositivist paradigms, such as medicine, natural science (e.g., biology), or some forms of psychology, objectivity is highly valued and desired. Therefore, quantitative data and experimental or quasiexperimental designs are favored over "soft" data and qualitative methods that are more common to social science fields (e.g., education or sociology). This favoritism toward quantitative methods comes from a desire to maintain a distance from the data and maintain objectivity throughout the study. You also will notice that researchers and evaluators who work in fields with traditional positivist or postpositivist lenses may apply these lenses when adopting qualitative methods. This practice may be

Table 7.1. MATRIX FOR A DATA COLLECTION PLAN THAT ALIGNS
WITH EVALUATION QUESTIONS

	1. Is the program successful?	2. Was the program implemented as planned?	3. Are parental stress levels related to the amount of family conflict?
Original Evaluation Question			
Analyzable Question	Are parental stress levels reduced by participating in the program?	Was the program implemented as planned?	Are parental stress levels related to the amount of family conflict?
Expected or anticipated answer (i.e., hypothesis), when applicable	Parental stress levels are reduced by the parenting program	The program was implemented as planned	Parental stress levels are strongly correlated with family conflict
Indicator or Evidence needed to answer the evaluation questions or test the hypotheses	Parental stress levels	How trainers implemented the program	Measures of Parental stress levels; Family Conflict
Data Source	Parents (participants and nonparticipant controls)	Trainers (i.e., program deliverers)	Parents
Data Collection Method	Stress Scale	Observations and self-reported checklists	Stress Scale; Family Conflict Inventory
Data Collection Points	Pre-, Post- and 6 months following the intervention	During program implementation	Pre-, Post- and 6 months following intervention
Analytical Design and Methods	Quantitative–RCT	Mixed Methods	Quantitative—Regression Model

RCT = randomized controlled trial

exhibited by an analyst's tendencies to quantify codes or impose categorical descriptions on data, rather than allowing the findings and their associated meaning to be inductively derived through the analysis.

Many social scientists value the opinions, ideas, experiences, and thought processes of participants and other stakeholders and use constructivist and transformative approaches when performing their work. Therefore, more subjective approaches that involve program participants and other stakeholders in an evaluation design and implementation are acceptable and desired. In other words, information obtained from participants and stakeholders constitute credible evidence in an evaluation. Participatory approaches to evaluation are, therefore, accepted, supported, and advocated among those who uphold this tradition.

These philosophically opposed traditions have created some tension among evaluators and funders and pose methodological challenges for evaluators in this era of accountability. These challenges are eloquently described by Jill Chouinard (2013) who discusses the dominance of "technocratic" approaches and how they hinder an evaluator's ability to select the best methods and approaches—especially those that support democracy, equity, and social justice—for answering evaluation questions. As evaluators, we must advocate for the approaches and methods most suitable for addressing stakeholders' needs for information and respect that what constitutes "credible" evidence among them will vary. Evaluation capacity building efforts can help to broaden these views and support the value of knowledge in many forms.

SURVEY DESIGN AND DEVELOPMENT

In this section, I begin my discussion about data collection methods by describing the most commonly used and overused data collection method in the evaluation field—surveys. I will describe, in detail, how to design a survey and review some of the pros and cons for the various ways (i.e., oral, written, electronic) to collect survey data. Many of the principles for designing a good survey will transfer to other data collection methods, such as psychometric instruments or guides used for interviews or focus groups.

Information from surveys can be collected in a variety of forms, including written, oral, and electronic. The most frequently cited reference for designing good surveys is a book by Don A. Dillman and colleagues titled, *Internet, phone, mail, and mixed-mode surveys: The tailored design method*, now in its fourth edition (2014). In this section, I will highlight some key lessons from Dillman's books and those by other authors who have addressed problems with surveys (Porter, 2004). In general, I like to think of survey questionnaires as having four general components. Surveys should begin with a brief introduction that describes the purpose of the survey, reason(s) the person has been asked to complete it, and approximate time it will take for the person to complete it. Any permissions needed to satisfy institutional review board (IRB) requirements must be contained as part of the introduction, and participants should be reminded that they can opt out of a survey at any time. Following the introduction, you will want to ask a few simple questions to familiarize the respondent with the style and format of the survey questions. These questions are then followed with the questions most relevant to the survey and questions of a sensitive nature (when applicable). When asking sensitive questions, rapport with a respondent must be built through early questions so sufficient trust can be established to obtain the most accurate responses as possible. The final items in a survey typically query the respondent for demographic information and thank them for their participation. The reason that demographic information is requested at the end of a survey is to be certain that needed information is obtained from participants, and they do not become disengaged early on by multiple demographic questions that seem irrelevant to the purpose of the survey (Dillman, 2000).

Question flow and response patterns are also important for obtaining complete information from a survey. If subject areas shift after a few or several items, insert one or two transition statements to guide the respondent through that change. It is also important that written surveys follow the same overall response pattern. In other words, if response items are to the right of a question, they should remain to the right of the question throughout the questionnaire. Shifts in questioning patterns may result in lost information. Questions requiring dichotomous (e.g., yes/no) responses and allow respondents to skip questions should be followed with queues, such as arrows or written phrases (e.g., "skip to question 6") that guide a respondent to the next appropriate question. I often am asked about the ideal length of a survey. In general, the fewer questions that will capture needed information, the better. Lengthy surveys, however, are not out of the question. Response rates tend to depend on the overall time it takes to do a survey and the interest level of respondents.

When wording questions and response items in a survey, the old expression "garbage in–garbage out," is highly relevant. Written items should be clearly articulated and worded in a way that is consistent with the language, linguistic patterns, and cultural backgrounds of the respondents. This could mean that your survey should be prepared in more than one language, delivered with two different linguistic patterns (e.g., those of academics vs. teens), or delivered in verbal form. I was recently reminded not to assume that a survey written in Spanish can be read by Spanish-speaking participants because illiteracy occurs in all languages. This experience provided an important reminder about how important it is to know the targeted respondents well in order to maximize response rates for surveys.

Dillman (2000) provides a list of 19 principles for writing questions and question items in order to avoid response problems (pp. 50–78). Table 7.2 highlights a few of them with examples.

Double-barreled items, or items that ask two questions at once, are a set-up for confusing responses, unless you are comfortable with a broad or ambiguous response. In most cases, however, they should be avoided. An example of a double-barreled item is, "What is your favorite food and how often do you eat it?" *Vaguely-worded* questions or items are also problematic because they open themselves to multiple interpretations and tend to elicit a range of responses that can result in lost or misleading information. *Wordy* items create confusion among respondents who may have to read them repeatedly to gain meaning or interpret them as intended. Keep items as

Table 7.2. EXAMPLES OF POORLY WORDED SURVEY QUESTIONS AND
EXAMPLES OF HOW TO CORRECT THEM

Common Problems with Survey Questions	Problem Example	Corrected Example
Double-barreled Questions	To what extent are you *tired and hungry* at the end of each day?	How *tired* are you at the end each day? How *hungry* are you at the end of each day?
Vague Quantifiers	On most days of the week . . . ❑ I am completely exhausted at the end of the day ❑ I am somewhat exhausted at the end of the day ❑ I am rarely or never exhausted at the end of the day	On at least five days of each week, how would you describe your level of tiredness? ❑ I am completely exhausted at the end of the day ❑ I am somewhat exhausted at the end of the day ❑ I am rarely or never exhausted at the end of the day
Wordy	Are you completely exhausted, somewhat exhausted, or rarely or not at all exhausted at the end of each day?	Which of the following items best describes your level of exhaustion at the end of the day?
Overly specific	How many days in the past month have you felt exhausted at the end of the day? _____ days	How many days in the past month have you felt exhausted at the end of the day? ❑ Less than 5 ❑ 6–10 ❑ 11–15 ❑ 16–20 ❑ More than 20

brief as possible, so that they are clear and solicit accurate responses. Wordy items are also likely to be double-barreled items, as the example in Box 7.1 illustrates.

Asking participants to provide specific information that is difficult to recall will likely result in less accurate information or questions that are skipped. It is important to find a balance between specificity and vagueness when writing questions and item responses.

Likert scales, as one type of response item, should be written along a continuum from positive to negative, with "no-opinion" or "undecided" responses placed last (Box 7.2). *Categorical* response items (e.g., apples, peaches, pears, etc.) run the risk of being overly or insufficiently comprehensive.

Box 7.1. AN EXAMPLE OF A WORDY AND DOUBLE-BARRELED SURVEY ITEM

On a scale of 1–10, please indicate your overall level of happiness with 1 being "not happy" and 10 being "extremely happy" and tell me why you selected your response.

Too few response items might cause respondents to skip the question because their response is not contained among the choices. Too many items are laborious to read and may cause items to be overlooked or a question to be skipped altogether. This problem can be avoided in two ways. First, an open-ended "other" category can be added that allows respondents to specify their response (e.g., "grapes"). This option, however, could result in multiple responses that are difficult to analyze and from which it would be difficult to derive meaning. Alternatively, a short list of response items could be provided and responses prompted with a question, "Which three of the following fruits do you like best?" This strategy reduces the number of possible responses to an item and maintains a focus on the most relevant information.

Other principles of survey design include avoiding questions that impose biases, hypothetical or objectionable questions, and talking down to respondents. Provide opportunities for a few open-ended responses whenever details would help to explain or describe a response and provide useful information for the study's purpose and guiding questions. Be certain, through a pilot study, that respondents are willing and motivated to answer each question and to reveal the type of information desired to answer the evaluation questions.

Box 7.2. EXAMPLE OF RESPONSE ITEMS ALONG A CONTINUUM

❑ Strongly agree
❑ Somewhat agree
❑ Neither agree nor disagree
❑ Somewhat disagree
❑ Strongly disagree
❑ No opinion

Pilot testing provides the means for an evaluator to maximize the quality of information obtained through a survey. Pilot surveys are typically performed with a small sample or subset of participants resembling the population of interest. Recruitment methods, time to response, proportion of questions answered, respondent characteristics, and clarity of questions, among other qualities and conditions, can be evaluated in a pilot survey. Cognitive interviews (Shafer & Lohse, n.d.; Willis, 1999) may be added to determine a respondent's interpretation of each item and whether questions have been worded or asked with an appropriate level of detail to solicit accurate responses.

When you are satisfied with your survey instrument, it can be given to the evaluation's participants. Surveys can be delivered in written, oral, or electronic form using e-mail or mobile devices. Written and electronic surveys are the most common form of delivery, and electronic surveys are the easiest and least expensive to deliver. Electronic surveys can make it difficult, however, to track nonresponders, and they require extra attention to maintain participants' confidentiality and anonymity. Oral surveys are time intensive because they require face-to-face or voice contact. They are also highly structured, and unlike interviews that are oriented around open-ended questions, they contain multiple close-ended questions.

Collecting survey responses can be very difficult. Response rates can be maximized with small incentives and correspondence (letters or e-mail) containing announcements and survey reminders. At least three attempts should be made to collect information using a survey. A single attempt will typically yield a response rate of less than 30% while three attempts will likely boost your response rate to over 60%. As you make multiple requests for survey responses, be sure to track those who have already responded, if possible, to avoid sending annoying communications.

Surveys are most useful when you would like to collect information from a large sample or you want to track and assess quantifiable information across time. They are also best utilized for describing a population's characteristics, opinions, or behaviors. Surveys are also most appropriate when collecting program outcomes, but are less suited for information regarding a program's process or when in-depth information is needed to understand a program, problem, issue, or phenomenon.

PSYCHOMETRIC TESTS

In program evaluation, two basic types of questionnaires are used. Each serves a different purpose—those designed to collect survey data and those designed to assess psychological constructs, such as cognition, self-efficacy, motivation, stress, well-being, and other types of psychological characteristics that cannot be easily measured. Most of the tips you learned for designing a good survey instrument also apply to psychometric tests (also known as scales or inventories). There are, however, additional processes and design elements that need attention when constructing these types of questionnaires. The steps for designing a psychometric test are listed in Box 7.3.

First, it is essential that the construct or attribute (e.g., motivation) you wish to assess be clearly defined and understood in terms of its various dimensions (Walsh & Betz, 2001). For example, several years ago when working on a study, our research team defined clinical research self-efficacy based on the following definition of clinical research.

> Clinical research is a component of medical and health research intended to produce knowledge essential for understanding human diseases, preventing and treating illness, and promoting health. Clinical research embraces a continuum of studies involving interaction with patients, diagnostic clinical materials or data, or populations in any of these categories: disease mechanisms; translational research; clinical knowledge, detection, diagnosis, and natural history of disease; therapeutic interventions including clinical trials; prevention and health promotion; behavioral research; health services research; epidemiology; and community-based and managed care-based research. (Association of the American Medical Colleges, 2002; Mullikin, Bakken & Betz, 2007, p. 372)

Therefore, we designed an instrument that would capture a person's self-assessed abilities to perform various tasks and activities needed to conduct clinical research. This construct was originally defined with ten dimensions, which later, through item analyses, was reduced to eight.

Box 7.3. STEPS IN TEST CONSTRUCTION (BETZ, 1996, PP. 241–242)

STEP 1. Carefully describe the attribute or construct to be measured.

STEP 2. Develop a large pool of items logically related to the attribute of interest.

STEP 3. Administer the items to a large sample of subjects (i.e., the development sample).

STEP 4. Refine the original item pool through item analysis and expert judgment.

STEP 5. Administer the revised test to a new sample of subjects.

STEP 6. Based on the new samples, examine evidence for reliability and validity and compile normative data.

After clearly defining a construct of interest, items that logically relate to the construct can be assembled (Step 2). For the Clinical Research Appraisal Inventory (CRAI; Mullikin, Bakken, & Betz, 2007), items were derived from our experiences, academic literature, and other published documents in the field. When constructing items, guidelines are the same as those provided in the previous section on surveys (e.g., avoiding double-barreled items). Regarding measures of self-efficacy, Bandura (1997) advises that items be posed in the context of a challenging situation because this construct is best exhibited when faced with obstacles. My point in mentioning this relevant detail is that some psychological conditions might be exacerbated or more or less pronounced under certain conditions that may be known or defined in the field, so it is important that items be sensitive to those conditions and worded accordingly. You might be asking yourself, "How many items do I need to create a sufficiently sized item pool?" As many items as possible within the boundaries of the construct's definition should be assembled as a first step in designing a psychometric questionnaire. When we designed the CRAI, we began with a pool of 200–300 items, which were reduced to 96 before we sampled our population of interest. This large pool of items was a first step toward establishing the instrument's *face* and *content* validity (i.e., operationalization of the construct in meaningful and logic terms).

The third step in designing a psychometric test is to have it completed by a relatively large and heterogeneous sample with the expectation of approximately 200–300 respondents. That sample should be based on the population for which you would like to make your final assessment. Simultaneously, you may wish to administer other psychometric instruments that assess related and unrelated constructs in order to assess the new instrument's *convergent* and *discriminant* validity, respectively (see Trochim, 2006). Once these responses have been obtained, you can begin the next step in the design process.

The next step (Step 4 in Box 7.3) requires that an item analysis be performed to determine how well the responses to each item individually and collectively correlate with the construct. The outcome of this analysis is a statistical term called, *Cronbach's alpha,* which is a measure of item correlation; therefore, the measure is a number between zero (no correlation) and one (full correlation). The higher its value, the stronger the items correlate. Item analysis produces correlation coefficients for each item and for the overall item pool. Item coefficients correspond with how well each item correlates with the overall construct (set of items), in contrast to the overall item correlation coefficient that represents how well the items "hang together" as a construct. Any item with an item-correlation of less than 0.3 should be removed from an item pool. You may want to remove items in a step-wise fashion and rerun the item analysis with each removal because item correlations will change with each analysis. When you have settled on a pool of items that are well-correlated to one another (or within a dimension of the construct) and to the overall construct (known as total item-correlation), you are prepared for the final two steps of the design process, which are to administer the refined questionnaire to a new sample and determine the validity and reliability of the instrument.

In psychometric test construction, a test's *reliability* is determined by assessing the previous sample's responses approximately two to four weeks following the original administration of the questionnaire. This step is known as test-retest reliability, and it is used to confirm that a measure is consistent over time, assuming all other conditions are held constant. When the second set of responses are obtained, the response sets are compared using a paired t-test to make certain there are no statistically significant differences between the two set of responses over the assessment period. Lack of statistical significance suggests a reliably performing instrument. Collectively, statistics reporting a test's validity and reliability are known as the instrument's *psychometric properties*. However, Nunnally and Bernstein (1994) note that an instrument's true psychometric properties are not based on a single sample or study, but are well established only after the instrument has been used and tested multiple times in a field. Regarding the Clinical Research Self-Efficacy Inventory, I continue to correspond with the inventory's users in other settings in order to track the instrument's overall performance and adaptations for similar populations. In the decade that has passed since we developed the instrument, I am continually impressed by its performance, and I have enjoyed many opportunities to be a part of those studies.

Program developers and coordinators tend to design data collection tools from scratch. I, therefore, encourage you to review instruments published in the literature, used by colleagues, or published by professional organizations, such as the American Psychological Association. Published instruments have typically undergone rigorous methods of development and evaluation to determine their validity and reliability. They can usually be obtained through written permission from the author or purchased through an online source and adapted for your own context. In doing so, it is important that the adapted instrument retains the original items' wording as much as possible. I also recommend that you perform tests for validity and reliability to demonstrate that the adapted instrument retains its original psychometric properties.

INTERVIEWS AND FOCUS GROUPS

Interviews and focus groups are best for collecting rich descriptive information and stories. Interviews are typically conducted face-to-face or by phone, but with more recent improvements in technology, they can be conducted electronically through e-mail or video communications (e.g., Skype). Interviews require strong communication skills that involve careful listening, as well as paraphrasing and clarifying what is heard. A skilled interviewer also avoids leading or judgmental remarks and expressions that could bias the participants' responses. These skills are important to practice and typically require several applications before they can be perfected. Audio-recordings of interviews help to hone these skills and serve as a source of written transcripts for a thorough analysis.

Focus groups add a level of complexity to qualitative data collection and optimally require two people—a facilitator and a recorder—to conduct them. The facilitator's role is to ask questions and probe for additional information that seeks clarification or adds depth to the participants' responses. As in interviews, facilitators need excellent communication skills to monitor the conversation and maximize opportunities for rich data collection. The recorder takes notes of the conversations, keeps track of time, and is responsible for focus-group logistics, such as making sure the recorders are turned on and recording. The ideal size of a focus group is six to eight participants, and the number you include depends on the heterogeneity of the participants, the scope of the evaluation, and the types of evaluation questions you are trying to answer. Focus groups typically last 60 to 90 minutes. Initial questions serve as icebreakers to discussion and are useful in creating a more relaxed atmosphere and opening a conversation. The facilitator must give careful attention to providing opportunities for all participants to be recognized and heard so that appropriate representation of participants' opinions and perspectives is obtained throughout the data collection process. Focus groups typically end by giving participants opportunities to express reflective thoughts or final comments. It is vitally important that in both interviews and focus groups, participants be thanked for their time and effort. Again, appreciation can be expressed with gift cards or other forms of recognition.

Interview and focus group guides contain a set of instructions, prompts, and questions that guide an interviewer or facilitator as he collects information from evaluation study participants. They can be used when collecting information in person, by phone, or electronically (e.g., e-mail). These guides can be structured, semistructured, or open-ended. *Structured* guides contain a list of questions to which wording and order are strictly adhered during the interview process. *Semistructured* guides provide a list of questions, too, but these can be worded somewhat differently, reordered, and supplemented with more probing questions during the interview process, depending on the flow of the conversation. These types of guides help to focus the interview while capturing in-depth information. *Unstructured* guides are used to solicit responses with minimal guidance (e.g., stories) and typically contain only a single question or instruction to get a conversation going. For example, you might ask a study participant to tell a story about their experience as a member of an activist group. Impromptu probes often are added during the conversation to solicit in-depth information from study participants.

Interview and focus group guides typically begin with a short introduction to the study and the reason why the participants' responses are important. As with a survey, you will inform the participant how long the interview will take, whether or not it will be recorded, and how it will be conducted. You also will want to remind participants of the voluntary nature of their responses and their ability to terminate the interview or leave the focus group at any time. When you are ready to begin the questioning period, I encourage you to use an audio- or video-recorder to record the participants' responses and accurately capture the information they provide. At the beginning of focus groups, ground rules are helpful in avoiding simultaneous dialogue, encouraging full participation, and controlling participants who tend to monopolize conversations. At the end of an interview or focus group, stop the recording and thank participants for their time and effort in contributing important information for the study. Detailed guidelines for developing, organizing, conducting, and analyzing focus groups can be found in Krueger (2002) and Krueger and Casey (2015).

OBSERVATIONS AND VIDEO-RECORDINGS

Our eyes can prove an extremely useful resource for data collection. Observation as a form of data collection can be used to understand behavior, interactions among people and their environments, a program or evaluation's context, and ways that knowledge and skills are applied in actual settings. Observations can be made directly in real time or indirectly through video-recordings. Observations in real-time require attentive note-taking or supportive record-keeping tools, such as checklists or rubrics. Notes and video-recordings can be qualitatively analyzed to yield rich information about an event or observed behaviors. Observing individuals or groups creates a sense of unease for participants, so initial observations may not yield very authentic or fruitful information. This situation can be reduced by observers who "blend" with or are unknown to the group, disappear into the background, or are invisible to participants through specially designed rooms with one-way windows. With additional time, however, participants often forget that they are being observed. In some cases, your purpose may be to observe a program's physical surroundings or other contextual elements that don't involve observations of people. In this case, it might be useful and appropriate to augment your observations with photographs, if permitted. Whether you are observing people, their surroundings, or a context, be sure to stay mindful of human-subject protections and seek permission to observe and record any people, events, or surroundings you are observing.

Observation guides are similar to those used for focus groups or interviews in that they provide a guide for making observations. For example, a guide might be segmented by time such that you would record your observations in the first five minutes of a dialogue and then record what you observe ten minutes later. Observations recorded at various points in time are useful for sampling a range of behaviors or events that are related to a specific phenomenon or process. An observation guide also might be designed to record the frequency of observed events, such as when a child strikes a playmate. A guide of this type also might include a space for the observer to describe an event that prompted the child's behavior. These are just some examples of how guides can be used to facilitate observations. The next section describes some additional methods of data collection, some of which have emerged in the field over recent years.

CHECKLISTS AND RUBRICS

Checklists and *rubrics* provide a simple way to capture data when an evaluator would like to track or quantify observed occurrences of specific characteristics, instances, or events. They are designed with a framework or list of concepts that adequately capture the attributes of interest. Often, theoretical or conceptual frameworks (e.g., Community Capitals Framework, Bourdieu, 1986) are used to specify the parameters or items to be captured by a rubric. Checklists are used to determine whether an attribute is present in the person, groups, or settings observed. Drawing from an earlier example in this chapter, I might use a rubric to track and quantify instances or characteristics of critical thinking in a one-hour discussion that is part of an educational intervention. Another way that checklists and rubrics can be used is to track events or other phenomena described in a group of reports or other documents. For example, you might wish to examine a group of clinical cases to determine whether high-risk prenatal patients received appropriate referrals or follow-up care and the type of care they received. Figure 7.1 provides an example of a rubric that was used to track and record social networks and relationships mentioned by members of listening sessions during community site visits. This is just one example of a way a rubric can be used in evaluation practice. I encourage you to think of other ways they may be useful in your work.

MAPS AND DRAWINGS

Maps and drawings are used to collect information that yields patterns and images not easily obtained through verbal communication. Maps are a great way to collect information about study participants' mental models or images, travel patterns, activities at various locations, communication patterns, or

Part B: Social Networks/Relationships
Directions: Identify and check each appropriate community characteristic. Include appropriate attendant documentation, if available, for further analysis (e.g., photographs, maps, graphs, and other visual aids).

Social Networks/ Relationships	Strong Presence (community networks have visible and material impact)	Intermediated Presence (community networks have emerging or minimal and impact)	Not Present (community networks have no visible or material impact)	Comment(s)
Community Organizations				
Community Programs				
Senior Housing				
Volunteer Network/ Group				
Community/ Government Boards				
Parent Network/Group				
Teachers Association/ Union				
Community Coalitions (e.g., block clubs)				
Friends & Neighbors				
Family/Extended Family Network				
Engagement with Unique Populations (e.g., Hmong, Tribal communities, Hispanic)				
Labor Force				
Other				
Total				

Figure 7.1. Example of a rubric that was used to track and record social networks and relationships.

social networks. They also may be used to focus the scope of an evaluation onto a specific geographic area, as the map in Figure 7.2 illustrates.

This map shows Wisconsin locations where factors related to food insecurity (e.g., high jobless rate, single mothers with children, high poverty rate, high proportion of elderly) were prominent in 2012 and 2013. Each star represents a factor and the more stars populating each county, the more likely assistance or services are needed. This map helped the evaluation team to establish a specific area to target for a study of the feasibility of expanding a food outreach program in this part of the state. Maps that illustrate a geographic

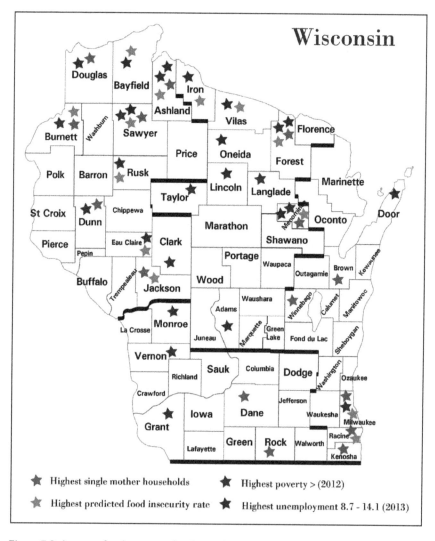

Figure 7.2. An example of a map used to determine target areas for an evaluation study. Stars represent factors that are associated with high rates of food insecurity.

location (e.g., a city or specific neighborhood) or physical structure also may be used to ask study participants to indicate with a sticker or marker their activities by location, such as where they go to shop or get gas. Maps, such as Ripple Effect Maps (Emery, Higgins, Chazdon, & Hansen, 2015; Hansen Kollock, Flage, Chazdon, Paine, & Higgins, 2012), may be used to determine changes to organizations or communities that resulted from a new program or intervention. Ripple effects maps are mind maps (Buzan & Buzan, 2010) that represent a program's collective outcomes and impact (Figure 7.3a). They are particularly useful for mapping the impact of a coalition or other group that has a specific mission to effect social change. Network maps (Figure 7.3b) are another type of map that provides a way to visualize a person's social or communication patterns and connections with other people in his or her community. They are useful for determining individuals or organizations that may be championing an effort or identifying where breakdowns in communication may exist.

Drawings and other visual illustrations are useful tools for acquiring participants' images of concepts or ideas. For example, one of my former doctoral students used drawings to collect information about how researchers viewed their communities of practice. These drawings allowed her to determine who was involved in those communities, how the researchers interacted with their communities, and why they interacted in the ways they did (Wang, 2005). Used as part of workshops or focus group activities, maps and drawings are an excellent way to encourage communication and group cohesion when that is a desired goal. Visual metaphors, for example, are useful for portraying ideas or concepts through common images, such as trees, rainbows, or butterflies. Coupled with photographs, maps can "come alive" by capturing facial expressions, activities, or meaningful structures and locations.

PHOTOGRAPHS

Photographic images are used to collect information about a participant's environment or life experiences as they occur. Photographs can be taken by program staff, evaluators, or study participants as a way to capture information in real time. As a method of data collection that engages participants, the act of collecting data through photographs often is referred to as "photovoice" (Bessell, Deese, & Medina, 2007; Hergenrather, Rhodes, Cowan, Bardhoshi, & Pula, 2009). Like other forms of visual data, photographs can be used to collect qualitative and quantitative information and are especially useful when working with youth. For example, youth could take photographs of places they "hang out" as a way to understand their social patterns and behaviors within a given context (e.g., a school or playground). These patterns and behaviors could then be quantified by counting occurrences of each or they could be

(a)

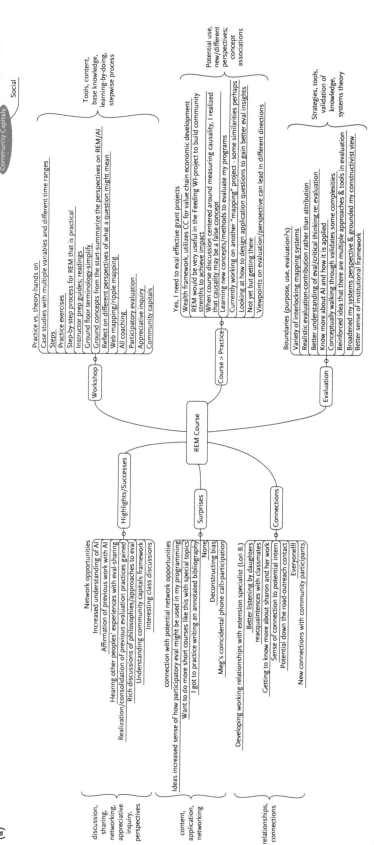

Figures 7.3a and 7.3b. Examples of a Ripple Effects Map (a) and a Network Map (b).

(b)

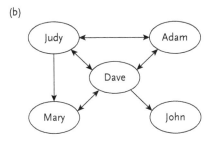

Figures 7.3a and 7.3b. Continued

qualitatively analyzed to determine the characteristics of the patterns and behaviors captured in the photographs.

Existing photographs also may be collected that represent an historical event, one's experiences or emotions, or a phenomenon. Qualitative analysis of existing photographs holds potential to reveal a story or a detailed description of a program or other evaluand (e.g., policy) as it was developed, implemented, and/or reported. Therefore, photographs provide a useful visual means of retrospective data collection that can capture processes or outcomes. In this era of cell phones, tablets, and other readily available electronic forms of communication, photographs (existing or new) are becoming a more prominent source of data in the evaluation field.

EXISTING SOURCES

Existing documentation, such as strategic plans, historical records, written reports, and websites, can also be sources of information for an evaluation study. These sources typically provide information about the context for an evaluation study. Existing documents can lend insight into organizational structures; power dynamics; an organization's mission, vision, and philosophy; ways of conducting business; and community influences and "champions," among other information. Typically, they are analyzed using qualitative methods to capture their content or meaning. Checklists and rubrics that quantify occurrences of information may be useful for evaluating the extent to which vision and mission statements appear on an organization's website, for example. As another example, discourse analysis may be used to quantity specific words or expressions used in text.

In the previous sections, I have described various ways to collect information for an evaluation study. In the remaining sections, I will discuss how reliable and accurate information is collected and how to record, track, and maintain the integrity of information throughout a study.

I already have described several ways that you can collect accurate and reliable information using surveys or psychometric tests. These included cognitive interviews, procedures to determine discriminate and construct validity, test-retest procedures for test reliability, proper ways to write items to obtain complete and accurate information, and photographs and audio- and video-recordings to capture accurate and "real-time" information. Valid and reliable quantitative information is obtained through well-designed instruments and study designs, as described in this and previous chapters.

Additional ways to ensure that qualitative information is collected with credibility are to use member checking, triangulation, and saturation. *Member checking*, a form of validation in qualitative evaluation, can be performed in several ways and at various points of data collection. For example, when conducting an interview, I could summarize what I heard and give the interviewee an opportunity to confirm or refute my comments and summary. Following an interview or focus group, I also could summarize the interview in written form and provide it back to participants for editorial comment and changes.

Triangulation is a method used to establish the credibility (i.e., validity) of qualitative information, and it can take multiple forms. One can triangulate data sources by collecting the same information from multiple sources (e.g., documents, program participants, and administrators); using multiple methods of data collection (e.g., face-to-face interviews, online surveys, and phone interviews) to collect identical information; or convening multiple analysts to code information (Patton, 2002). The goal of triangulation is to cross-check information collected in one way with that collected or analyzed in another way or by another person.

Saturation of information obtained through interviews, focus groups, or other qualitative data collection methods is important for valid information. It is reached when an evaluator is repeatedly obtaining the same information from data sources and no longer acquiring new information when collecting and analyzing data. Premature attempts to reach saturation, or a limited sample composition, threaten an evaluator's ability to obtain credible information by limiting the type and amount of information from which conclusions are drawn.

The *academic literature* can be used as an external form of validation for both qualitative and quantitative studies. Studies published in previous reports can verify or explain findings from an evaluation study, thereby lending legitimacy to the work. In qualitative evaluation studies, *reliable* information is primarily established through multiple analysts. Analysts should agree on naming and defining codes, as well as on categories and themes derived from information collected in an evaluation study. They also should apply codes consistently over time. This process is known as *inter-rater reliability*.

Last, but not least, accurate findings are derived through not only the accurate collection of information, but accurate recording of it, too. The next section will address ways that data is recorded and maintained to ensure that its integrity remains throughout an evaluation study.

DESIGNING DATABASES FOR ELECTRONIC STORAGE

Whether you collect data electronically or in pen and paper form, you likely will want to store it in an electronic database (e.g., spreadsheet, qualitative software, or statistical software) for analysis. How data is recorded and organized in an electronic form has a great bearing on how easily it can be analyzed. In this section, I will provide some tips for recording and organizing electronic data, so it can be efficiently and properly analyzed. I will begin with data collection using quantitative methods (e.g., surveys) and then provide some tips for electronically storing qualitative information.

A first consideration is to have a clear understanding of your unit of analysis. A *unit of analysis* is the object (e.g., persons, places, or things) on which you conduct the evaluation (Hoy & Adams, 2016, p. 28). In program evaluation, the object of an inquiry is typically a program, or, using a more generic term, an "evaluand." In order to make judgments about a program, however, we typically collect data from program participants and other data sources (e.g., program coordinators, program documents, or associated stakeholders). So, it is important to have a clear understanding of the evaluation's data sources and how each source will contribute information that will allow you to evaluate a program or other unit of analysis (e.g., project, policy, or a coalition's activities). Have you collected data from individual participants? Have you collected data from an organization's or a community's members? Do study participants and the data collected from them represent subsets of a population or group? How do you wish to analyze the data? By participant? By participant's age, community membership, or other demographic characteristic? According to information you collected on each participant over time? Answers to these types of questions have bearing on how you will structure an electronic database and how data will be recorded and organized for analysis.

Each record or row in an electronic data file should pertain to a single data source (e.g., a participant) and a single method of data collection (e.g., a survey questionnaire). Each column of your database will contain "fields" or "cells" that correspond to specific demographic information, group characteristics, and responses to individual items in a questionnaire. Figure 7.4 illustrates what a typical record might look like for quantitative data collected from each of three participants.

Participant I.D.	Gender	Age Group*	Site	Study Group	Pretest	Posttest
001	F	1	1	I	5	16
002	F	2	2	C	8	10
003	M	2	1	C	6	7

*1= 20-29 yrs.; 2= 30-39 yrs.; 3= 40-49 yrs.; 4= 50-59 yrs.; 5= >59 yrs.

Figure 7.4. An example of a typical structure for a database.

Notice that for age group and site, categorical responses are represented by numbers. When recording categorical responses, it is important to assign numbers to each category so that statistical software can appropriately analyze that information. Also notice that pretest and posttest response are recorded in separate columns. Each response must be recorded in separate columns or *cells* corresponding to a participant. Multiple responses in a single cell create extra and often laborious steps for statisticians and data analysts, and they will for you, too, if you are your own data analyst or statistician, as many of us are. Spreadsheets and statistical software treat information in each cell separately, so if a cell contains multiple responses, it cannot be analyzed appropriately. Like multiple responses to a single item, time series data also must be contained in separate cells. So, if you collect data before, immediately after, and three or six months following an intervention, your data file will have columns for pretest, posttest, and three-month posttest data. Often, evaluators like to maintain participants' demographic identifiers in files that are separate from data files. When analyzing data, however, you often will want to perform an analysis according to participants' demographic information. To do so, you must have at least one column in each data file that is identical and unique to a corresponding record in the second file. In the example shown in Figure 7.5, and in most databases, that column is "Participant ID." By recording electronic information in this way, the records can be linked, matched, and analyzed as if they were a single record (Figure 7.5). One word of caution, however, data in each row must correspond with a single record for this to work. If, for example, one data file contained information in each column that corresponded to a different participant (information contained in columns instead of rows), the data would have to be converted to rows before the files could be linked accurately. Most statistical software is designed to analyze data recorded in this way (see Chapter 2 in Abu-Bader, 2011).

To keep track of how you name fields and record data in a database so that other (or new) members of your evaluation team can understand the information, it is important to develop and maintain a *coding dictionary*. Coding dictionaries simply provide a list of codes, their meanings and the various ways that information is recorded in a database (Table 7.3) so that you can identify it in the output from a statistical analysis.

(a)

Demographic Data File		
Participant ID	Gender	Study Group
001	F	I
002	F	C
003	M	C

Results Data File		
Participant ID	Pretest	Posttest
001	5	16
002	8	10
003	6	7

(b)

Merged Data File				
Participant ID	Gender	Study Group	Pretest	Posttest
001	F	I	5	16
002	F	C	8	10
003	M	C	6	7

Figure 7.5. Examples of separate and merged data files.

Table 7.3. A SIMPLE EXAMPLE OF CODING DICTIONARY FOR AN EVALUATION STUDY

Code	Code Meaning	Response Type	Response Options and Identifiers
Participant ID	The unique identification code assigned to a study participant	Numeric Indicator (not quantity)	Assigned
Gender	The gender indicated by a respondent	Categorical	F = 1
			M = 2
Study Group	The group that the participant was randomized to for the study	Categorical	I = 1
			C = 2
Pretest	Respondent's test score prior to the intervention	Continuous	Computed Score
Posttest	Respondent's test score immediately following the intervention	Continuous	Computed Score

Similarly, you can store transcriptions or other documents (e.g., photographs or video recordings) in qualitative data analysis software and perform an analysis directly on those sources. You also can use word processing software in combination with spreadsheets to analyze many of these sources. In this case, a spreadsheet might contain the information, such as the data source ID, collection date, type of data source, and the outputs of your analysis (e.g., codes, coded excerpts, and categories). Coding dictionaries may be created for qualitative data; however, their purpose is not to decipher information, but to facilitate the analysis. In qualitative evaluation and research, coding dictionaries help to establish reliability across analysts and maintain consistency among members of the evaluation team throughout the analytical process. This process and the function of a coding dictionary are described in detail in Chapter 9.

TRACKING INFORMATION

Accurate records of data collection and analysis are extremely important for tracking the progress of your study and making sure that all information is obtained and appropriately processed for analysis. I recommend that this information be stored in an electronic spreadsheet, database, or table in an electronic document. For each study participant or unit of analysis, you will want to track the following information.

Participant identifiers
Date of study enrollment
Whether or not a consent form is on file
When data were collected and in what form
The date the participant's information was uploaded to or recorded in a database
The date of data analysis and who on the evaluation team performed the analysis, and
Other information that might be important for tracking, such as group membership.

For qualitative information, such as interviews, you will want to record the date the interview was conducted, who conducted the interview, whether or not a recording exists (sometimes we have equipment malfunctions), if and when the recording was uploaded or sent for transcription, the date of the transcription (and when received by study personnel), and, finally, the date the transcript was analyzed and the person who analyzed it. This tracking information is critical for accurate record keeping and complete data analysis. Remember, a tracking record for missing data is important for making inferences or drawing conclusions about the data when it is analyzed, so complete records are essential. If, for any reason, data is missing (e.g., an incomplete survey), this information must be recorded, because it, too, has bearing on data analysis and interpretation. Complete and accurate tracking data is also essential for reporting your study's activities to an IRB.

SUMMARY

This chapter has equipped you with a variety of data collection methods commonly used in evaluation studies. It also has provided tips for organizing and recording information that facilitates tracking and data analysis. Your choices and decisions about data collection methods will be driven by the evaluation's questions and the types of evidence considered to be credible among its stakeholders. In the next two chapters, I will delve into data analysis, thereby, furthering your understanding of the importance of quality data collection and accurate record keeping.

REFERENCES

Abu-Bader, S. H. (2011). *Using statistical methods in social science research* (2nd ed.). Chicago, IL: Lyceum Books.

Association of American Medical Colleges. (2002). *Information technology enabling clinical research. Findings and recommendations from a conference sponsored by the Association of American Medical Colleges with funding from the National Science Foundation.* Retrieved from http://www.aamc.org/members/gir/clincalresearchreport.pdf.

Bandura, A. (1997). *Self-efficacy: The exercise of control.* New York, NY: W. H. Freeman.

Bessell, A. G., Deese, W. B., & Medina, A. L. (2007). Photolanguage: How a picture can inspire a thousand words. *American Journal of Evaluation, 28(4),* 558–569.

Betz, N. E. (1996). Test construction. In F. Leong & J. Austin (Eds.), *The psychology research handbook* (pp. 239–250). Thousand Oaks, CA: Sage Publications.

Bourdieu, P. (1986). The forms of capital. In J. G. Richardson (Ed.), *The handbook of theory: Research for the sociology of education* (pp. 241–258). New York, NY: Greenwood Press.

Buzan, T., & Buzan, B. (2010). *The Mind Map Book: Unlock your creativity, boost your memory and change your life.* Edinburgh Gate, Harlow, England: BBC Active.

Chouinard, J. A. (2013). The case for participatory evaluation in an era of accountability. *American Journal of Evaluation, 32(2),* 237–253.

Dillman, D. A. (2000). *Mail and Internet surveys: The tailored design method* (2nd ed.). New York, NY: John Wiley & Sons.

Dillman, D. A., Smyth, J. D., & Christian, L. M. (2014). *Internet, phone, mail, and mixed-mode surveys: The tailored design method* (4th ed.). New York, NY: John Wiley & Sons.

Emery, M., Higgins, L., Chazdon, S., & Hansen, D. (2015). Using Ripple Effect Mapping to evaluate program impact: Choosing or combining the methods that work best for you. *Journal of Extension 53*(2). Available for download at http://www.joe.org/joe/2015april/tt1.php.

Hansen Kollock, D.A., Flage, L., Chazdon, S., Paine, N., & Higgins, L. (2012). Ripple Effect Mapping: A "radiant" way to capture program impacts. *Journal of Extension, 50*(5). Available for download at http://www.joe.org/joe/2012october/tt6.php.

Hergenrather, K. C., Rhodes, S. D., Cowan, C. A., Bardhoshi, G., & Pula, S. (2009). Photovoice as community-based participatory research: A qualitative review. *American Journal of Health Behavior, 33(6)*, 686–698.

Hoy, W. K., & Adams, C. M. (2016). *Quantitative research in education* (2nd ed.). Thousand Oaks, CA: Sage Publications.

Krueger, R. A. (2002). *Designing and conducting focus group interviews*. Available for download at http://www.eiu.edu/ihec/Krueger-FocusGroupInterviews.pdf.

Krueger, R. A., & Casey, M. A. (2015). *Focus groups: A practical guide for applied research* (5th ed.). Thousand Oaks, CA: Sage Publications.

Mullikin, E. A., Bakken, L. L., & Betz, N. E. (2007). Assessing research self-efficacy in physician-scientists: The Clinical Research Appraisal Inventory. *Journal of Career Assessment, 15*(3), 367–387.

Nunnally, J. C., & Bernstein, I. H. (1994). *Psychometric theory* (3rd ed.). New York, NY: McGraw-Hill.

Patton, M. Q. (2002). *Qualitative research and evaluation methods* (3rd ed.). Thousand Oaks, CA: Sage Publications.

Porter, S. R. (2004, Spring). Pros and cons of paper and electronic surveys. *New Directions for Institutional Research, 121*, 91–97.

Shafer, K., & Lohse, B. (n.d.). *How to conduct a cognitive interview: A nutrition education example*. Available at: www.au.af.mil/au/awc/awcgate/usda/cog-interview.pdf.

Trochim, W. M. K. (2006). The research methods knowledge base (2nd ed.). Retrieved from: www.socialresearchmethods.net/kb/measval.php.

Walsh, W. B., & Betz, N. E. (2001). *Tests and assessment* (4th ed.). New York, NY: Pearson Education.

Wang, Min-fen. *Physician-scientists' learning in communities of practice*. Order No. 3186050 The University of Wisconsin—Madison, 2005. Ann Arbor: *ProQuest*. Web. August 8, 2016.

Willis, G. B. (1999). *Cognitive interviewing: A "how to" guide*. Available at: http://www.hkr.se/pagefiles/35002/gordonwillis.pdf.

Analyzing and Interpreting Quantitative Data

VIKRAM KOUNDINYA, CONTRIBUTOR

Chapter 8 begins as if you had a quantitative data set in front of you ready for statistical analysis. Therefore, I begin by describing some common techniques for cleaning data and handling missing data. I then cover some basic concepts and definitions that apply to statistical analyses and lay the groundwork for analysis by discussing the importance of getting acquainted with your data set through plots and descriptive statistics. Next, I describe various types of evaluation questions and how they inform hypotheses testing and inferential statistics.

Box 8.1 lists the general steps for performing a statistical analysis. This chapter covers the information needed to perform each of these steps and builds your understanding of statistics, so that you can apply them in practice. I conclude this chapter with strategies for gaining a better understanding of statistics, so you will feel more confident in designing an analytical plan for your evaluation studies.

CLEANING DATA AND HANDLING MISSING DATA

Before quantitative data can be analyzed, it should be examined for accuracy and missing information and "cleaned" in preparation for your specific analysis. In my 25-plus years as a researcher and evaluator, I have never witnessed a complete data set. For various reasons, study participants either overlook

> **Box 8.1. GENERAL STEPS FOR PERFORMING A STATISTICAL ANALYSIS**
>
> STEP 1. Clean data and prepare it for analysis
> STEP 2. Specify your hypotheses
> STEP 3. Select a statistic test
> STEP 4. Diagram your analytical plan
> STEP 5. Run the statistical analysis
> STEP 6. Interpret the statistical analysis
> STEP 7. Run any post-hoc analyses and interpret
> STEP 8. Prepare a summary and report

items or choose not to respond to them. Therefore, it is important that data be carefully examined for omissions or responses that have been entered into a database more than once in order to avoid biases in your analysis due to incomplete or missing data. A few other tasks to consider while cleaning data are:

> Eliminating duplicate responses,
> Removing "speeders" (those who complete the survey too quickly),
> Copying your raw data set and using the copied version for cleaning,
> Conducting cleaning trials with a subsample of your data set (saves time while working on big data sets), and
> Identifying the crucial outcome variables to give adequate attention to the information that you would define as a complete data set. (Bainbridge, 2009)

Another important aspect to consider would be the elimination of responders who provide nonsensical answers to open-ended questions (a probable indication of inattentive or careless response). Tabachnick and Fidell (2001) provide an excellent chapter on how to screen and handle data prior to analysis. I will highlight some of their most useful tips in this section.

It is important to track nonresponders and take into account missing records in your analysis. Missing responses may represent a specific sector of your sample, which, if present in your data set, may have influenced the results of your analyses. Although you cannot account for this missing data, you should acknowledge missing records as a limitation that may have influenced your final results and interpretation. Therefore, it is important to know demographic characteristics of nonrespondents whenever possible, so that you can explain potential biases in the limitations section(s) of your study reports.

Sometimes, the number of nonrespondents is small and will not affect your findings; however, if you have a small data set to begin with, as often happens in evaluation, a few missing records may make a major difference in your data analysis and interpretation.

Occasional missing data from a set of responses, such as when a respondent overlooks a question or item, also could have a major effect on your data analysis and results, especially if such occurrences are frequent in your data set. One way to handle this problem is to substitute missing data with the average response of the sample or subsample (i.e., average imputation). If your sample is heterogeneous, it becomes very important to substitute missing data with a subgroup mean that closely represents the demographic characteristics of the respondent whose record is incomplete. Caution must be exercised when taking this approach because, if missing responses are frequent in your data set, you are, in essence, altering or fabricating your data set, which is a serious violation of ethical practice.

Other ways of handling missing data are summarized in Box 8.2 and include deleting all data from any respondent with missing data (listwise deletion), recovering data from respondents if it was not an anonymous survey, making educated guesses based on the response pattern, using the middle point or the mostly common chosen value (common-point imputation), and using multiple linear regression analysis to predict the missing value (regression substitution) (Sauro, 2015).

In addition to handling missing data, inattentive or careless responses are also a concern. Some ways to identify careless responses include considering the response time (observing how much additional time a respondent is taking than the average time taken by all the respondents), analyzing the outliers (e.g., Mahalanobis distance can identify inattentive responses), performing a consistency analysis between items with similar content, and examining response patterns (checking whether respondents are consistently responding in the same way) (Mead & Craig, 2012).

Box 8.2. PROCEDURES FOR HANDLING MISSING DATA

Substitution with mean
Listwise deletion
Data recovery
Response pattern substitution
Common-point imputation
Regression substitution

MATCHING STATISTICS TO QUANTITATIVE STUDY DESIGNS

In order to select the appropriate statistical tests for your study design, the first thing you need to know is the type of independent and dependent variables with which you are working. Table 8.1 adapted from Hoy (2010, p. 64) provides a useful guide to these decisions.

With nonexperimental designs (descriptive or one-shot study designs) you will generally use descriptive statistics (e.g., means, medians, frequencies) or chi-square tests (for inferences to populations) to analyze your data. When a control group is added to a one-shot design, you can compare the groups with statistical tests that are appropriate for independent comparisons, such as an *independent* t-test or chi-square analysis, which allow you to analyze outputs *across* independent groups. When a pretest is added to a one-shot design, you are now inferring a change between baseline and postprogram measures of an outcome. To analyze that change, you will need to use a *paired* t-test (assuming the outcome is measured as a continuous or ordinal variable) because the change you are assessing is occurring *within* a group of participants for which you are pairing pretest assessments with posttest assessments. If you combine pre- and posttests with a control or comparison group, your study design represents what statisticians refer to as a general linear model (GLM). For this design, you will likely be using statistics such as analysis of variance (ANOVA), analysis of co-variance (ANCOVA), or the corresponding nonparametric test. These statistics assume measures of a single short-term outcome or dependent variable. When

Table 8.1. TYPES OF VARIABLES AND APPROPRIATE STATISTICS TESTS[a]

Independent Variable	Examples of Independent Variable Types	Dependent Variable	Statistical Test
Dichotomous	men/women; visual/verbal	Continuous	Independent t-test
Categorical	Pretest/posttest; Pre/post/ 6-mo; < 5 yrs, 5–10 yrs, > 10 yrs	Continuous	Paired t-test (two paired measures) or F test (ANOVA)
Categorical	Fruits, Vegetables, Protein, Grains	Categorical	Chi-square (χ^2)
Continuous	Ounces of fruits and vegetables consumed in a day	Continuous	Correlation (r)
Multiple and continuous	Program, Demographic characteristics, Psychological constructs	Continuous	Multiple correlation (R)

[a] Adapted from Wayne K. Hoy, *Quantitative research in education: A primer*, Sage Publications, Thousand Oaks, CA, Copyright © 2010.

you assess within group changes over time, such when baseline, short-term, and long-term outcomes are assessed, you will use a time-series ANOVA or similar time series statistical test. You also can use ANOVA to compare means across three or more independent groups in a similar way to using the independent t-test to compare two independent groups. When your designs involve the assessment and analysis of complex associations among a program's short- and long-term outcomes and impacts, the statistical models become more complex and involve multivariate tests, such as various forms of regression, path analysis, or structural equation modeling, which are designed to assess relationships among several variables. Multivariate statistical methods are also necessary to perform cluster analyses, such as when examining parent and child relationships within family clusters. A cluster analysis, however, is controlled by the investigator's definitions of clusters, and it is an exploratory technique, so inferences cannot be made to a population based on this type of analysis (Hair & Black, 2000).

In practice, I often observe that simpler types of statistical analyses, such as t-tests, are used for designs that require more sophisticated statistical models. I encourage you to develop your professional skills and get well acquainted with statisticians or other knowledgeable professionals who can guide you through your analytical designs and provide assistance when needed.

VARIABLES, CONSTANTS, AND LEVELS OF MEASUREMENT

As Dr. Abu-Bader (2011) points out,

> The main purpose for conducting any statistical analysis is to examine if relationships exist among two or more variables under investigation and whether these relationships can be generalized to the population from which the sample is drawn. *Variables* [emphasis added] are, thus, anything that can vary among subjects, events, or objects. (p. 5)

Common examples typically include demographic variables such as gender, race, age, income, or education, but they also can be psychometric variables, such as levels of stress, anxiety, well-being, and other psychological constructs (e.g., attitudes, perceptions, opinions, beliefs). Variables also can be behaviors we count; for example, trips to a grocery store or the types of food items we purchase in a grocery store. However, *constants*, as their name implies, are characteristics that remain unaltered or are not variable in a population of interest; therefore, they do not need to be included in your analysis. For example, if you were to study only 10-year-olds, age would not be a variable in your analysis unless incremental age by month had a relationship with your dependent variable.

Quantitative variables are those that are "measured using numerical values and, thus, have numerical meanings"; in contrast to *qualitative variables*, which are "classified into groups or categories" (Abu-Bader, 2011, p. 5). These terms should not be confused with quantitative and qualitative *analytical methods,* which refer to the overall philosophical and methodological ways that data are collected and analyzed.

Variables also can be classified according to their type and level of measurement. There are four general types of variables: *independent, dependent, extraneous,* and *control.* In program evaluation, the *independent* variable of interest is typically the program or intervention you are studying. Sample demographics are independent variables because they can influence your outcome, or *dependent* variable. Hence, they must be controlled for in your analysis and are referred to as *control variables,* because you are interested only in the relationship of your intervention to the outcome or dependent variable. In other words, any measured factor that could influence your dependent variable (i.e., outcome) is a potential *control* variable in your statistical analysis. *Extraneous* variables are those that have not been part of your analysis and provide an alternative explanation for the observed relationship between the independent and dependent variables. A common example is a similar educational program or intervention that a participant may attend while simultaneously participating in the program being evaluated.

Variables can be measured in several different ways, which are referred to as *levels of measurement. Nominal* variables are those that represent exhaustive and mutually exclusive (i.e., discrete) categories or groups, such as gender, country of birth, or religious belief. They are qualitatively rather than quantitatively different. The relationship between the categories (i.e., groups) is that they differ from one another, but one is not quantitatively more or less than the others (Ary, Jacobs, Razavieh, & Sorenson, 2006). For example, if you assign a code of "1" for female and "2" for male during data entry, it doesn't mean male (code = 2) is greater than female (code = 1).

As their name implies, *ordinal* variables are variables that can be rank-ordered, such as the numbers in a Likert or Likert-type scale or dress sizes (XS, S, M, L, XL). They have arbitrary values that cannot be meaningfully quantified, but can be ordered in a way that makes sense and creates groups of information that are exhaustive and mutually exclusive. *Interval* variables are similar to ordinal variables (exhaustive, mutually exclusive, and rank-ordered), except that the differences between intervals are constant and have meaning, such as temperature differences of 10, 20, and 30 degrees. There is no true zero for interval variables. In other words, a zero doesn't mean the absence of the variable you are measuring.

Ratio variables are less intuitive and include examples such as age, weight, and annual salary, because they can be associated with values for which zero has meaning (i.e., no salary). Again, ratio variables have all the other characteristics of other levels of measurement (exhaustive, mutually exclusive, rank-ordered, and equal distance). Why is it important to know the levels of measurement for each type of variable (independent, dependent, control) in your analysis? Because this information determines, in part, the statistical method you will select for your data analysis.

DESCRIPTIVE STATISTICS

Descriptive statistics are the statistics that describe a data set. They include measures of central tendency (mean, median, mode), frequencies, percentages, and measures of variability (range, variance, and standard deviation) (Abu-Bader, 2011; Hoy & Adams, 2016). The *mean* is simply the average of all values in the data set. The *median* is the midpoint value which half of the data set's values fall below and half fall above. The *mode* is the most frequently occurring value in a distribution. The more symmetrical or normally distributed the data, the more identical the mean, median, and mode values. A distribution that is not symmetrical is called a skewed distribution. The values of central tendency differ in skewed distributions. A distribution is positively skewed if the mean is more than the median and mode, and negatively skewed if the mean is less than the median and mode. The *minimum* is the lowest value and the *maximum* is the highest value in a data set. It is useful to compute the *range* of these values to determine how broadly data are distributed; however, this range can be misleading if the lowest or highest value is an *outlier* (i.e., a lone ranger). Therefore, the *standard deviation* around the mean, or value for which 68% of the data falls above or below the mean, is a useful statistic. *Standard deviation* summarizes the data in the same unit of measurement as the original data; hence, it is the most commonly used measure of variability (Ary et al., 2006). The standard deviation is an interval or ratio level variable, like mean.

Table 8.2 summarizes these descriptive statistics and their definitions. You will want to know and study these statistics before you analyze data. These

Table 8.2. DESCRIPTIVE STATISTICS AND THEIR DEFINITIONS

Statistic	Definition
Mean	The average of a set of numbers or scores.
Median	The middle number in a set of numbers after they are ranked from low to high.
Mode	The most frequent number in a set of numbers.
Frequency	The number of times an item is selected among several items.
Percent	A number expressed as a fraction of 100.
Range	The difference between the highest and lowest number in a set of numbers.
Variance	The variability of a set of measures in relation to their mean (i.e., average)
Standard Deviation	The amount that a set of numbers or scores vary or deviate from the mean

statistics provide clues about the data set that will help you decide whether any transformations or specific analyses will be needed before you statistically test any hypotheses. For example, if the mean and median are far apart, you are likely working with a skewed data set. If the range is broad, the data set may have a relatively "flat" or bimodal (two most commonly occurring values) distribution. The next section will describe a few plots that will help you to visualize data and make sense of the data's descriptive statistics.

SIMPLE PLOTS

Years ago, when I was an undergraduate in my first statistics course, my professor taught me that the most important first step in analyzing data is to plot it and look at its characteristics. This step is important because it provides the first glimpse into how well data holds up to assumptions of the statistical tests you plan to perform. Histograms, boxplots, and scatterplots are the most common plots for visualizing a set of data.

Ideally, data points should distribute themselves evenly around the sample's mean in a nice bell-shaped curve as shown in Figure 8.1. So, the first question to ask is, do the data resemble a bell curve and thus have a *normal*

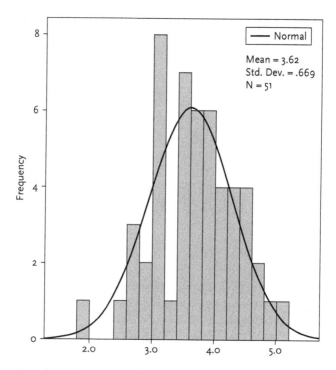

Figure 8.1. Example of a histogram with a normal distribution.

distribution around the mean? With a normal distribution, the mean, median, and mode of a data set are equal (Hoy & Adams, 2016). Most of the time, however, those values will not be the same, so you need to determine how non-normally the data are distributed. A *histogram* is one way to visually assess the distribution of a data set. A histogram represents the frequency of each number in a data set, and it is especially useful for plotting item scores or total scores. Histograms allow you to visualize how well the data set conforms to a normal distribution around a mean, as represented by a bell-shaped curve (Figure 8.1).

Box plots (Figure 8.2) are a useful way to view two or more subsets of a data set. The horizontal line within the boxes in Figure 8.2 represents the mean and the box represents the range and distribution of numbers around that mean. As you will notice in Figure 8.2, the box on the right represents a skewed data set relative to the mean. If each set of data were normally distributed, the vertical line would fall somewhere near the middle of the box, as can be seen in the box on the left in Figure 8.2. In this figure you also can notice the difference between two means and how much overlap there is in the two distributions.

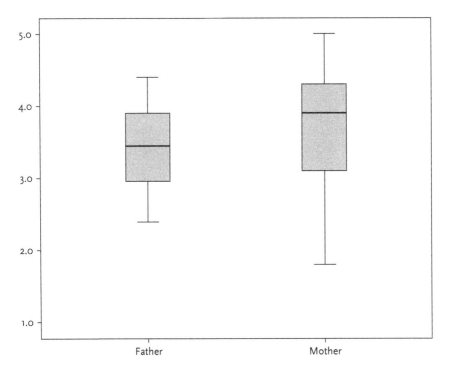

Figure 8.2. Example of a boxplot illustrating the mean and distributions of two groups of data.

Scatterplots help to visualize the correlation between two sets of numbers or variables in a data set. Figure 8.3 illustrates two types of scatter plots—one representing a positive correlation and one representing no correlation between variables *x* and *y*. If two variables are well correlated, the points form a fairly tight line in either the positive or negative direction (Figure 8.3a). If they are not correlated, then the points scatter across the plot in a loose or unclear arrangement (Figure 8.3b). This is important information because as stated earlier, statistical analyses assess the relationship between the independent and dependent variable, so these plots become especially important when analyzing a bivariate correlation or conducting a regression analysis—a point I will return to later in this chapter.

All of these plots can be easily generated for data using Excel or statistical software. When viewing these graphs, several questions should come to mind. Is the distribution skewed in one direction? Is the distribution single or bimodal? Does the distribution of data appear relatively flat in appearance or is it quite sharp (the difference between a hill and a mountain)?

Figure 8.4a illustrates an example of a skewed distribution. You will notice that the frequency of responses is higher at low values than at high values along the *x* axis. Figure 8.4b represents a contrast between peaked and relatively flat distributions across three groups. If you were to calculate only a mean for each of these distributions, the calculation would provide no information about how data are distributed around that mean. Furthermore, having information about the range in which your data is distributed (e.g., minimum value, maximum value, or standard deviation) would only provide information for the data displayed by the images in Figure 8.4b and would not provide information about the modality or skewness of the data. Adding a median to your calculations would provide hints about skewness, because as a median gets further from the mean, the more skewed the data is likely to be. However, it would not give you information about a bimodal distribution as suggested by Figure 8.4c. It is only through plots that this characteristic of your data can best be revealed.

Another question to ask is, "Are the data distributed differently for different subgroups, such as gender, race, ethnicity, age, or geographic location?" Figure 8.5 provides an example of what your data might look like if you plotted it by group membership. As shown in this figure, the data for each group has a different mean and distribution. In one group (bell-shaped curve on the left), the data appears to be distributed more broadly and has a lower mean (approximately 4.0 units) than the other group, which has a relatively higher mean (approximately 4.3 units) and narrower distribution; however, the curve on the right also appears higher than the one on the left, which suggests a more homogenous sample (or subsample) than the curve on the left.

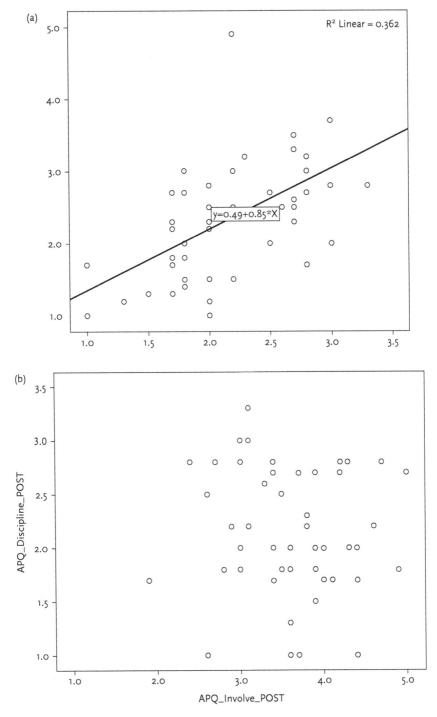

Figure 8.3a and 8.3b. Examples of scatter plots with positive correlation (a) and no correlation (b).

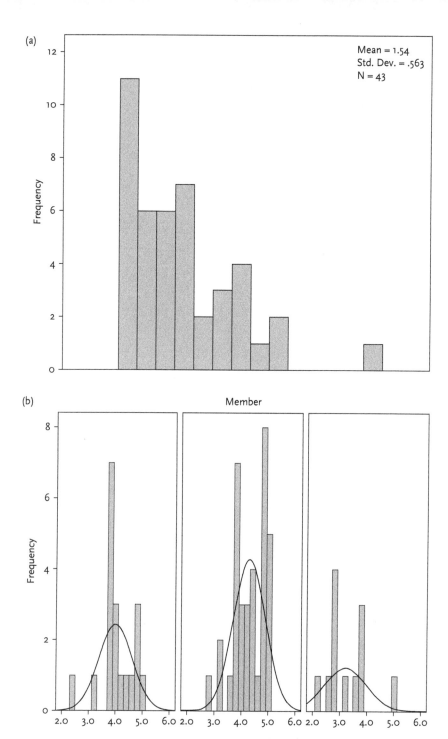

Figures 8.4a–c. Examples of histograms for skewed (a), peaked, flat (b), and bimodal (c) distributions.

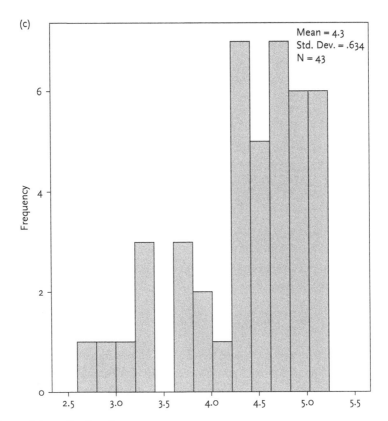

Figures 8.4a–c. Continued

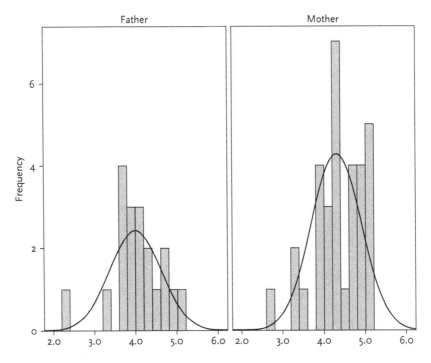

Figure 8.5. Histograms comparing two groups.

If data are not normally distributed around the mean, why does it matter? It matters because parametric statistics (e.g., t-test, analysis of variance) assume that data are normally distributed around the mean. Let's pause for a moment to examine this and other assumptions of parametric statistics.

STATISTICAL ASSUMPTIONS

Parametric statistics are based on the following primary assumptions (Abu-Bader, 2011).

The sample is representative of the population to which generalizations will be made;

The sample size is sufficiently large to run the analysis (usually ≥ 30);

Data representing the dependent variable are normally distributed around the mean; and

The dependent variable is measured at the interval or ratio levels.

Some statistical tests are based on additional assumptions, as listed in Table 8.3, so it is important to know them prior to conducting an analysis. I will mention those unique assumptions as I describe each type of statistical analysis covered in this chapter; however, for a comprehensive list, I recommend that you consult a statistician or statistics textbook. Some of my favorites are listed at the end of this chapter.

If statistical assumptions are ignored or violated, then you are essentially unable to make accurate inferences about the data. What's an inference? An *inference* is a claim about a sample of data that is inferred to a population of interest, such as participants' increased knowledge of various food groups following a nutrition education program. "Hmm . . . , " you may be thinking, "But that's why I am doing this program and what I hope to show by my data analysis!" How do you avoid violating statistical assumptions so you can make inferences from data? You typically will not have adequate resources or time to collect additional data or begin collecting data all over again. If you did, you might be faced with the same problems, given that you would be sampling from a similar population. Table 8.4 lists some basic procedures that can be performed to prepare data for analysis, so that you don't violate statistical assumptions. These procedures will vary somewhat according to your sample's size and the specific statistical test you wish to perform, but overall, they accomplish the same goal. I will not cover these procedures in this chapter, so I encourage you to consult a statistician or the sources listed in the reference section for further guidance.

Table 8.3. ASSUMPTIONS FOR COMMON STATISTICAL TESTS

Statistical Test	Assumption
Independent samples t-test (comparing two different samples)	Independent variable is dichotomous Dependent variable is based on simultaneous observations Variances of both groups on the dependent variable are equal Sufficient sample size to compare means of both groups (usually ≥ 30)
Paired samples t-test (same sample compared at two different time points)	Independent and dependent variables must be continuous data and must be an interval or ratio Dependent variable is measured twice Both repeated measures should approximate normal distributions Both measures must have equal possible ranges Sufficient sample size to compare paired measures (usually ≥ 30)
F-test (One-way ANOVA (comparing more than two samples), ANCOVA)	Nominal independent variable All measures must be collected at the same time Dependent variable must be continuous and measured at the interval or ratio level Dependent variable must approximate a normal distribution The variances of all groups on the dependent variable should be equal Sufficient sample size to make group comparisons on dependent variable
Chi-square	Variables are measured at the nominal level For tests of association, two variables must be independent Data must be frequencies, not scores No more than 20% of the cells should have an expected frequency of less than 5 Sample size must have sufficient power for the analysis
Multiple regression	Sample must represent the population to which generalizations will be made Dependent (criterion) variable must be continuous data and measured at the interval or ratio level Distribution of dependent variable should approximate a normal distribution Independent variables can be measured at any level and categorical variables must be recoded as dummy variables Residuals must be normally distributed

(Continued)

Table 8.3. CONTINUED

Statistical Test	Assumption
	The relationships among the criterion and factor variables are assumed to be linear
	For each value of the independent variables (factors), the dependent variable should be normally distributed (i.e., equal variances of independent variables)
	Independent variables are not highly collinear (multicollinearity)
	Sample size is sufficient, generally 50 + 8(# of factor)

Table 8.4. COMMON CHARACTERISTICS OF DATA THAT REQUIRE MANIPULATION PRIOR TO STATISTICAL ANALYSIS

Characteristic of Data Set	Preparation for Statistical Analysis
Skewed data	Transformation to normal distribution (e.g., z-score)
Outliers	Correction factors
Multimodal distributions	Determine what creates the groupings and then controlling for it.
Flat data	Indicates large confidence intervals or heterogeneous sample; may have to consider subgroups
Peak data	Small confidence intervals; tight; may suggest too much homogeneity of sample; may need to continue sampling or sample a different group

Procedures typically performed at the time of analysis (e.g., tests for equality of variances or multicollinearity among independent variables) are described in the references listed at the end of this chapter. After you have adequately prepared the data for analysis, you can run the appropriate statistical procedures to test your inferences. Inferences take several general forms that can be stated as hypotheses that you will test in your statistical analysis.

EVALUATION HYPOTHESES

In a typical evaluation study plan, you may not have specified a set of hypotheses statements to guide a data analysis or developed (or been handed) a detailed analytical plan. However, hypotheses are implied by the evaluation's purpose statement and questions. For example, if the purpose of a study were to determine a meditation program's effectiveness in reducing parents' overall stress levels, and the evaluation question was, "Has this meditation program reduced parents' overall stress levels?", one could hypothesize that "The meditation program reduces stress levels in parents." In this statement, the independent variable is the meditation program and the dependent variable is the parents' stress levels. Therefore, I am interested in the reduction of stress levels as an effect of the program. A *hypothesis statement* is "an assumption about the relationship among two or more variables under investigation" (Abu-Bader, 2011, p. 10). Another way of defining a hypothesis is as "a conjectural statement that indicates the relation between key ideas in a researcher's formulation of an answer" (Hoy & Adams, 2016, p. 7). In practical words, a hypothesis is an educated guess about how a program will be related to its outcomes. Said another way, a hypothesis is an expected answer to an evaluation question. To assess parents' stress levels (a psychometric construct) and test my hypothesis, I would use a validated metric in a pretest/posttest design, preferably with a comparison group that receives no intervention, an intervention different from the experimental group, or a control group that does not receive the intervention. The *null hypothesis* (H_0) or *hypothesis of no difference* assumes that there is no difference in the dependent variable based on pre- and posttest measures. In this example, then, the null hypothesis (H_0) is that parental stress is not significantly reduced by the meditation program. The statistical test, then, determines if I can reject the null hypothesis in favor of the *alternative hypothesis* (H_a), which is that parental stress levels are reduced by the meditation program. Statistical tests assume that the test is being performed against the null hypothesis (null hypothesis assumed), so it is important to articulate the distinction between the null and alternative hypothesis before conducting an analysis. Examples of the way that hypotheses statements are typically written and interpreted are shown in Table 8.5.

Table 8.5. EXAMPLES OF HYPOTHESIS STATEMENTS FOR PARENT
MEDICATION PROGRAM

Hypothesis	Hypothesis Statement
There is *no statistically significant* difference between parental stress levels before and after the meditation program.	H_0 (null): Posttest Mean (X_1) = Pretest Mean (X_2)
Parental stress levels following the meditation program will be *statistically significantly* lower than their levels before the meditation program.	H_a (alternative): Posttest Mean (X_2) < Pretest Mean (X_1)

> **Box 8.3. SIX STEPS FOR ANALYZING HYPOTHESIS STATEMENTS**
>
> ---
>
> STEP 1. Identify the independent and dependent variables by name
> STEP 2. Determine the variable type—categorical or continuous
> STEP 3. Elaborate each variable by describing what the numbers mean
> STEP 4. Specify the relationship between the variables in hypothesis statements
> STEP 5. Determine the appropriate unit of analysis (object of the evaluation)
> STEP 6. Select the appropriate statistical test

Note that I hypothesized only a reduction of parental stress levels. Because I hypothesized a change in only one direction (i.e., reduction in stress level), the hypothesis is *one-tailed*. This means that I am interested in only one half of the bell-shaped curve around the mean parental stress level. This is an important point when it comes to interpreting statistical output from a software program. Typically, software programs report two-tailed statistics, so the p-value (probability of detecting a significant difference in means) should be reduced by half for an interpretation of a one-tailed test. Hypothesis statements are helpful for clarifying and focusing a data analysis plan, as well as the types of statistical analyses you will use to answer the evaluation questions.

Hoy and Adams (2016) recommend that hypotheses be analyzed using the six steps listed in Box 8.3 and diagrammed in a *Hypothesis Diagramming Table* (p. 76), so that you have clarity about your analytical plans. Table 8.6 provides an example of a Hypothesis Diagramming Table for the meditation program evaluation. For each hypothesis, a similar table would be created to specify the statistical analysis. Later in this chapter, I will discuss how to select a statistical test according to your hypotheses, the types of variables with which you are working, your sample size, and how well your sample adheres to statistical assumptions.

SAMPLE SIZE, POWER, AND EFFECT SIZE

If you prepared a thorough analytical plan as part of your evaluation plan, you may have computed an appropriate sample size for your anticipated statistical analyses, referred to as "a priori" or before an analysis is conducted. In evaluation, sample size computations are frequently overlooked, typically because we "take what we get" and do not have the resources to offer programs

Table 8.6. HYPOTHESIS DIAGRAMMING TABLE FOR THE MEDITATION
PROGRAM EVALUATION

Hypothesis: Parents' stress levels will be significantly reduced by the meditation program.		
	Independent Variable (X)	Dependent Variable (Y)
Name of Variable	Meditation program	Parental Stress Levels
Kind of Variable (Continuous or Categorical)	Dichotomous (Participate or not participate)	Continuous
Elaboration of Variable	Intervention or cause	Varies with intervention or effect
Specify Relationship	Posttest < Pretest	
Unit of Analysis (Object of Study)	Parents	
Null Hypothesis	Mean posttest (Y_2) = Mean pretest (Y_1)	
Statistical Test	Paired t-test; F-test (ANOVA) when using a comparison or control group	

frequently or on a broad scale. So, we have two strategies. One of them, non-parametric analysis, will be discussed later in this chapter. The other, post-hoc power analysis, will be discussed now. Let's assume I had been able to implement the meditation program with approximately one hundred parents, and I want to know whether that sample size is sufficient to detect an observed reduction in parental stress levels or if the reduction is due to chance. I can conduct a *post-hoc* power analysis to determine the power of detecting a reduced parental stress level (when it is truly present) in a sample of one hundred parents who actually participated in the meditation program. I can do this in a statistical program or power calculator, such as GPower (Erdfelder, Faul, & Buchner, 1996), by providing the appropriate parameters, such as actual sample size, desired p-value, and descriptive statistics (e.g., pre- and posttest sample means, control group means). And, indeed, a sample size of one hundred is more than adequate to detect a significant statistical reduction in parental stress levels with a *p-value* of .05. What does "with a p-value of .05" mean? What it essentially means is that I am 95% confident that when I obtain a significant difference in pre- and posttest values, the difference really exists and is not due to chance (Type I error).

When performing statistical analyses, it is important that you stay mindful of two types of error, because statistics are based on probability. The first type (i.e., Type I error, represented as "α") is the probability of detecting a statistically significant finding when none actually exists. It is basically a false alarm (Ary et al., 2006). The second type of error (Type II error, represented as "β") is the probability of not detecting a significant finding when it exists. Most of the time, we are concerned with Type I error, because it may lead to changes or decisions that are unwarranted. There is always some chance of error in statistical calculations, which can be reduced by deciding on the acceptable level of significance before a null hypothesis can be accepted or rejected. I can upgrade the precision of a statistical test by running it at a predetermined p-value (e.g., .01 or .001). In the social sciences, we generally use a p-value of .05 and aim for a power of .80 or greater, but those parameters depend on the type of intervention being evaluated.

Now, let's ask ourselves whether any difference matters or whether a difference of a certain magnitude matters to us? *Effect size* estimates the difference between means, so the larger the effect size, the more powerful the statistical test (Abu-Bader, 2011). Effect size has "universal meaning to assess both the direction and strength of a difference between two means" (Ary et al., 2006, p.155). It is the ". . . difference between experimental and control groups divided by the standard deviation of the control group or the difference between two groups divided by the estimated population standard deviation" (Ary et al., 2006, p.186). So, for example, if I were to test for significant differences in pre- and postprogram stress levels of a magnitude of 20 units (big effect), the power to detect that difference would be .99 (based on a SD = 5 units, calculated effect size = 4). If, however, I lowered that difference in mean values to 10 (all other factors held constant), the power to detect that difference in mean values would be .90 (SD = 5; calculated effect size = 2). It is also worth noting that as the power to detect that difference declines, the size of sample necessary to test a hypothesis increases. It is up to evaluators or researchers to decide, based on the goals of their projects, what they would consider to be a meaningful effect size. Cohen, however, has suggested some interpretations of what can be considered to be a reasonable distinction between meaningful and inconsequential differences between groups. According to Cohen (1988), an effect size of .20 is *small*, .50 is *medium* and .80 is *large*.

Now let's examine a somewhat different scenario. If, for practical reasons, I needed to limit the number of parents who participate in the meditation study, I would want to determine the minimum sample size needed to test my hypotheses in advance (a priori) of the program's implementation. So, I would again use appropriate software to estimate the sample size. For this example, a simple paired samples t-test of the difference between pre- and posttest stress levels (no controls or comparison groups) would require an estimated minimum sample size of 30 participants (GPower calculation). If I were to add a comparison or control group, I would need a sample size that is slightly higher (n = 34) to account for the group comparison (GPower: using ANOVA and a Cohen's effect size estimate = .5). This increased sample size exemplifies a general rule about sample size and statistics. The more variables in an analysis, the larger the sample size needed to test the hypotheses. For some general guidelines regarding sample sizes, see Abu-Bader (2011) and Mertens and Wilson (2012).

ALIGNING STATISTICAL ANALYSES WITH
ANALYTICAL DESIGNS

Multiple inferences can be made about the population from which a sample is drawn. These commonly include a targeted benchmark (e.g., 80% of respondents reported using a financial planning tool); a change in respondents' knowledge, attitudes, or behaviors after an intervention or over time (e.g., increased knowledge of factors affecting health); a difference between two or more groups (e.g., crime rates in a westside neighborhood compared with those in an eastside neighborhood); a relationship between two or more variables (e.g., parenting skills and child behaviors that impact school performance); or whether one intervention predicts a better outcome than another (e.g., an online degree program predicts a greater proportion of degree-earners than a face-to-face program).

Most tests of interest to you will involve just *one dependent variable* and one or more independent variables, such as when assessing parental stress following an intervention. In this case, you will want to perform a *univariate* statistical analysis. When you have only a postintervention measure of a dependent variable, your analysis will be limited to descriptive statistics or a Chi-square Goodness-of-Fit test, depending on your level of measurement. For this analysis, you will need to know the expected frequency of your dependent variable in the population from which you sampled. This information can often be found in journal articles or reports.

If you wish to add a pretest measure of your dependent variable, pre-/posttest differences in means would be analyzed using a *paired* t-test. If you wish to test differences between two groups for which you have obtained only posttest measures, you would use an *independent* t-test. A one-way *analysis of variance* (i.e., ANOVA), or *F test*, is used to test the differences in posttest means of the dependent variable among more than two groups, such as three or more sites (e.g., schools) in which a program is implemented. You also can test the differences between two groups and simultaneously look at changes in scores (pre/post differences). This design is referred to as a General Linear Model, for which a two-way ANOVA is used to compare two groups simultaneously (i.e., cross-group comparisons) and measure across two time points (i.e., within group comparisons). A statistical test called *analysis of covariance*, or ANCOVA, provides a way to control for differences in baseline or pretest measures and until recently, was commonly used to do so; however, *propensity scores* are gaining popularity as a way to manage differences in baseline data. The primary advantage of propensity scores is that they address the selection bias that may result when individuals are not randomly assigned to groups (intervention and comparison or control groups) (Coffman, 2011). If you wish to examine measures of your dependent variable at several time points (e.g., pretest, posttest, and at six months following), a time series ANOVA (assumes measures of a continuous variable) is likely the statistical test you will use to do so. Results of a time series ANOVA, however, will only tell you that a difference exists between two or more measures. It will not tell you when that difference occurred (i.e., between pretest and posttest, or between posttest and 6months following, or between six months following and pretest); therefore, *post-hoc* analyses are needed to determine at which time points the difference(s) occurred. Examples of post-hoc analyses (assuming homogeneity of variances) for this purpose include the Least Square Difference (LSD), Bonferroni, Scheffe, and Tukey tests (Abu-Bader, 2011).

None of the statistical tests described so far are appropriate for analyzing a dependent variable that is categorical (i.e., nominal). This is typically the case when surveys are used to collect data that reflects choices or other groups of information (e.g., range of income). The *Chi-square test* (designated χ^2) is the statistic of choice when we are interested in the relationship between two categorical variables where one is the independent variable and one is the dependent variable (e.g., gender and range of income). There are two types of chi-square tests—the Chi-square Goodness-of-Fit Test and the Chi-square Test of Association. The Chi-square Goodness-of-Fit Test provides a way to determine how well a sample represents the population to which we make our inferences. So, we compare the frequency of a categorical variable (e.g., gender) in our sample (i.e., actual frequency) with the frequency of the same variable in the population of interest (i.e., the expected frequency). For example, the proportion of people in Wisconsin receiving federal food benefits in 2016 compared to the proportion receiving those benefits nationwide during that same year.

Alternatively, the Chi-square Test of Association provides a means of determining whether differences in frequencies or proportions of two categorical variables (independent and dependent variables) are statistically significant. In other words, a Chi-square test of association examines the association between an independent and dependent variable when both are categorical (i.e., nominal). This test would likely be used, for example, when we want to study observed aggressive behaviors (dependent categorical variable) in boys compared to girls (independent categorical variable). Your evaluation question would be, "Are aggressive behaviors associated with gender?" To perform a chi-square test, you begin by constructing a contingency table. A contingency table (also known as a cross-tabs or two-way table), "is a frequency table that presents the observed frequencies of one categorical variable (dependent variable) as a function of another categorical variable (independent variable)" (Abu-Bader, 2011, p. 286). It, therefore, displays the frequencies of two categorical variables (e.g., aggressive behavior and gender) as shown in Table 8.7.

When a Chi-square test is performed, the probability of the observed frequencies compared to the expected frequencies for the population of interest are tested. What differs between the Goodness-of-Fit test and the

Table 8.7. OBSERVED FREQUENCIES
OF AGGRESSIVE BEHAVIORS FOR BOYS AND GIRLS

	Girls	Boys	Total
Aggressive behaviors	7	15	22
Nonaggressive behaviors	13	5	18
Total	20	20	40

Test of Association is that in the Goodness-of-Fit test, we need to know the actual frequencies of the variable in the population of interest. In a Test of Association, we examine the null hypothesis that the observed frequencies are no different than what we would find by chance (Hoy & Adams, 2016). For more information about Chi-square tests and how to perform them using SPSS software, consult the references listed at the end of this chapter.

MULTIVARIATE ANALYSES

Program planners and directors are increasingly being asked to report multiple indicators for variables associated with broad level change. Analysis of the effects of multiple variables on one or more changes is complicated and typically requires multivariate analyses. The most commonly used multivariate statistical analysis in evaluation is multiple regression. Multiple regression allows you to *predict* or *explain* the relationships of several independent variables to a single dependent variable. Independent variables (X) are referred to as factors or predictors and the dependent variable (Y) is referred to as the criterion or, familiar among evaluators, the outcome. In practical terms, it provides a way to assess the contributions of multiple programs or program activities and other independent variables (e.g., personal demographics or environmental conditions) to a single expected outcome or impact. In analytical terms, regression computes the degree of variability that each independent variable in your model contributes to an outcome (or total variance in the model), or dependent variable. Said more simply, it determines the strength and extent of the contributions of the independent to the dependent variable. Therefore, the analysis "tests" how well the hypothesized model predicts or explains the variance in an outcome.

Before beginning a regression analysis, factors (independent variables) must be selected. These factors should be highly and significantly correlated with the outcome, so bivariate correlations between each factor and the outcome variable should be computed in order to select the appropriate factors for the analysis. There are various types of regression models and your selection of one will depend on the evaluation's questions and purpose, as well as the

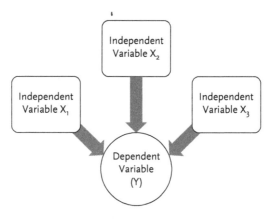

Figure 8.6. Illustration of a general model for multiple regression.

type of dependent variable (outcomes) you are evaluating. If you are assessing the contributions or relationships among multiple independent variables on a single dependent variable or outcome that is dichotomous, such as whether a program participant remains incarcerated, then you will use *logistic regression*. *Multiple regression* is a way to test several independent variables simultaneously in no particular order of importance and see which ones have the strongest relationship or predictive or explanatory effect on your dependent variable, as modeled in Figure 8.6.

Hierarchical regression, as its name implies, assumes a hierarchical order of the independent variables (Figure 8.7). The variable correlating most strongly with the dependent variable is typically entered as the first variable in the regression model, followed by other variables with declining correlation coefficients. As each factor is entered into the analysis, all other factors remain constant. Because an analyst enters the independent variables in the order of correlation magnitude based on theory or past research, hierarchical regression is used to explain the variance in a dependent variable.

In *step-wise regression*, factors are entered into the model by a computer software algorithm based on the size of their partial correlation coefficients. Each time a new factor is entered into the model, the contribution of the factor in the analysis is reassessed. Factors that no longer contribute significantly to the variance in the outcome are removed, and the process continues

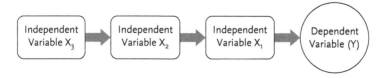

Figure 8.7. Illustration of a general model for hierarchical regression.

until no more factors contribute significantly to the variance in the outcomes (Abu-Bader, 2011).

These models may resemble, or remind you of, logic models you have seen. In fact, regression can be used to assess the relationships among program activities, outputs, outcomes, and impacts. Regression provides a more accurate assessment of a program's causal relationship to an expected outcome or impact. But, in practice, we often assume that these relationships are true and proceed to tests of a program's direct effects on a particular outcome.

STATISTICAL TESTS FOR MULTIPLE DEPENDENT VARIABLES

By now, some of you may be asking, "What if I am interested in how my program effects multiple outcomes?" (i.e., effects more than one dependent variable). If you find yourself in the position of needing to analyze multiple dependent variables, you likely will need a statistician to help you. Due to the complex nature of these designs, their statistical analyses are also complex. Typically, path analysis, structural equation modeling, or some other multivariate statistical procedure (or combination of them) are used to analyze these complex designs. In essence, they are similar to regression and allow us to model the best predictors of our expected outcomes; however, the mathematics behind them are more complicated and difficult to interpret. Some of the best and most interesting examples of these study designs and their corresponding analyses can be found in the counseling psychology field.

Table 8.8 summarizes the parametric tests described in this chapter and how to base your selection on levels of measurement. I strongly recommend

Table 8.8. PARAMETRIC STATISTICAL TEST SELECTIONS BASED ON LEVELS OF MEASUREMENT

Independent Variable	Dependent Variable	Statistical Test
Dichotomous	Continuous	t-test
Two time points		Paired
Two groups		Independent
Categorical	Continuous	F-test (ANOVA, ANCOVA)
Categorical	Categorical	Chi-square (χ^2)
Continuous	Continuous	Correlation (r)
Multiple, continuous, and nested	Categorical	Logistic regression
Multiple, continuous, and nested	Continuous	Step-wise or hierarchical Regression or hierarchical linear Modeling (HLM)

that you consult one or more of the texts listed at the end of this chapter for further reading. It is also extremely wise to consult a statistician when you design a quantitative analytical plan and before you begin your statistical analysis.

NONPARAMETRIC STATISTICS

You may be wondering what to do when your sample size is small (< 30), the distribution of your data is unclear, and the data violates many statistical assumptions. Now what? Nonparametric statistics are evaluators' friends when working with small sample sizes or uneven distributions of data. Nonparametric statistics are a group of statistical analyses that were designed for use on small or unevenly distributed samples (Pett, 1997). For each parametric statistical analysis, there is a corresponding nonparametric test, as shown in Table 8.9.

Programs that you typically evaluate often contain a small number of participants (often less than 20), who may not be representative of their population, and it would not, therefore, be appropriate to generalize findings. In such cases, nonparametric statistical procedures are often more appropriate to use than their parametric counterparts when conducting an evaluation. By having both skill sets in your evaluator's toolbox, you will be better equipped to analyze a variety of analytical challenges faced in evaluation practice.

The next section moves away from application and use of statistics to highlight some important points about reporting statistics and statistical analyses. Over the years, I have accumulated some tips through my various experiences with statisticians and study designs, and I would like to share them with you.

Table 8.9. PARAMETRIC TESTS AND THEIR NONPARAMETRIC ALTERNATIVES[a]

Type of Problem	Parametric Test	Nonparametric Alternative
Repeated Measures		
2 time periods	Paired t-test	Sign; Wilcoxon signed ranks
> 2 time periods	Repeated-measures ANOVA	Friedman
Independent Samples		
2 groups	Independent t-test	median; Mann-Whitney U
> 2 groups	One-way ANOVA	median; Kruskall-Wallis
Measures of Association	Pearson r	Spearman's rho; Kendall's tau

[a] Adapted from Majorie A. Pett, *Nonparametric statistics for health care research: Statistics for small samples and unusual distributions.* Thousand Oaks, CA: Sage Publications, Copyright © 1997.

The first point I would like to highlight is the difference between *statistical* significance and *practical* significance. Just because the difference between two values has statistical significance, does not mean it has practical significance. For example, a correlation *r* value of .3 (remember, it can range from –1 to +1) can be statistically significant if you have a sufficiently large sample size, but in reality, it is predicting only 9% [r2 (coefficient of determination)] of the variance in another variable, which doesn't have a lot of practical significance.

How we report statistics is important, too. I have learned that descriptive language related to statistics has no universally accepted meanings among statisticians, so interpretations can be misleading; for example, it is important to emphasize that a difference is *statistically* significant at a predetermined *p* level and not just significant. There is always a margin of error in a calculation, and a statistically significant difference may not be practically important. It is also important not to get too hung up on numbers that are close to cut-off points, such as a p-value that is .055 instead of .05 (which rounds to point .06 to indicate a nonsignificant value). Remember, these values are obtained through *sampling* and a different sample, especially when small, may yield different results. So, keep your eye on the big or practical picture and remember that statistics are tools.

When reporting p-values, I have heard conflicting arguments for reporting a p-value of less than .05 (p < .05) in contrast to an actual p-value. I was taught to report actual values, so readers of my report can make value judgments about those values on their own. This approach does and should not, however, preclude me from making my own interpretations and judgments about my statistical results in the body of the report. Also, be clear on whether a reported p-value is two-tailed or one-tailed (e.g., p < .05, one-tailed) and when to use two-tailed or one-tailed values.

It is also important to report statistics in standard formats and in sufficient detail so that a reader is clear on the approach to and findings from an analysis. For example, when reporting the results of an ANOVA, a table should be provided that includes sample sizes, means, standard deviations, confidence intervals, p-values, and eta values. Most statistics books, and often style guides (e.g., American Psychological Association [APA] or Modern Language Association [MLA]), will include this information. In text, you should always carefully describe the statistical procedures you followed and include any procedures for handling missing data, performing corrections, making transformations, testing assumptions, and running post-hoc analyses, along with explanations for why you did them. Reports of regression analysis should always include a table of correlation coefficients. Figures illustrating a path analysis or structural equation model should contain correlation coefficients and any corresponding markers of significance (i.e., "*" or "**") that indicate the strengths of relationships among variables. Both tables and figures should augment, not duplicate, the information provided in text. Because we can't assume that people have or will print a report in color, always prepare your tables and figures in black and white.

WORKING WITH STATISTICIANS AND BUILDING YOUR OWN CAPACITY

As evaluators and other social science professionals, we often enter our fields with limited statistical backgrounds. I took three statistics courses (in addition to research methods courses) as an undergraduate and graduate student, and I had difficulty applying what I learned until I had to design statistical plans for my own studies and teach research methods and evaluation courses. I also have taken a few workshops on statistics since that time. Over the years, I have become comfortable with univariate statistical analyses and to some extent, multivariate statistical analyses. My increasing knowledge in and confidence with statistics has developed because I make deliberate attempts to design data analyses before I consult with a statistician whom I ask to "check my work" and provide further guidance. As a result, I have had very positive experiences with statisticians who respect my attempts to design an analytical plan and to learn through my experiences. This approach saves a statistician time, places him or her in an instructional role (which they tend to like), and helps to build my capacity to do quantitative data analysis. A statistician's time is in high demand, so anything you can do to make a statistician's time more efficient is greatly appreciated. I highly recommend this approach if you wish to build a strong relationship with a statistician and improve your own knowledge and skills in statistics.

It is also helpful to enroll in courses and workshops on statistics as often as possible if you are routinely performing and interpreting statistical analyses. The American Evaluation Association offers statistics workshops at its annual meeting and frequently addresses statistical topics in its online instructional forums. The Evaluator's Institute also provides excellent workshops on statistics as part of its offerings each year (usually about two to three times per year in Chicago, Washington, DC, or Claremont, California). Other workshops on statistics, but not necessarily contextualized for evaluation, are offered through universities and popular online educational sources as Massive Open Online Courses (MOOCS) (e.g., Coursera, edX, Udacity). Graduate students have found these online tutorials to be extremely informative and helpful when learning about specific topics.

SUMMARY

Chapter 8 described basic statistical terms, concepts, plots, analytical techniques, and procedures that are commonly used in evaluation practice.

Knowledge of statistical terms and concepts is critical for designing evaluation studies and selecting appropriate statistical tests. Types of variables (independent, dependent, extraneous, and control) and their levels of measurement (nominal, ordinal, interval, and ratio) inform hypothesis testing and determine appropriate statistical tests, data analysis, and reporting. Accurate data analysis begins with techniques for cleaning data and handling missing data, which should be conducted as a first step in the analytical process. Plots and descriptive statistics are essential for getting acquainted with data, informing the extent of your statistical analysis, and taking any necessary steps to analyze data that may violate statistical assumptions. Parametric and nonparametric statistical tests (along with the assumptions that need to be fulfilled for selecting these tests) provide options for analyzing data that ultimately inform answers to the evaluation questions. Strategies for gaining a better understanding of statistics help you to gain confidence in designing an analytical plan for your evaluation studies. Because not all evaluation questions can be answered with quantitative designs and analyses, however, the next chapter guides you through the process of analyzing qualitative information.

REFERENCES

Abu-Bader, S. H. (2011). *Using statistical methods in social science research* (2nd ed.). Chicago, IL: Lyceum Books.

Ary, D., Jacobs, L. C., Razavieh, A., & Sorenson, C. (2006). *Introduction to research in education* (7th ed.). Belmont, CA: Thomson Wadsworth.

Bainbridge, A. (2009). Survey data cleansing: Five steps for cleaning up your data. MartizCX. Retrieved from https://www.maritzcx.com/blog/survey-data-cleansing-five-steps-for-cleaning-up-your-data/

Cohen, J. (1988). *Statistical power analysis for the behavioral sciences* (2nd ed.). Hillsdale, NJ: Erlbaum Associates.

Coffman, D. L. (2011). Estimating causal effects in mediation analysis using propensity scores. *Structural Equation Modeling, 18*(3), 357–369.

Erdfelder, E., Faul, F. & Buchner, A. (1996). GPOWER: A general power analysis program. *Behavior Research Methods, Instruments & Computers, 28*(1), 1–11.

Hair Jr, J. F., & Black, W. C. (2000). Cluster analysis. In L. G. Grimm & P. R. Yarnold (Eds.), *Reading and understanding more multivariate statistics* (pp. 147–206). Washington, DC: American Psychological Association.

Hoy, W. K. (2010). *Quantitative research in education: A primer*. Thousand Oaks, CA: Sage Publications.

Hoy, W. K., & Adams, C. M. (2016). *Quantitative research in education: A primer* (2nd ed.). Thousand Oaks, CA: Sage Publications.

Meade, A. W., & Craig, S. B. (2012). Identifying careless responses in survey data. *Psychological Methods, 17*(3), 437–455.

Mertens, D. M., & Wilson, A. T. (2012). *Program evaluation theory and practice: A comprehensive guide*. New York, NY: The Guilford Press.

Pett, M. H. (1997). *Nonparametric statistics for health care research: Statistics for small samples and unusual distributions*. Thousand Oaks, CA: Sage Publications.

Sauro, J. (2015). 7 ways to handle missing data. Measuring U website. Retrieved from http://www.measuringu.com/blog/handle-missing-data.php.

Tabachnick, B. G., & Fidell, L. S. (2001). *Using multivariate statistics* (4th ed.). Needham Heights, MA: Allyn & Bacon.

CHAPTER 9

Analyzing and Interpreting Qualitative Data

You have collected a set of documents, recorded interviews or focus groups, obtained a set of video-recordings, recorded notes from observations, or all of the above. Now what? How does all this information get processed and analyzed in order to make sense of it? "The process of bringing order, structure, and interpretation to a mass of collected data is messy, ambiguous, time-consuming, creative and fascinating. It does not proceed in linear fashion; it is not neat." (Marshall & Rossman, 2006, p. 154). In this chapter, I will guide you through the process for managing, analyzing, and interpreting qualitative information. The goal of qualitative data analysis is to "pull it apart and put it back together" (Stake, 1995, p. 75) in order to gain the perspectives of program participants or other stakeholders associated with a study and derive meaning from the information that informed it. When using qualitative methods, data collection and analysis is iterative and, as Marshall and Rossman (2006) describe, is not step-wise or linear. It is a process in which you refine data collection strategies, continually learn, and use new information to inform subsequent data collection and analysis. Hence, an evaluator will rely upon and use several forms of qualitative thinking to guide an analysis.

QUALITATIVE THINKING

Qualitative analysis is not simply a process of sorting, organizing, and summarizing information to achieve the goals and purpose of an evaluation study. It involves curiosity and an ability to ask questions about the information from a variety of perspectives in order to derive meaning through the analysis. It also engages four forms of analytical thinking that enable an evaluator to probe information in great depth and detail (Saldaña, 2015). *Deductive* thinking draws from preexisting ideas, organizational structures, concepts, or theoretical frameworks to guide, focus, and organize the analytical process. In contrast, *inductive* thinking is applied when we allow information to "talk to us" and tell us what those ideas, structures, concepts, or theories are and mean. When we look across information, we use *abductive* thinking to identify categories, patterns, or hierarchies that are embedded in that information. Lastly, when we reflect on what we learn from the information and notice themes and various types of relationships among categories, patterns, or hierarchies, we are using *retroductive* thinking. All forms of thinking are utilized in qualitative data analysis and are important for assuring the quality of an evaluation's findings.

METHODOLOGICAL APPROACHES AND ANALYTICAL STRATEGIES

In Chapter 6, I described four major methodological approaches to qualitative data analysis—narrative inquiry, phenomenology, grounded theory, and ethnography. For the purpose of this chapter, I also will include qualitative case studies among those four approaches. These methodological approaches are executed in different ways depending on the philosophical orientations that govern an analyst's values and ways of thinking and knowing. These orientations also influence the extent to which evaluators use qualitative methods and how they position themselves during a qualitative inquiry. Expanding from the ideas of Crabtree and Miller (1999), Marshall and Rossman (2006) described approaches to qualitative analysis along a continuum from that of "prefigured technical" to "emergent intuitive" (Figure 9.1). Those who approach their work from a technical perspective tend to use a "quasistatistical analytic style"; whereas, those who adapt intuitive approaches use an "immersion/crystallization style." Others will adopt approaches somewhere between those two extremes (Crabtree & Miller, 1992; Marshall & Rossman, 2006). The point,

Figure 9.1. A Continuum of Analysis Strategies. Reproduced by permission from Catherine Marshall and Gretchen B. Rossman, *Designing qualitative research*, Sage Publications, Inc., Thousand Oaks, CA, Copyright © 2006.

however, is that philosophical perspectives influence how one approaches a qualitative analysis.

Based on my experiences, positivists and postpositivists tend to gravitate toward deductive forms of thinking and count occurrences of information that help to establish causal or explanatory relationships among outcomes. They also may use qualitative methods and approaches to support or better understand quantitative findings, and they tend to remain highly objective in their approaches. In other words, they tend to use "prefigured technical" approaches when analyzing qualitative information. Humanists, constructivists, and transformativists gravitate toward the other extreme of the continuum to varying degrees. Humanists will rely more heavily on inductive forms of thinking and give voice to the perspectives and thought patterns of those who participate in an evaluation study. They also may gravitate toward narrative forms of inquiry or phenomenological studies. Evaluators who tend toward constructivist and transformative approaches will emphasize co-constructed knowledge and the importance of deriving the study's findings through the forms of thinking that dominate those who are key to informing the evaluation. Therefore, they may place their own thinking patterns aside and occupy a facilitative or fully engaged role in an evaluation. They may advocate for any of the four methodical approaches, but it will be clear that key stakeholders are both involved in and inform the evaluation's findings to the extent possible.

Different approaches to qualitative analysis are also evident in the academic literature. If you look across disciplines, such as medicine, psychology, education, and sociology, you will likely discover that qualitative data analysis is described, approached, and performed in various ways. For example, Strauss and Corbin's book on grounded theory (Strauss & Corbin, 1990) evolved from a disagreement that Strauss had with his colleague, Barney Glaser, about the appropriate extent to which grounded theory could be informed by pre-existing theory and conceptual frameworks. More broadly, some qualitative researchers (e.g., Hill, Thompson & Williams, 1997 or Grbich, 1999) incorporate code or category counts as a strategy to focus the analysis and identify major concepts of importance. These variations in qualitative data analysis largely stem from philosophical origins of disciplines or, in contrast, adaptations of methods that increase their receptivity and use in disciplines that have positivist origins. Notwithstanding these variations, Creswell (2013) identified several characteristics that are common across qualitative research studies (Box 9.1).

My personal bias favors constructivist and inclusive approaches to qualitative inquiry; however, in my own evaluation practice, I have combined more than one approach to perform an analysis in a way that was suitable for the purpose of the study and resonated with the philosophical perspectives of my clients and collaborators.

- It typically occurs in natural settings as opposed to "laboratories"
- The researcher is a key instrument for data collection
- Multiple data sources and data collection methods are used
- Researchers use complex reasoning through inductive and deductive logic
- It focuses on participants' perspectives and meanings
- The study design is typically emergent and cannot be fully described in advance
- Is reflexive and interpretive, so it is sensitive to the researcher's identity and background
- It represents a holistic account or complex picture of the problem, phenomenon, or issue studied.

[a] *Adapted from John W. Creswell,* Qualitative Inquiry & Research Design: Choosing among five approaches *(3rd ed.). Sage Publications, Thousand Oaks, CA, Copyright © 2013.*

QUALITATIVE APPROACHES AND HOW THEY INFLUENCE AN ANALYSIS

Table 9.1 compares characteristics of the five approaches to qualitative study design discussed in Chapter 3 and how each of them influence data analysis. Notice that each approach has a different focus and purpose for the analysis. If the goal of the analysis is to create or reconstruct a story that reflects the experiences of individuals (e.g., an historical event) across time, then narrative inquiry will be used to capture individual stories of study participants during an analysis. Phenomenology differs from narrative inquiry in that information is analyzed to capture the essence of a lived experience (e.g., a mild brain injury), independent of chronology. In other words, the goal of phenomenology is to understand what it is like to experience a phenomenon, rather than to capture a story about what happened when a specific situation or event was experienced. Using a grounded theory approach, an analyst will develop a theory about a process, action, or interaction among individuals (Creswell, 2013). Ethnography, in contrast to the other approaches, specifically focuses on culture and what it's like to be directly embedded in that culture, so the analysis typically will involve multiple forms of data collection and will seek a rich description of that culture during an analysis. Finally, if the purpose of an

Table 9.1. COMPARING CHARACTERISTICS OF FIVE QUALITATIVE APPROACHES AND THEIR INFLUENCES ON ANALYTIC APPROACHES AND STRATEGIES[a]

Characteristic	Narrative Inquiry	Phenomenology	Grounded Theory	Ethnography	Case Study
Focus	Exploring the life of an individual	Understanding the essence of the experience	Developing a theory grounded in data from the field	Describing and interpreting a culture-sharing group	Developing an in-depth description and analysis of a case or multiple cases
Purpose of the Inquiry	To tell stories of individual experiences	To describe the essence of a lived phenomenon	To ground a theory in the views of participants	To describe and interpret the shared patterns of a group's culture	To provide an in-depth understanding of a case or cases
Unit of Analysis	One or more individuals	Several individuals who have shared an experience	A process, an action, or an interaction involving many individuals	A group that shares the same culture	An event, program, or activity, or more than one individual
Data Analysis Strategies	Analyzing data for stories, "re-storying" stories, and developing themes, often using a chronology	Analyzing data for significant statements, meaning units, textual and structural description, and description of the "essence"	Analyzing data through open coding, axial coding, and selective coding	Analyzing data through description of the culture-sharing group and themes about the group	Analyzing data through description of the case and themes of the case as well as cross-case themes
Analytical Goal	Developing a narrative about the stories of an individual's life	Describing the "essence" of lived experiences	Generating a theory illustrated in a figure	Describing how a culture-sharing group works	Developing a detailed analysis of one or more cases
Unique Characteristics	Highly contextual, occurring within specific places or situations; often contain turning points	Detailed descriptions of a phenomenon that focus on what was experienced and how it was experienced by a group of individuals	Focus and process for developing a theory	Researcher is embedded in the culture being studied; dependent on field work and relationships with key informants	Intent to illustrate a unique case or understand a specific issue, problem or concern; multiple data sources and collection methods

[a] Adapted from John W. Creswell, *Qualitative inquiry & research design: Choosing among five approaches*. Sage Publications, Thousand Oaks, CA, Copyright © 2013.

inquiry is to gain an in-depth understanding of a case or several cases (i.e., a business going through a reorganization or a group of people responsible for a specific outcome), the analysis will seek a rich description of those cases for the purpose of the evaluation. This process, however, will differ according to the design's focus, purpose, and analytical goal.

ETHICAL ISSUES IN QUALITATIVE ANALYSIS

One of the major ethical concerns in qualitative data collection and analysis is respecting the privacy of those who participate in an evaluation study. This can be challenging, especially when participants are well known in their community or occupy positions that are unique among stakeholders. Therefore, it is important to de-identify qualitative information by using pseudonyms and generic titles (e.g., "a community leader" as opposed to "the mayor"), and removing contextual identifiers (e.g., a name of a town) that may reveal a participant's identity. This issue becomes even more challenging when you are engaging study participants in data analysis. By creating "composite profiles" (Creswell, 2013) or "case reports" (e.g., in case studies) you can maintain the privacy of those who participate in a qualitative study. Other concerns in qualitative data analysis include siding with a participant or reporting only positive or favorable findings. These concerns can be avoided by obtaining and analyzing multiple perspectives and reporting contrary information obtained during an analysis.

PREPARING FOR THE ANALYTICAL PROCESS

A set of documents, such as meeting notes, recorded observations, written stories, or other such recorded text are usually ready for analysis as collected. If you plan to analyze them by hand or using a word processor (vs. using qualitative analytical software, such as NVIVO), it would be helpful to put them in an electronic form with large (two-to-three-inch) right margins and line numbers. This margin will provide you a space to record codes that relate to segments of the document's text. Alternatively, you can use a word processor's "comment" feature to record codes. If you are using electronic software that is designed for qualitative analysis (e.g., NVIVO, MAXQDA, ATLAS), an electronic file (typically a Microsoft Word or text file) will import directly into the software for analysis. Check the software's specifications to be certain about the types of file formats that can be imported into the software.

Recorded interviews or focus groups are best analyzed by converting them to written text. You can transcribe them yourself, which can be a rewarding and interesting process, or you can use a transcription service. Transcription services are provided by individuals who have this skill and are "for hire" or available through online services. Typical cost for a one-hour, two-person recording is approximately $120 (±$30) in today's currency. When selecting a transcription service, be sure that transcribers who have familiarity with the language typical to the field or culture that you are studying are available. For example, there are transcribers who specialize in foreign languages, specific accents, and medical, financial, and legal terminology. Hiring a specialized transcriptionist will help to improve the accuracy of a transcript and will save you significant time that may be needed for corrections due to misunderstood terms or contextual unfamiliarity.

Video-recordings can be analyzed as is, but it is easy to get caught up in analyzing what is heard as opposed to what is viewed, especially if you also are analyzing transcripts from interviews or focus groups. So, if you are interested only in what is said, skip the video-recordings and use audio-recordings. Video-recordings are most appropriate when observing behaviors, communication patterns, or environmental factors alone or in relation to other factors or conditions that must be analyzed. Rubrics or checklists containing some basic items or categories may be used to capture qualitative or quantitative information during data collection. Alternatively, an evaluator could observe a video segment and record codes that describe her observations. This coding process is described in the section that follows.

QUALITATIVE ANALYSIS

Before I describe the analytical process used in qualitative evaluations, I define a few terms that are key to understanding qualitative data analysis (Table 9.2). In my experience, I have learned that these terms, if not well understood, can lead to misunderstandings about how qualitative analysis is performed.

Table 9.2. COMMON TERMS USED IN QUALITATIVE DATA ANALYSIS AND THEIR ASSOCIATED DEFINITIONS

Term	Definition
Code	A descriptive label that is given to a segment of information (e.g., image from a photograph, clip from a video, or a section of text from an interview transcript).
Subcode	A code that is applied to a segment of information that is related to another code.
Category	A group of codes that form a category of information that can be labeled by a unique code.
Theme	A general idea or concept that emerges through the analytical process when comparing findings across participants, data sources, codes, and categories.

Qualitative data analysis involves eight major steps as listed in Box 9.2. With any of the five evaluation approaches, you will begin your analysis the same way. Figure 9.2 provides a schematic illustration of the first six steps for conducting qualitative data analysis. It begins by coding segments of information contained in source documents (e.g., interview transcripts, video clips, or historical documents). In general, coding (i.e., process of assigning descriptive codes

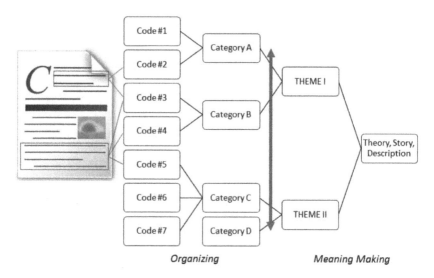

Figure 9.2. Schematic of qualitative data analysis process.

to your data) can be approached from two perspectives, as illustrated in Figure 9.3. *Deductive* coding uses predetermined frameworks, theories, concepts, or other such structures, along with deductive thinking to initially focus and organize information in the data source. In other words, information is categorized by some predetermined structure and subsequently coded in more detail; for example, when an evaluator divides evidence of faculty performance into the categories of "research," "teaching," "and service/outreach." Many evaluators working in positivist or postpositivist traditions, such as medicine or psychology, favor this approach. In contrast, *inductive* coding is a process in which the source of information "talks" to the analyst. In other words, the analyst does not impose a specific set of concepts (i.e., conceptual framework) or assumptions on the information, but allows codes to emerge from what is viewed or read in the data source; for example, when I am reviewing a group of manuscripts written by a professor on a specific topic and I decide to categorize them into evidence of "area of expertise" instead of "research." This category also might include evidence of teaching specific to the faculty member's expertise and be differentiated from evidence of "committee leadership." You can see, then, that the categories are defined differently based on the analyst's approach to coding.

Personally, I prefer inductive coding for two major reasons. First, it is consistent with the humanistic origins of qualitative methods, and second, based on my experience, it typically reveals more rich and accurate findings. For inexperienced analysts, however, this is often a challenging task that may lead to frustration and blank gazes. Tentative or "loose" coding structures can be helpful in guiding a novice analyst. I will also, at times, use an initial deductive coding process to focus an analysis on evaluation questions or retain concepts in a conceptual framework that guided the study. The main point is that when

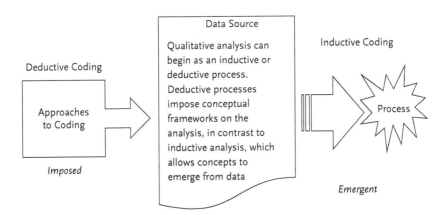

Figure 9.3. Illustration of the difference between inductive and deductive coding.

you begin the coding process be sure it has focus and direction; otherwise, you may be analyzing information in ways that are not useful. It is also OK to abandon a strategy that is leading you off track or not providing useful information. You would then "recode" the information utilizing a new strategy. This process is time consuming, however, so think through your analytical strategies very carefully before you begin an analysis. It often helps to fore-shadow the findings using a specific strategy or perform a pilot analysis on a small data set to avoid extra work. With that said, it is helpful to include as much detail as possible about your analysis in an evaluation plan; however, many evaluations do not proceed exactly as planned, so it is important to be flexible and adaptable in your approaches and strategies during qualitative analysis.

Before coding a data source, it is best to read or view it in its entirety to gain a sense of the information it contains. This step will help you to decide what fragments of text (i.e., sentences, phrases, or paragraphs) to code and provides a context for your analysis. To code information, you will begin with segments of text or video that are large enough to capture meaning, yet sufficiently small to be distinct from other segments. Coded segments typically range from a single sentence to two or three paragraphs. Personally, I typically code between two sentences to a single paragraph. For each segment, your goal is to record a word or short phrase, a *code*, that best captures the information in the segment (Figure 9.4). For example, the following segment of text could be coded as "fetching game," "curious behaviors," and "human-dog interactions."

> My dog enjoys a game of "fetch the squirrel" at the beginning of each day. On the first toss of his toy squirrel, he anticipates its landing and spends a few moments arranging it with his paws before picking it up and returning it to me. In subsequent fetches, he just picks it up and delivers it to me. This behavior is curious to me.

After a few data sources are analyzed, you will begin to notice that several codes are related and fall within one or more *categories* of information. This is the time when you should begin to develop a list of categories and the codes associated with them. It is helpful to think about properties and dimensions when building your categories. *Properties* are "attributes or characteristics pertaining to a category" and *dimensions* are "location of properties along a continuum" (Strauss & Corbin, 1990, p. 61). From the previous example, properties of "human-dog interactions" could be "games" and "curious behaviors." Dimensions of "games" based on several segments of data could be "fetching," "tugging," and "teasing." Although dimensions and properties are typically used when developing a grounded theory, I find these concepts to be useful for all approaches to qualitative data analysis.

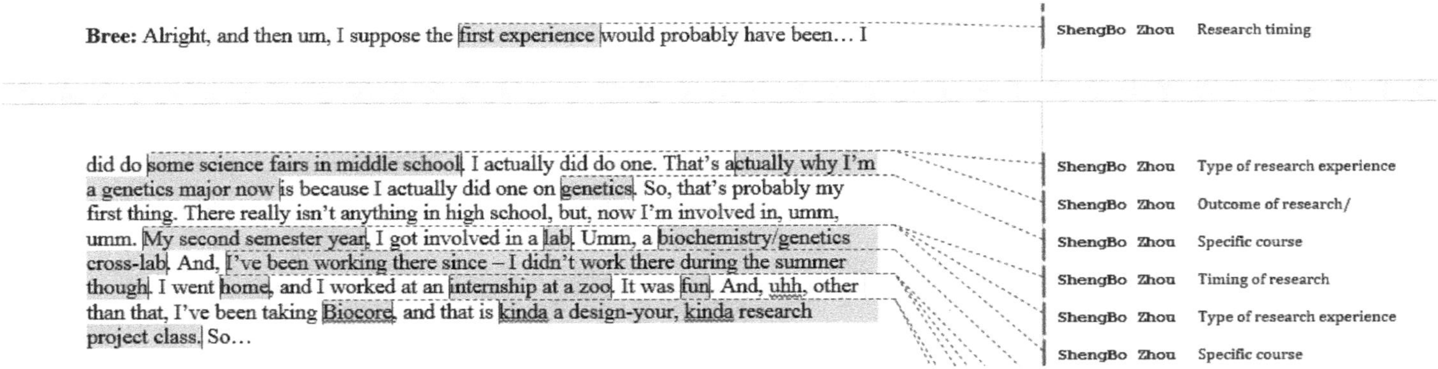

Bree: Alright, and then um, I suppose the |first experience |would probably have been… I

did do |some science fairs in middle school| I actually did do one. That's actually why I'm — ShengBo Zhou — Type of research experience

a genetics major now |is because I actually did one on genetics| So, that's probably my — ShengBo Zhou — Outcome of research /

first thing. There really isn't anything in high school, but, now I'm involved in, umm, — ShengBo Zhou — Specific course

umm. |My second semester year| I got involved in a lab. Umm, a biochemistry/genetics

cross-lab| And, |I've been working there since — I didn't work there during the summer — ShengBo Zhou — Timing of research

though| I went home| and I worked at an |internship at a zoo| It was |fun| And, uhh, other — ShengBo Zhou — Type of research experience

than that, I've been taking |Biocore| and that is |kinda a design-your, kinda research — ShengBo Zhou — Specific course

project class.| So…

ShengBo Zhou — Research timing

Figure 9.4. Example of a transcript coded in Microsoft Word.

By thinking about the properties and dimensions of categories, you are able to build a much richer description and understanding of the information you are analyzing. This process of coding and categorizing information is generally referred to as *open-coding* or simply, *coding* because you are freely assigning labels to and organizing segments of information. As you proceed through this process, your mind will start generating questions and ideas that are important to your analysis and that you will want to capture in *notes* or *memos*. You likely also will begin to think about the data across sources or units of analysis that will prompt you to generate new codes and *categories*. When using a grounded theory approach, this type of analysis is called *axial* coding. In a case study analysis, this process is referred to as *cross-case* analysis. When approaching your study as a narrative inquiry, this stage of the analysis will involve *chronologically ordering a set of experiences* that are derived through an analysis across participants' stories. Phenomenologists, in contrast, will organize significant statements and capture meaningful units that describe a phenomenon as they analyze their data across a set of sources.

Throughout the analysis, you will continue to record notes containing reflective thoughts and ideas. These notes, along with the codes and categories you've developed, will eventually reveal *themes* about the data that can be organized to align with the goal of your analysis. These themes may be related through linear, causal, cyclical, or complex webs of relationship (Saldaña, 2015). Hence, it is through the evolution of themes that you are able to develop a theory, rich description of a phenomenon, a collective story, or cultural understanding of the object of your evaluation. In evaluation, an emergent theory, description of a phenomenon, collective story, or cultural understanding should be oriented toward answering an evaluation question. For example, if an evaluation question were, "How and where do impoverished community members access food?" a phenomenological study using interviews with impoverished people might reveal an answer that suggests a variety of ways (e.g., rides with neighbors or family members), sources (e.g., church dinners) and locations (e.g., convenience stores and food pantries). If, however, the evaluation question were, "How do people cope with job loss?" a narrative inquiry could reveal an overall story that describes a process involving multiple emotions, coping strategies, and action steps, for example.

At this point, you may be asking yourself, "How long does the analytical process proceed and how many data sources do I need to analyze when doing a qualitative evaluation?" You will continue this process until you reach the point when you are acquiring no new information from your data sources. This stopping point is referred to as *saturation*, and it is typically reached when approximately 10 to 50 data sources have been thoroughly analyzed, depending on your approach (Mertens & Wilson, 2012).

To confirm or "validate" your findings, common practice is to provide the results of your analysis to your study participants or informants and ask them whether the information rings true for them. This procedure is called *member checking,* and it can be done with your analysis following each interview, for example, or it can be done at the completion of your study. To cite one example, when I did my dissertation research, I interviewed physicians. Following each interview, I transcribed the recording and analyzed the transcript. I then wrote short one- to two-page summaries of what I learned and understood them to say, so that I was certain I interpreted their information as each of them had intended. As another example, I assisted a colleague with a qualitative study in which her team performed interviews with students and then transcribed and analyzed those interviews. When they completed their analysis, it revealed a small number of (four to five) case scenarios describing the students' experiences. Subsequently, they convened focus groups of students who participated in the study and asked them to confirm their findings. These examples represent just a couple of ways qualitative findings can be confirmed.

As mentioned in a previous chapter, *triangulation* provides a way to establish the trustworthiness or credibility of the findings from your data analysis. Triangulation is a word that is used to describe the use of multiple data sources, methods, and analysts to corroborate information. For example, an evaluator who uses annual performance reviews and interviews to study the work of faculty. *Peer reviews, external audits,* and *debriefings* provide external forms of validation through critical and ongoing questioning. In essence, a person or group of people who are external to the evaluation study serves as a critical lens and holds an evaluator accountable to the analysis and its associated findings (Creswell, 2013). It is also important that an *evaluator clarify and make explicit their own biases* when conducting an evaluation study. Often, these biases influence an analytical approach and strategies for conducting an evaluation, so it is essential that they be made explicit from the beginning of a study. Finally, it is crucial that evaluators engage with study participants over prolonged periods of time and with persistence in order to gain the trust and rapport needed to acquire accurate and reliable information that yields rich and substantial descriptions of the findings (Creswell, 2013).

To acquire *reliable* information, it is important that the analytical process include multiple coders who have established agreement and consistency among them. Through the process of gaining clear and consistent agreement on code assignments, analysts work through discrepancies that result from their individual perspectives. This process minimizes the potential for inconsistent findings across time. Coding dictionaries (described in a subsequent section) and frequent debriefings among coders during the analytical process are ways to establish the reliability of an evaluation study's findings. For more information, I encourage you to consult the references cited in this chapter.

Because many of you may be working with small data sets or do not have affordable qualitative analysis software readily available to you, I would like to spend some time talking about how to manage qualitative data using a word processor (e.g., Microsoft Word) and spreadsheet (e.g., Excel). To code information using a word processor, simply highlight the text you wish to code and use the comments tool to record your code as illustrated in Figure 9.4. Once your document is completely coded, your codes and textual elements (i.e., excerpts) can be copied and pasted into separate cells of a spreadsheet. You also will want to record the file source of the text excerpts and corresponding page numbers in that document as illustrated in Figure 9.5. These records are important for retrieving information when the context of the comments is not clear or is incomplete.

After you have coded several sources and you begin to notice that the codes can be grouped into categories, you can add an additional column to

	A	B	C	
	G79	▾ : ✕ ✓ fx		
	A	**B**	**C**	
1	Category	Descriptive Terms/Codes	Reference	Trans
2	Attitude toward research with people (ε	working with people is undesirable; prefers independe	Adele, p.16	
3	Attitude toward research with people (ε	"better" and more connected or fulfilling	Josie, p.16	
4	Attitude toward research with people (ε	more benefit to work	Josie, p.16	
5	Attitude toward research with people (ε	clearer benefit	Curtis, p.16	
6	Attitude toward research with people (ε	direct application to person	Curtis, p.16	
7	Attitude toward research with people (ε	research for communities is beneficial	Josie, p.16	
8	Attitude toward research with people (ε	more motivating	Josie, p.17	
9	Attitude toward research with people (ε	more pressure	Josie, p.17	
10	Attitude toward research with people (ε	disease related research is "depressing"	Curtis, p.17	
11	Attitude toward research with people (ε	"positive" research and direct interactions with people	Curtis, p.17	
12	Attitude toward research with people (ε	directly helping people is a "huge motivator"	Josie, p.17	
13	career choice, research as	If "I fall in love with it"	Adele, p.12	
14	characteristics of research experience	helped PhD	Adele, p.2	
15	characteristics of research experience	"structured", "controlled"	Josie, p.2	
16	characteristics of research experience	team	Isaac, p.2	
17	characteristics of research experience	"awesome" program	Isaac, p.3	
18	characteristics of research experience	"fun"	Isaac, p.3	
19	characteristics of research experience	"crazy", "absurd"	Isaac, p.3	
20	characteristics of research experience	handed down	Isaac, p.3	
21	characteristics of research experience	passed through multiple students	Isaac, p.3	
22	characteristics of research experience	"not doable", inappropriate level	Isaac, p.3	
23	characteristics of research experience	"good experience"	Isaac, p.3	
24	characteristics of research experience	"joyful"	Isaac, p.3	
25	characteristics of research experience	micro scale; not something you can see	Adele, p.4	
26	characteristics of research experience	"scary" questioning by more senior investigtators	Josie, p.5	
27	characteristics of research experience	"overwhelming"	Josie, p.5	
28	characteristics of research experience	"wanted in lab", helper	Adele, p.5	
29	characteristics of research experience	"connected to something"; "good"	Adele, p.5	
30	characteristics of research experience	"overwhelming" talks (lab meetings)	Adele, p.5	
31	characteristics of research experience	"cool"	Curtis, p.5	

| ◄ ► | **Sheet1** | Sheet2 | Sheet3 | ⊕ |

Figure 9.5. Example of a spreadsheet in which coded data is captured and collated according to sources.

your spreadsheet, which contains the category names for each code in your file, as shown in the first column of Figure 9.5. You can also create additional sheets that contain your coding dictionary and notes. The sheet containing your coding dictionary should contain the name of each category, a clear definition of each category, and a list of codes associated with each category, which all members of your analytical team agree to and are using to assign codes to data sources (Figure 9.6). Early attempts to create a coding dictionary will help you to visualize inconsistencies among coders that can be cleared up at a timely point in the analytical process. A separate sheet of coding notes should, at a minimum, contain the date a note was entered, any source or code it references, the note, and any action steps (e.g., interviewing more participants with specific characteristics) that should be taken to enrich your analysis.

Spreadsheets make it easy to assign categories to each code and record their corresponding properties, dimensions, or other related information. These data can then be organized in ways that make them easy to find and organize around central themes. If you are a novice to qualitative analysis, I can think of no better way to learn how to do it and not be overwhelmed by all the features of sophisticated software. I am aware, however, that those much younger than I are technically savvy and may find software packages "a piece of cake."

The process for managing qualitative data in electronic software is very similar; although somewhat more complex. Electronic software will organize and store text excerpts, codes, categories, notes, themes, and other information, sometimes with names unlike those to which you are accustomed. It can be tremendously powerful and helpful when searching, selecting, and comparing information across sources, records, text excerpts, codes, categories, notes, or other forms of data, but electronic software can be daunting for a novice user. Therefore, I recommend that you learn to code and analyze qualitative data using simple tools, such as Microsoft Word and Excel, and progress to more sophisticated software packages when you have done at least one small study, for which you have learned to apply the basic concepts, methods, and strategies of qualitative analysis. I also recommend that you participate in a tutorial or workshop to learn the electronic software you plan to use.

SUMMARIZING, ORGANIZING, AND DESCRIBING QUALITATIVE INFORMATION

Summarizing, organizing, and describing the findings from a qualitative analysis can be challenging. Findings can be organized by individual participants (e.g., in the case of interviews), participant groups, cases (as are case studies), document type, emergent themes, or any other way that makes sense to you

UPSTAR Coding Dictionary

Category	Description	Examples of codes
Attitudes toward research with people	This category characterizes students attitudes or feelings toward conducting research with people	Undesirable; "better"; more connected; more benefit to work; clearer benefit; direct application; more motivating; beneficial; more pressure; "depressing"; "positive" with direct interactions/help
Career choice, research as	This category describes how students react to research as a career choice.	If "I fall in love with it". Depends on what excites you and connection to benefits
Characteristics of research experience	Describes the characteristics of the students' prior research experiences	"structured", "controlled", "handed down"; passed through multiple students; "not doable", inappropriate level; "good"; micro scale, not something you can see; questioning by senior investigators; wanted in lab, helper"; connected to something"; not official, helped brother; computer "less glorious" than clean room; "in front of a computer and data analysis"; still "interesting"; "work intensive"; requires background knowledge; group discussions; "crunching numbers"; "just an intern", abrupt stop/halt to project that was not funded; "abstract" work with no clear benefit
Feelings associated with students' research experiences	Captures the feelings students articulated when describing their research experiences	"fun", "crazy", "absurd", "joyful", "awesome", "scary" (questioning), "overwhelming", "cool", "good", "not glamorous", "moving", "traumatic" (presentation); can be "frustrating"

Figure 9.6. Example of a coding dictionary excerpted from the UPSTAR project.

and the evaluation report's key audiences. Once you have decided how to organize your findings, your aim is to tell the data's story in a narrative that is supported by quotations, illustrations, video clips, or other information from your data sources. Drawings and notes used to illustrate and record ideas and concepts during the analytical process also will facilitate this narrative, so be sure to incorporate them. The final section of the findings should contain a description of the theory, narrative, phenomenon, or personal experience that emerged from the analysis. For an evaluation, I typically present the findings using quoted materials or examples to justify and support each claim and summarize them by answering each evaluation question that was posed for the study.

SUMMARY

Chapter 9 began with the type of thinking, methodological approaches, and analytical strategies needed for qualitative data analysis. You learned that qualitative analysis can be performed inductively or deductively. You also learned about how different evaluation purposes influence whether you will use an ethnographic, phenomenological, narrative inquiry, or grounded theory approach to an evaluation and how that approach influences an evaluator's position for data collection and analysis. Ethical issues in qualitative data collection were highlighted and emphasized the importance of and strategies for protecting participants in your evaluation studies. I walked you through an analytical process that included coding, categorizing, theming, and making sense of the information. Along the way, I provided suggestions for tools that can facilitate the analytical process. This chapter concluded with tips for how to summarize, organize, and describe findings from a qualitative analysis to support your conclusions. The next chapter begins the final part of this book and describes the reporting and dissemination process, including various ways that qualitative information can be meaningfully expressed and described to answer the questions and achieve the evaluation's purpose.

REFERENCES

Crabtree, B. F., & Miller, W. L. (Eds.). (1999). *Doing qualitative research* (2nd ed.). Thousand Oaks, CA: Sage Publications.

Creswell, J. W. (2013). *Qualitative inquiry & research design: Choosing among five approaches* (3rd ed.). Thousand Oaks, CA: Sage Publications.

Grbich, C. (1999). *Qualitative research in health: An introduction.* Thousand Oaks, CA: Sage Publications.

Hill, C. E., Thompson, B. J., & Williams, E. N. (1997). A guide to conducting consensual qualitative research. *The Counseling Psychologist, 25*(4), 517–572.

Marshall, C., & Rossman, G. B. (2006). *Designing qualitative research* (4th ed.). Thousand Oaks, CA: Sage Publications.

Mertens, D. M., & Wilson, A. T. (2012). *Program evaluation theory and practice: A comprehensive guide.* New York, NY: The Guilford Press.

Saldaña, J. (2015). *Thinking qualitatively: Methods of mind.* Thousand Oaks, CA: Sage Publications.

Stake, R. E. (1995). *The art of case study research.* Thousand Oaks, CA: Sage Publications.

Strauss, A., & Corbin, J. (1990). *Basics of qualitative research: Grounded theory procedures and techniques.* Newbury Park, CA: Sage Publications.

PART FOUR

Report and Prepare Again

Part Four concludes the evaluation process by describing various ways that an evaluation's findings are reported and disseminated. This part of the book also closes out the evaluation process by discussing some trends in evaluation that you may encounter as you conduct program evaluations. Chapter 10 covers how the evaluation's findings are reported and disseminated to meet stakeholders' needs for information about the program. You not only will learn how to craft a written evaluation report, but you will learn about other ways to report an evaluation's findings based on the context of a program and the types of information that stakeholders find meaningful. Throughout these chapters, examples from practice are included to bring relevance and understanding to the chapters' contents.

The final chapter of the book is about your continued learning and the knowledge and skills demanded by emerging trends in the field. You will learn how trends are shifting from an emphasis on programs to an emphasis on systems and how that change affects the way you think about evaluation. Among the various evaluation approaches discussed are realistic evaluation, developmental evaluation, and movements toward social justice and inclusive evaluation practice. Hence, you may want to tackle new challenges or prepare for an evaluation in new ways by continuing your learning and professional development.

CHAPTER 10

Reporting and Disseminating Findings

This chapter covers a variety of ways that an evaluation's findings can be reported and disseminated. Written reports are the most common way to report an evaluation's findings and they often contain lengthy details about how the evaluation was planned and conducted. The report's content, length, and organization, however, will vary, depending on its audience. For certain audiences, it may be better to convey the evaluation's purpose, questions, methods, findings, interpretation, and conclusions by means other than a written report. It also may be more appropriate to prepare a brief report containing only a few elements of a full report. Alternative forms of reporting will be covered in later sections of this chapter. These forms of reporting are more commonly used for communicating an evaluation's findings in specific cultures, such as indigenous tribes, or among certain groups, such as those who are illiterate.

WRITTEN EVALUATION REPORTS

The purpose of a written evaluation report is to summarize all elements of the evaluation with the goal of answering the questions originally posed. Some audiences (e.g., program directors or funders) may require a full and detailed report, which is typically quite lengthy. Others (e.g., community stakeholders) may want only the final answers to the evaluation questions and not care as much about the elements and processes of the evaluation that helped to provide those answers. Fact sheets also can be produced to convey the key findings of an evaluation and provide a reference to the full report (Mertens & Wilson, 2012). Overall, a written evaluation report contains a description of each element of the evaluation process and includes the sections listed in

Box 10.1. CONTENTS OF A WRITTEN EVALUATION REPORT

1. Cover page
2. Table of Contents
3. Executive Summary
4. Description of context and object of the evaluation
5. The purpose, goals, and scope of the evaluation
6. The evaluation's key stakeholders and questions
7. The approaches and methods used to answer the questions
8. The findings of the evaluation (including unanticipated findings)
9. Limitations of findings and approaches
10. Interpretation of findings
11. Recommendations
12. Appendices

Box 10.1. These sections are quite common among evaluators and vary somewhat according to the report's audience (Brun, 2014; Fitzpatrick, Sanders, & Worthen, 2011; Mertens & Wilson, 2012).

Ultimately, your goal is to convey sufficient information that demonstrates to the reader why the evaluation study was conducted, how the study was conducted, who was involved, what was found, how the findings addressed the evaluation questions, and how the information will be used and disseminated. A written report can vary from just a few pages to more than one hundred pages in length, depending on its audience and the duration and scope of the evaluation. Often, reports include several appendices, which contain copies of consent forms, data collection instruments, logic models, and other materials produced for the evaluation. If you prepared a memo of understanding, or an evaluation proposal, plan, or contract before you began your study, the first six components of your report may have been written, but they will likely need to be edited to account for information that was gleaned after you wrote the original proposal or be tailored to specific stakeholder audiences.

Cover Page and Table of Contents. The cover page of a written report should convey the words "Evaluation Report" or more specifically, a short title communicating the overall message of the evaluation's findings, such as "Facilitating a System of Support." A byline containing the name of the object of the evaluation (e.g., Evaluation Training Program) should be included below the report's title. The authors' names and affiliations, along with the date of the evaluation report also should be included on the cover page. The names of evaluation team members who contributed to the report or study may be added, too. Photographs or other visual images help to add interest to

Facilitating a System of Support
Report of a Feasibility Study to Expand Food Assistance Outreach

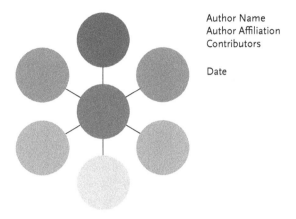

Author Name
Author Affiliation
Contributors

Date

Figure 10.1. An example of a cover page for an evaluation.

the cover page and can convey the topic of a report. Figure 10.1 illustrates a cover page containing these elements.

Because evaluation reports can be quite lengthy, it is important to add a Table of Contents as the next page of your report. A table of contents will simplify efforts to seek information during discussions about the evaluation and when conveying key information to stakeholders. The Table of Contents should be kept simple and page numbers should be aligned at the right-hand margin. Word processing software often contains a feature to generate a Table of Contents, but be sure it is correct when you distribute the final report. Because your stakeholders' need for information and their interest in the evaluation's details will vary, executive summaries are the next important component in your evaluation report.

Executive Summary. Executive summaries can be organized in several ways, but my preference is to focus its content on answering the evaluation questions. I also like to write this section as a stand-alone piece that could be provided to stakeholders who require limited information about the evaluation study. This is also the place to take advantage of photographs and infographics so that your findings are expressed clearly and succinctly through visual representations. I typically begin with a brief description of the situation or context that prompted the evaluation, the object of the evaluation, and the evaluation's purpose and use. In the next paragraph, I briefly mention the methods and approaches used to conduct the evaluation and provide a graphic, if helpful. I then provide a transition sentence that keys the reader into the next section, which lists each evaluation question one-by-one and provides a short descriptive paragraph that answers each question. I conclude the executive summary with a brief synopsis and concluding remarks followed by a list of recommendations (in a table format, if possible) that stem from the study's findings (i.e., answers to the evaluation questions).

Context and Object of the Evaluation. This section can vary in length from a single paragraph to several pages. It should contain a description of the community, organization, or other context in which the program you evaluated resides. This description may include a brief historical account, demographic characteristics, political climate, values held by stakeholders, and other information that helps to situate the evaluation in the context in which it was performed. This section also includes a description of the situation or need that led to the evaluation and a detailed description of the program or object of the evaluation. It also may contain the results of any assessments (e.g., a needs assessments or logic analysis) that were completed prior to and for the purposes of informing the evaluation described in the report.

Purpose, Use, and Scope of the Evaluation. As in your evaluation plan, the purpose, use, and scope of the evaluation are conveyed in clear and concise statements that easily can be found and identified in the report. I typically include them as separate sections so that they stand out among other sections of the report and are easily found.

Key Stakeholders. This section of the report lists the evaluation's key stakeholders and briefly describes them. In your description, it is important to identify each stakeholder's interests in the program (and/or evaluation) and how those interests were recognized and accounted for in the evaluation. Your philosophical approach to the evaluation likely will dictate how and the extent to which stakeholders were engaged in the evaluation process. This section affords an opportunity to make your approach explicit and provide a rationale for including or excluding various stakeholders. If you attempted to involve specific stakeholder groups and were not successful, your efforts should be documented.

Evaluation Questions. In this section, you will not only list the evaluation questions, but you may provide a description of the process by which you obtained and prioritized them. If several key stakeholders were involved in this process, their involvement will provide readers with knowledge of the range of perspectives that influenced the evaluation's questions and associated design. Typically, the evaluation will be focused on one to three main questions with subquestions that help to focus the study. At the reporting stage of an evaluation, it is not necessary to list all subquestions, unless it helps to clarify in advance how the findings will be reported. It is much easier for a reader to follow the findings associated with a short list of questions than a more detailed report involving answers to subquestions.

Approaches and Methods. This section describes your overall approach and strategies for addressing the evaluation questions, sampling methods, and methods used for collecting information, as well as the methods and approaches you used for analyzing data and interpreting the evaluation study's findings. It is helpful to illustrate the overall description in a figure, and perhaps, use the figure to organize this section. For example, a sequential mixed methods study that begins with interviews that are followed by a survey. For each phase of the study, you could then describe the sampling strategy and data collection methods used. This section also can be organized by starting with a description of your population and sample followed by data collection methods and the analytical methods and procedures used to answer each evaluation question. As illustrated in Figure 10.2, a matrix provided in the body of the report or an appendix can be helpful when describing how the sampling strategies, data collection methods, and approaches to data analysis were aligned with each evaluation question. In this section, it is also important to include the standards and criteria for judging the value, merit, or worth of a program.

Depending on your audience, it may be desirable to keep this section quite short and provide more detailed information in an appendix. Some readers may get bogged down with these details and lose interest in the report. Alternatively, you may wish to present the findings first, followed by the approaches and methods used to arrive at those findings. This saves the reader from having to slog through the details of data collection and analysis to get to the heart of the report.

Findings. Detailed reports of the evaluation's findings are important but can become overwhelming for most readers. Therefore, it is important to use graphs, tables, and other illustrations as often as possible to summarize and convey findings in simple and readable form. It is vitally important to ensure that findings are reported with accuracy. Standard A8 of *The Program Evaluation Standards* (Yarbrough, Shulha, Hopson, & Caruthers, 2011) states that "evaluation communications should have adequate scope and guard against misconceptions, biases, distortions and error" (p. 217). This means that members of the evaluation team reveal their own backgrounds and biases and attend to cultural norms, differences, and languages when reporting an evaluation's findings. Furthermore, evaluators should use alternate reporting approaches (e.g., film, dramatizations, and photography) when these more appropriately convey stakeholders' experiences, program outcomes, or other

Evaluation Question	Indicators or Information Needed to Answer the Question	Data Collection Methods	Data Analysis Procedures

Figure 10.2. Matrix for aligning data collection and analysis with evaluation questions.

important processes and findings (Yarbrough, Shulha, Hopson, & Caruthers, 2011, pp. 219–220).

In recent years, techniques for data visualization have become extremely popular among evaluators, thanks to the work of Stephanie Evergreen and others (Azzam & Evergreen, 2013; Azzam, Evergreen, Germuth, & Kistler, 2013; Bessell, Deese, & Medina, 2007; Evergreen, 2014; Henderson & Segal, 2013; Hergenrather, Rhodes, Cowan, Bardhoshi, & Pula, 2009). Visual displays, such as maps, matrices, word trees, and work clouds, among others can be used to effectively convey qualitative information, often more clearly and efficiently than traditional forms of display, such as quoted text (Henderson & Segal, 2013). Tables and bar graphs, for example, can be enhanced through simple techniques (e.g., removing horizontal lines on bar graphs) that improve their readability and focus an audience's attention on the main message being conveyed. Dr. Evergreen has dedicated books and a website to describing how best to communicate evaluation findings in clear and concise visual forms. Some examples from my own work are shown in Figure 10.3.

For written reports, Dr. Evergreen recommends that evaluators follow her checklist of best practices when selecting a typeface, arranging the report, and using graphics and color (Evergreen, 2013). A helpful *Research and Evaluation Report Layout Checklist* also is provided as an appendix to her book (Evergreen, 2014, p. 173). These techniques go a long way toward conveying information in a comprehensible form, but they do require specialized skills and time.

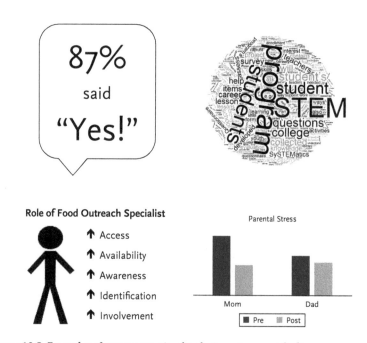

Figure 10.3. Examples of ways to use visual techniques to report findings.

So, when, or if, you can't take the time to prepare a report of this standard, I encourage you to get training or seek the assistance of professionals when needed. These efforts will go a long way toward a reader's ability to understand an evaluation's findings and capture the main messages from a report (Azzam, Evergreen, Germuth, & Kistler, 2013).

Unanticipated Findings. It is likely that some unanticipated findings may have emerged from the evaluation. These findings should be noted, explained, and discussed in terms of their relative importance in answering the evaluation's questions and gleaning new insights. These findings may have significant influence on the way that one or more of the evaluation's questions are answered, so take adequate time to explore them. For example, we conducted a feasibility study to expand a program that facilitated access to government food assistance. During our context analysis, we discovered the food systems that operated in the small rural communities in which we were interested. This information was critical to one of our subquestions, which was directed at understanding the role of an outreach specialist in these communities. The clients had assumed to some extent that the program would operate in the same way that it had in larger communities, but with this finding they quickly realized that their assumption was not valid.

Summary and Conclusions. By the time your readers reach this part of the report, they likely will be fatigued, so it is important to keep your summary and concluding remarks short and pointed. Therefore, the summary of the evaluation's findings should be brief and highlight conclusions from the main findings of the evaluation. What is the bottom line message you wish to convey to your readers about this evaluation? The answer to this question should be the focus of this section. Typically, I like to organize this section by repeating the purpose of the evaluation and providing brief statements about how the findings were helpful in addressing that purpose. For example, when we reported on the feasibility study mentioned earlier, we concluded with a section about whether it was feasible to expand the program to the area of interest and how the evaluation helped to inform the likelihood that expansion efforts would be successful. It is helpful to end the report on a positive note, so you may wish to summarize a few "next steps" to provide direction and encourage use. For example, I recently concluded an evaluation report with a quote from a participant and summarized the actions needed to reduce the community's problem successfully. By ending the report this way, I was engaging the reader's emotions and optimism for change.

Limitations. Any evaluation study has limitations and those limitations should be made explicit in any report. Examples include limitations posed by the sample, data collection methods, types of questions posed for the study, availability of information, and scope of the study (which is often influenced by the budget). With a description of the study's limitations, the reader is provided with guidance on how and to what extent he or she can interpret and extrapolate the finding beyond the present study. Describing limitations also reveals information about how the findings might have been different if they had not been influenced by the limitations reported.

Interpretations and Recommendations. As an external evaluator, you may not be sufficiently familiar with the context or subject matter of the program you are evaluating, so it is important to include key stakeholders when interpreting the findings of an evaluation. Engaging them in the interpretation and reporting of the evaluation's findings increases the likelihood that they will use and disseminate the information found. For example, when I and my students worked with social workers to evaluate their organization's parenting program, we learned that their efforts were not being sustained several months after the program. Although this was very disappointing to them, engaging them in a discussion about those findings and exploring reasons for them empowered the social workers to change their approach to the program's delivery in ways that would improve the sustainability of its effects.

Recommendations typically surface throughout the evaluation process, so if you have adequately documented the evaluation's process, you should have a list of recommendations for the final report. Typical recommendations include ways that tracking and data collection methods can be improved to yield better quality information, ways to sustain assessment and evaluation in the organization, training needs, suggested approaches for addressing emergent findings, or alterations in program theory. Recommendations also may involve a decision about whether a program should be continued. In this situation, the results must be reported carefully, because an evaluator is typically not the person in a decision-making role. We must be careful to adhere to and explicitly note the criteria established when the evaluation was planned, stick closely to the evaluation's findings (let the data talk), and frame any interpretations and recommendations in the context of the study's limitations. If you have engaged with key stakeholders during the process, the recommendations will be of no surprise to them. If, however, their engagement has been limited, recommendations may be received with some surprise and even defensiveness. If this happens, it is important to frame those reservations within the context of the evaluation and its associated limitations, focus on evidence, and emphasize the importance of learning and program improvements.

Appendices. Appendices typically contain documents that were created and used in the planning and execution of the evaluation. Examples include logic models or other conceptual models, consent forms, data collection forms, summaries and/or bibliographies of literature reviews, relevant policy documents, or other documents that are referred to in the main body of the report.

BRIEF WRITTEN REPORTS

Brief reports should not be mini versions of the full report, but instead include only information that conveys key elements that are important to the report's audience. Because brief reports are typically written for public audiences, community members, or administrators who may have limited time or understanding of evaluation, it is important that the report be written in a language and presented in a form that is easily understood by them. Brief reports typically include a short description or statement about the object of the evaluation, the evaluation's purpose, and key findings for each question. If desired, the findings may be limited to answering one or two of the most important evaluation questions or to the one or two questions of most interest to the report's readers. Again, visual representations (e.g., photographs or graphs) are important and helpful in conveying a message simply, quickly, and understandably. Brief written reports also should be translated into languages and forms that can be understood by different cultures, such as through stick drawings or other visual representations. One important thing to keep in mind is that even a translated report (or data collection form) will not be understood by a person who is illiterate, so verbal or visual representations of the evaluation report may be necessary to communicate its findings.

Short flyers and other brief reports (e.g., newsletters and interim reports) can augment oral presentations, be posted in strategic locations to facilitate organizational learning, be used to disseminate information quickly to large audiences or send key messages when time is limited. Sometimes a simple graphic illustration with a few call-outs can convey the most relevant findings of an evaluation. Other times, a short series of pictures may tell a story to illustrate an evaluation's findings. These forms of reporting also can be used to inform key stakeholders about benchmarks and other important information as an evaluation's findings unfold. Be careful, however, that premature release of information does not convey findings that are contradicted in later releases or final reports.

Written reports constitute only one of several ways that findings from evaluation studies can be reported and disseminated. Other ways that evaluation findings can be shared with key stakeholders are through oral presentations, brief flyers (e.g., news briefs), visuals (e.g., photographs or journey maps), storytelling (oral or visual), and acting. However, these forms of reporting and disseminating an evaluation should augment rather than supersede a written report. Written reports are necessary for thoroughly documenting the evaluation process and findings (see Standard E1, Evaluation Documentation, in Yarbrough, Shulha, Hopson, & Caruthers, 2011). In the following sections, I will describe the various ways, beyond written reports, that evaluation findings can be reported and disseminated and discuss for which audiences these are most appropriate.

ORAL PRESENTATIONS

Oral presentations are a common way to present evaluation findings. However, they often are done with little attention to effective ways of communicating information through visual representations. How many times have you sat through numerous PowerPoint slides in which information is provided in lengthy bullet points? Again, the work of scholars who specialize in visual and oral presentations is helpful. Ten tips are listed in Box 10.2.

It is also important to time your presentation so that you do not exceed your limits. For a 10-minute presentation, I generally aim for no more than 10 slides. The longer the presentation, the fewer slides per minute can be presented, so a 60-minute presentation should be limited to 30 to 40 slides. These rules of thumb assume that you will engage with your audience and fill in details with your knowledge of the evaluation. Slides should not substitute for your knowledge about the evaluation. They should support what you say.

Box 10.2. TEN TIPS FOR GIVING EFFECTIVE POWERPOINT PRESENTATIONS

1. Include no more than three to four words in a bullet point and highlight (with a change in color or animation) each bullet point when you refer to it.
2. Place no more than three to five bullet points on a single slide.
3. Make sure that your text optimally contrasts with the slide's background. For example, dark-colored text (e.g., black, navy, forest green, or brown) should be placed on a white background and white text should be placed on a dark blue background.
4. Use photos or pictures as much as possible to illustrate concepts and ideas.
5. Make the main point the largest element on the screen.
6. Keep quoted material to a minimum.
7. Simplify graphics by combining categories, using color and bolding, and limiting the number of elements in the illustration.
8. Be sure that textual elements are readable, which usually means that font size is no less than 20 points.
9. Augment slides with handouts when visuals are complicated or difficult to read.
10. Use san sarif fonts (no tails on letters) to aid readability. This is a **Sans Sarif** Font.

The pace, volume, and clarity of your voice are very important in conveying information effectively. Older adults process information more slowly and often have some loss of hearing, so use a microphone to help project your voice when necessary and deliver your message more slowly than usual. Also, avoid fancy lingo and acronyms that may be unfamiliar to your audience. When conveying information to multicultural audiences who may speak different languages, be sure that the information is translated in ways that can be understood by them. Better yet, have a key stakeholder who is also a member of your audience, convey the information to their peers. By engaging them in the presentation, you are more likely to empower them to use the findings in ways that are beneficial to them. Often, evaluators will prepare short presentations that stakeholder groups can give to their peers. This effort not only saves the stakeholders' time and effort, but helps in conveying accurate and appropriate information.

STORYTELLING

Some cultures, such as tribal communities, convey information through storytelling or dance. Stories can be shared verbally or through pictorial representations. Journey maps, such as the one illustrated in Figure 10.4, are pictorial representations that tell a story frame-by-frame through drawings or photographs. They are highly effective for conveying evaluation findings, especially when written language is a barrier.

Photographs or drawings are another way to convey a story and may be particularly helpful when working with youth or illiterate populations (Bessell, Deese, & Medina, 2007; Hergenrather, Rhodes, Cowan, Bardhoshi, & Pula, 2009). Often, you will have to engage local community members in this way to convey findings from an evaluation study. This is an excellent strategy for involving them in reporting and disseminating an evaluation's findings.

ELECTRONIC AND SOCIAL MEDIA

Electronic (e.g., e-mail or websites) and social media provide yet another way to report and disseminate an evaluation's findings. We must be mindful, however, that this form of dissemination is typically very public, so it is important that the evaluation's findings be conveyed in a way that is easily understood and not misinterpreted by multiple audiences. One of the best examples that I've seen are video documentaries of an evaluation's findings on YouTube. Again, this is most effective when the means of dissemination not only represent but *involve* key stakeholders. Short video-clips also can be inserted into oral presentations to help convey findings in a convincing manner. Websites

Image #1   Image #2

Image #3   Image #4

Figure 10.4. This figure provides an example of a journey map containing four photographs. Image #1 illustrates the study team walking toward the mural shown in Image #2. Images #2 and #3 illustrate a mural that reflects this rural town's mining history. Image #4 displays rocks containing minerals that were mined. Photographs by David Lee (with permission).

can be used to access evaluation reports, videos, and other information that is relevant to an evaluation project, making the information readily available to a larger audience.

ACTING

Artistic expression, specifically acting, is yet another way to report the findings of an evaluation, although much less popular than other forms of reporting. Through acting, emotions can be conveyed, chronological events can be replicated, and context can be communicated. In essence, actors tell an evaluation's story. Imagine, if you will, a key informant describing what it is like to be food insecure in a small isolated rural community. You are told that this person must rely on friends, relatives, and neighbors for transportation to a local food pantry (that is open only once a week) and an occasional meal that is offered. You also learn about making choices between paying your heating bill and buying food that will last you through the end of the month. This situation may be further complicated by other family members, such as children, who rely on you for support and are involved in the choices you make between feeding them and feeding yourself. Now imagine how this story would be told through acting as compared to a written report. Would the words on paper (or a video-taped interview) tug at your heart the way an acted scenario would? Would you be able to grasp the contextual elements and hardships of being isolated and unable to access food because you relied on others who may not be available in a timely manner to help? Would you feel the joy of having choices about the foods you eat, rather than being told what and how much you could take at a local food pantry? Acting provides a compelling option for reporting an evaluation's findings. Consider it an option in your portfolio of reporting formats. Like other forms of evaluation reporting, acting is most effective and applicable under specific conditions and for specific audiences. It is limited by the number of talented people needed to convey an evaluation's message, and it depends on those who are available to hear that message during a specific day and time. Nonetheless, when words on paper or other forms of communication are not sufficiently effective for conveying an evaluation's findings, acting is another form of expression.

PUBLICATIONS IN PROFESSIONAL JOURNALS

You and/or other members of your evaluation team may wish to report an evaluation in a professional journal after spending considerable amounts of time planning, implementing, analyzing, and reporting it. To do this, an evaluation should make a significant contribution to research or practice in the evaluation field or in a field that relies on evaluation as a form of applied research to advance practice. Examples of journals in the evaluation field include the *American Journal of Evaluation, Evaluation and Program Planning*, and *Evaluation Practice*. Examples of journals emphasizing evaluation in specific fields include *Assessment and Evaluation in Higher Education, Educational Evaluation and Policy Analysis, Engineering Evaluation*, and *Evaluation and the Health Professions*. When reporting an evaluation study in a professional journal, a manuscript's typical organization would include an introduction, methods, findings, and discussion containing the conclusions and major contributions to the field. You also may wish to report on a novel evaluation teaching approach, conceptual model, data collection method, or other topic that may be relevant and important to advancing the field. Not all journals accept a range of manuscript types, so check the journal's authorship guidelines before submitting a manuscript for publication. Sometimes, the publication's editor may be willing to review an abstract and answer questions about a manuscript's appropriateness for a journal before you submit a manuscript. This effort may save you a tremendous amount of time and effort, especially if you are inexperienced.

SUMMARY

The final evaluation report marks the culmination of an evaluation study. Various forms of reporting, such as written reports, fact sheets, and newsletters can be used to convey the findings and conclusions of an evaluation study. Forms of expression, such as acting, storytelling, and photovoice are powerful ways to capture an audience's emotions and attend to visual forms of learning when reporting and disseminating an evaluation's findings. Techniques that enhance data visualization help to improve comprehension and meaning so that an evaluation's findings and ultimate message are accurately understood. Evaluation reports can be tremendously powerful and often serve as a basis for decision-making. Therefore, an evaluator must accurately and clearly convey the evaluation's findings and report any limitations that influence its conclusions. By including key stakeholders in this process, an evaluation report does a better job of meeting an audience's needs for information and conveying its message in a way that improves buy-in, comprehension, and acceptance when findings may not be as favorable as expected. So, be certain to allow adequate time for preparing an evaluation report and disseminating it to its intended users.

By now, you should have acquired the fundamental knowledge and skills to prepare, design, conduct, and report a program evaluation. In the final chapter of this book, I will describe major trends in the evaluation field that provide insights to some of the challenges you may encounter when evaluating programs. The knowledge and skills needed to tackle these challenges are also briefly described to give you an appreciation for some of the limitations of program evaluation. The chapter concludes with the implications of these trends and how you can play an instrumental role in contributing to evaluations of social change.

REFERENCES

Azzam, T. & Evergreen, S. (Eds.). (2013). *Data visualization, part 1. New Directions for Evaluation* (Vol. 139). San Francisco, CA: Jossey-Bass.
Azzam, T., Evergreen, S., Germuth, A. A., & Kistler, S. J. (2013). Data visualization and evaluation. In T. Azzam & S. Evergreen (Eds.), *Data visualization, part 1. New Directions for Evaluation, 139,* 7–32.

Bessell, A. G., Deese, W. B., & Medina, A. L. (2007). Photolanguage: How a picture can inspire a thousand words. *American Journal of Evaluation, 28,* 558–569.

Brun, C. F. (2014). *A practical guide to evaluation.* Chicago, IL: Lyceum Books.

Evergreen, S. (2013). *Evaluation report layout checklist.* Retrieved from http://stephanieevergreen.com/wp-content/uploads/2013/02/ERLC.pdf).

Evergreen, S. D. H. (2014). *Presenting data effectively: Communicating your findings for maximum impact.* Thousand Oaks, CA: Sage Publications.

Fitzpatrick, J. L., Sanders, J. R., & Worthen, B. R. (2011). *Program evaluation: Alternative approaches and practical guidelines.* Upper Saddle River, NJ: Pearson Education.

Henderson, S., & Segal, E. H. (2013). Visualizing qualitative data in evaluation research. In T. Azzam & S. Evergreen (Eds.), *Data visualization, part 1, New Directions for Evaluation, 139,* 53–71.

Hergenrather, K. C., Rhodes, S. D., Cowan, C. A., Bardhoshi, G., & Pula, S. (2009). Photovoice as community-based participatory research: A qualitative review. *American Journal of Health & Behavior, 33*(6), 686–698.

Mertens, D. M., & Wilson, A. T. (2012). *Program evaluation theory and practice: A comprehensive guide.* New York, NY: The Guilford Press.

Yarbrough, D. B., Shulha, L. M., Hopson, R. K., & Caruthers, F. A. (2011). *The program evaluation standards: A guide for evaluators and evaluation users* (3rd ed.). Thousand Oaks, CA: Sage Publications.

CHAPTER 11

Preparing for Complexity in Evaluation

In Chapter 11, I bring you back to the preparation stage by describing some emergent trends in the evaluation field and how they are affecting evaluation practice. These trends create challenges for evaluators that provide you with opportunities to expand your knowledge of and skills in evaluation so that you are better prepared to tackle these challenges when encountered.

One of the most remarkable changes in the field in recent years occurred when Michael Patton published his book, *Developmental Evaluation* (Patton, 2011). This book captured a need for an evaluation approach that could address emergent and complex social issues and problems. Moreover, it underscored a trend in the evaluation field from an emphasis on *program* evaluation to an emphasis on *systems* evaluation. Systems approaches to evaluation highlight adaptive processes that are responsive to and proactive toward emergent change. We also began to hear the phrase, *collective impact,* which has become an especially popular concept among nonprofit foundations and government organizations who typically fund a significant number of partnerships and broad-scale efforts toward social change.

What is common among these trends is a shift away from thinking about programs and program evaluations as isolated activities to thinking about programs as part of larger systems. As described in earlier chapters, the field is experiencing a shift away from evaluations of *predicted* outcomes and *attributions* of a program toward evaluations of program *contributions* to *actual* outcomes (Mayne, 2001). Realistic Evaluation (Pawson & Tilley, 1997) was an early response to this trend by emphasizing the mechanisms and conditions that contribute to *actual* outcomes across multiple system layers. Consequently, outcomes are not only thought of as short-term changes resulting from a program's activities, but as changes that can be monitored and promoted within systems to evaluate broad-scale social impact involving multiple organizations, community stakeholders, and societal sectors.

These trends in the evaluation field also strengthened the field's focus on evaluation practices that advocate a more equitable and just society. This latter shift creates a greater need and emphasis on participatory approaches to evaluation, such as Empowerment Evaluation (Fetterman, 1994; Fetterman & Wandersman, 2005), Transformative Evaluation (Mertens, 2009), and Deliberative Democratic Evaluation (House & Howe, 1999, 2002). Given these trends, recent literature is combining systems thinking and theory with previously established evaluation approaches that engage greater stakeholder involvement, such as complex adaptive systems theory and utilization-focused evaluation (Patton, 2011), critical systems theory and developmental evaluation (Reynolds, 2014), and culturally responsive evaluation and systems-oriented evaluation (Thomas & Parsons, 2016).

FROM PROGRAM THEORY TO SYSTEMS THEORY

For decades, the evaluation field has been dominated by program theory and evaluations that emphasize the study of outcomes and impacts of a program's activities. As our country simultaneously shifted toward demanding greater accountability, program funders, including but not limited to major foundations and government, quickly began to require that their grantees conduct program evaluations based on sound theory and evidence that anticipated outcomes were achieved. Consequently, program evaluations based on randomized controlled trials and quasiexperimentation became the desired standard. Decades later, it was realized that although program outcomes were often achieved (or not), significant and much needed changes in organizations and communities, more broadly, were not occurring to the extent anticipated. With the increased popularity of collective impact and associated shared measurement systems (Kania & Kramer, 2011), this realization caused funders to create their own set of outcomes and impacts with which grantees needed to align in order to be funded. Communities and organizations driven by grass-roots efforts also were realizing that to be most effective, collective efforts were needed for social change (Cook, 2014; Sheldon & Wolfe, 2015). Hence, efforts to align programming with a collective set of activities within organizations and communities emerged and evaluations of collective impact became more popular.

The consequence of this collective approach, however, has raised issues about a single program's actual significance toward contributing to the desired outcomes and impacts. Therefore, a dialogue about measuring a program's contributions, instead of attribution to an organizational or community impact, has gained momentum (Mayne, 2001). Before I describe various evaluation approaches that have emerged in response to more collective ways of working and demonstrating impact, however, it is important to distinguish among the types of problems and situations we typically encounter in evaluation practice.

SIMPLE, COMPLICATED, AND COMPLEX SITUATIONS AND PROBLEMS

In his book on *Developmental Evaluation*, Michael Patton (2011) distinguishes among simple, complicated, and complex situations along two dimensions—certainty and agreement. In simple situations, there are high levels of both agreement and certainty about a situation or problem among stakeholders; for example, a program, such as a nutrition education program, that instructs a group of parents about the nutrition pyramid and how to select healthful food groups when preparing meals for children. There is a high level of agreement that the nutrition pyramid provides good dietary guidance and a high certainty that a person who follows it will receive balanced nutrition—it is *simple*. We all know, however, that even those who are knowledgeable of the food pyramid and try to follow it most of the time, don't always do so. We also know that cultural backgrounds influence dietary choices. Factors such as culture and human behavior often *complicate* a situation, so that outcomes are less certain and predictable. Although there is still high agreement that the food pyramid provides guidance for good nutrition, there is a great deal of uncertainty that it will actually be followed as a function of the factors just mentioned.

A situation becomes *complex* when there is great disagreement and high level of uncertainty about a situation. For example, although the food pyramid provides good nutrition guidance, it becomes almost meaningless for those who are food insecure and not able to purchase "good food" because it is either unavailable or not affordable. Those providing services may not agree on whether to provide nutritious food or just focus on providing any type of food whether it is nutritious or not. There is also a great deal of uncertainty about how food choices are made. In other words, there is a great deal of disagreement among stakeholders about what foods can be purchased, and there is a high level of uncertainty about whether these foods can consistently be purchased—the situation is complex.

The contrast among these three situations is important, because in simple situations, relationships between cause and effect are clear and predictable—a nutrition education program teaches people about the food pyramid and they learn it. Program theory has typically assumed very simple causal relationships between programs and outcomes as evidenced through logic models and evaluation designs, such as quasiexperimental designs and randomized-controlled designs. In recent years, however, evaluation approaches and designs have shifted to ones that can handle complicated and complex situations. Change takes various forms, which can provide direction for designing evaluations in various situations and when encountering different types of problems. The next section describes these various forms of change, so that you can recognize them when you confront them.

STATIC, DYNAMIC, AND DYNAMICAL CHANGE

Static change is a form of change that is easily predicted and controlled, such as acquired skills or knowledge gained through a single educational program (e.g., a nutrition education program) or social intervention (e.g., an inmate transition program). *Dynamic* change is quite predictable, but difficult to control. For example, weather forecasters can do a pretty good job of predicting tomorrow's weather, but they can't control whether or not we will get a storm. Finally, *dynamical* change is neither predictable nor easy to control. For example, a crowd of spectators that suddenly surges onto a football field after a major and unexpected win. This form of change is associated with several autonomous actors who come together in complex situations and their collective dynamics lead to emergent (and sometime rapid) change (Cabrera & Cabrera, 2015). These different forms of change are reflected in what is known as the Cynefin Framework (Kurtz & Snowden, 2003; Snowden, 2002) as illustrated in Figure 11.1.

As you will note from this illustration, *chaos* is described as another form of change. Chaos is recognized when complex situations have gotten seemingly out of control. Change appears to be random and disordered. It also signifies an opportunity to shift from traditional linear ways of knowing and doing to those that are more adaptive (Eoyang, 2009). If an evaluator is faced

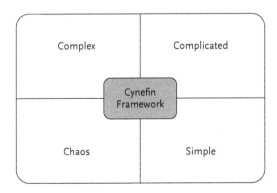

Figure 11.1. A simplified illustration of the Cynefin Framework (Snowden, 2002).

Table 11.1. SEVEN CHARACTERISTICS OF COMPLEX ADAPTIVE SYSTEMS
(EOYANG, 2009)

Characteristic	Description
Butterfly effects	Small effects that lead to big changes; for example, a leaky faucet that creates a flood.
Boundaries	Mark the distinctions between and among systems components. Communication is critical across boundaries in a system.
Transforming Feedback	A change-causing exchange of information across boundaries in a system.
Fractals	Patterns that repeat at multiple scales in a system.
Attractors	Recognizable patterns of change across time (Human Systems Dynamics Institute, 2016).
Self-organization	A property that is inherent in any system. When disorganized, a system will find ways to reorganize itself.
Coupling	The attachments between subsystems within a complex system.

with a chaotic situation, he or she can be helpful in assessing the situation and recommending strategies that alter one of the seven characteristics of complex adaptive systems (Table 11.1) and help to regain order. For example, an evaluator could evaluate how much communication is occurring across a system's boundaries and, if determined to be insufficient, could recommend that mechanisms be implemented to improve communications.

An evaluator's ability to recognize various forms of change and assess characteristics of complex adaptive systems is a tremendous asset in evaluating an organization or community's collective efforts toward favorable social change. By recognizing forms of change as part of a situational or contextual analysis, evaluators are better able to make decisions about what approaches and methods are needed to evaluate large-scale impacts. Program theory has served and will continue to serve us well for evaluating static change, but other approaches are needed for evaluating dynamic and dynamical forms of change.

REALISTIC EVALUATION FOR COMPLICATED SITUATIONS AND DYNAMIC CHANGE

Realistic evaluation was originally introduced to the evaluation field by Ray Pawson and Nick Tilley in 1997 as an attempt to move away from causally oriented program theory to evaluation theory that embraced the reality of complicated factors inherent in social problems. This approach is a sharp contrast to program theory based in logic models and assumptions of causal relationships. By emphasizing the underlying mechanisms and context of *actual* change (i.e., outcomes), Realistic Evaluation can help to understand an intervention's contributions to social impacts based on this simple formula:

Context + Mechanism = Outcomes (Pawson & Tilley, 1997)

This formula provides a structure for helping to answer the question, "What works for whom and under what conditions?" (Pawson & Tilley, 1997, p. xvi). The authors argue for an evaluation approach to assessing change that is grounded in scientific realism. This approach assumes that programs are not static, and that causation is *generative* (p. 59). So, in order to assess outcomes, evaluators must drill down to the mechanisms and context that influence the relationship between cause (a program) and effect (one or more outcomes). So, if a nutrition education program resulted in outcomes for which some participants altered their healthy eating behaviors and others did not, it would be important to know the mechanisms and contexts that led to those outcomes and to what extent the program contributed to them.

Realistic evaluators, therefore, assess the conditions for various outcomes (desired or not) and seek to understand the mechanisms and context that generated them. By looking at patterns across several outcomes, or changes, throughout the "stratified layers" of a system, one can understand the optimal conditions for change. In essence, the role of an evaluator when using a realistic approach to evaluation is to use an appropriate array of data collection and analysis methods to unpeel the layers of change within a system and identify the mechanisms and conditions that generate an impact.

Realistic evaluation has provided valuable contributions to the evaluation field through its emphasis on mechanisms and context in relation to dynamic change; however, this approach is limited by its heavy focus on program/intervention (vs. other change mechanisms), a dilution of agency as part of mechanism (Porter, 2015), and the value it places on evaluators and clients' knowledge over that of participants and other stakeholders (Gregory, 2000). To evaluate the highly dynamical change that characterizes complex social situations, more adaptive, participatory, and robust theories, approaches, and methods are needed. Complex situations require systems thinking and theory that provides evaluators the means of assessing change under highly complex conditions.

SYSTEMS THINKING AND COMPLEXITY

Over time, the necessity to think about and evaluate a program as part of a larger *system* of activities and events that lead to social impact has increased. In other words, the system, not necessarily a program, becomes central to evaluation. Cross-organizational and cross-sector stakeholders, however, do not share the same stake in solving a problem. Issues of equity and power can potentially create controversy that may stymie their collective efforts (Reynolds, 2014). The stakeholders' mental models for how a collective change can be achieved and who should benefit are typically different and sometimes opposed. They are thinking as autonomous agents. To transition their thought patterns to work more collaboratively, they must develop a shared mental model for collective change (Cabrara & Cabrara, 2015; Kania & Kramer, 2011).

Stakeholders, however, often are challenged when asked to think about programs as part of a collective striving to make large systems change. To test this notion, I and a colleague asked over one hundred people (coalition members, students, and evaluation professionals) to draw pictures of their vision of a collective change (i.e., impact). The result was over one hundred different illustrations that could be organized into three general categories: *circular* (e.g., an ecological model or Venn diagram), *linear* (e.g., logic model), and *foundational* (e.g., tree or building) (Figure 11.2; Bakken, in progress).

So, how does an evaluator convening a group of stakeholders help them to create a shared mental model that will guide an evaluation of a collective and dynamical change within a complex situation?

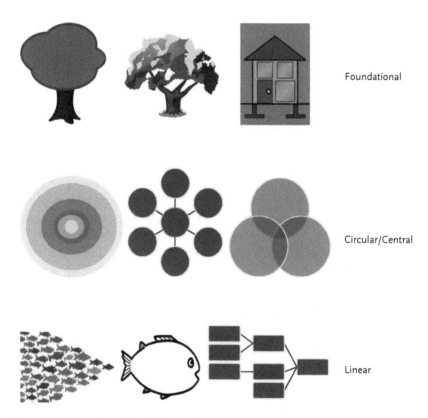

Figure 11.2. Mental models of collective impact.

If you were to look across the three categories of mental models that emerged from our inquiry, the illustrations share some common characteristics of systems. Each have distinct *elements*, the elements are *interrelated*, and they represent multiple *perspectives*. They also are *bounded* in some way. These similarities are known as simple rules of systems, and they can be used to understand a culture, shift a group in a new direction, or create a shared model for change (Cabrara & Cabrara, 2015; Eoyang & Holladay, 2013; Williams & Hummelbrunner, 2009). "Simple rules help with a flexible balance between the collective systems and the single actor because they support the choice of the individual while serving the shared purpose of the whole" (Eoyang & Holladay, 2013, p. 97). However, a traditional emphasis on evaluations based on program theory has conditioned us to think of programs as autonomous agents of change, so when we work as part of collaborations attempting to make collective changes to solve complex social problems (e.g., obesity), we are typically challenged not only by the complexity of the issue but by the emergent and complex dynamics that are shaped by similarities and differences among the stakeholder groups represented. *Patterns* observed in systems help evaluators identify and manage complexity, so it can be evaluated.

Systems that run smoothly are *adaptable* to change and run transparently (Eoyang & Holladay, 2013). When systems are not adaptable or are chaotic, they break down. It is when systems break down that we notice a problem. When a system is not adaptable and could benefit from innovation, it's helpful to "shake things up" by purposefully creating instability in the system (Eoyang & Holladay, 2013). Alternatively, when a system needs more stability, it helps to identify and resolve one of its tensions. For example, when I ride my bicycle, I move along smoothly and at a steady pace, only pausing for stop signs or difficult hills. As I continue my bicycle journey, I can adapt to various changes in terrain because my bicycle, a complex mechanical system, is designed to adapt to those changes through its gears and other components. I can continue my bicycle journey in a reliable and dependent fashion because the brakes and gears are working well for me. If, however, my chain derails during a gear shift on a hill, I am suddenly faced with the problem of losing my ability to transcend the hill in an easy manner—I and the bicycle are not able to adapt. If my chain derails several times over the course of my journey or every time I get on my bicycle, I notice a *pattern* that suggests that my bicycle is likely in need of repair. Alternatively, if my bike is performing well, but seems to be "doggish," especially in high winds, I might get innovative and streamline it in some way. An evaluator, therefore, can serve the role of a troubleshooter or mechanic by assessing a system for patterns.

Returning to the previously mentioned drawings of collective impact (Figure 11.2), we can recognize several patterns as we look across the mental models that represent multiple perspectives. For example, we see a central or focused target that typically represents the desired impact (a distinct element). We also may observe stick drawings of people (another element) and their relationships to other people and other elements of the drawing (relationships among elements). We may see patterns across mental models, such as those illustrated as a set of concentric circles or those displayed in a linear pattern (some distinctions). In other words, we can identify a set of "simple rules" specifically related to these drawings of collective impact (Cabrara & Cabrara, 2015; Williams & Hummelbrunner, 2009; Eoyang & Holladay, 2013). Patterns, then, are a useful way to define a system and assess its functioning. They also can provide useful information about how a system can be modified to run more favorably. When a system starts to breakdown or a problem emerges, *tension* is created in that system. These tension points can serve as indicators and opportunities for change.

In social systems, we notice complex problems, such as increased rates of food insecurity, because there is a breakdown or tension in the system (e.g., job loss, grocery store closures, lack of transportation) that supports food security. As evaluators, we must gain an understanding of these systems through thorough and systematic situational or context analyses. Furthermore, because we may be asked to evaluate a single program within a systems context, it is important for us to assess the ways that a program contributes to the system's functioning. If we are asked to evaluate the impact of a system on a social issue (e.g., food insecurity), we must be able to identify and assess its boundaries, distinct perspectives (e.g., activities, groups of people, organizations), and their interrelationships and how they function to create an impact. Evaluators of programs within complex systems, therefore, must pay attention to, assess, and document patterns and tensions in a system in order to provide useful information about a program's functions and contributions to broad impacts within that system.

Within an organizational or community system, desired impacts (e.g., reducing food insecurity) often are shared among stakeholders, but the ways to achieve those impacts (i.e., activities) and the priorities given to them may not be clear, and they may differ depending on a stakeholder's perspective. Stakeholder perspectives are influenced by cultural backgrounds, life experiences, values, ideologies, and the situation or context in which stakeholders reside. These differences can create tensions among stakeholders that challenge the functioning of a system. Tensions are normal and can signal separations among stakeholders or vast differences in opinion or ideology that can render a system unable to adapt to change. In the absence of tension, too much homogeneity among stakeholders may exist. Systems thinking and inclusive practices help us to embrace diversity and remain adaptive to the complexity of social change.

DEVELOPMENTAL EVALUATION

Developmental evaluation (Patton, 2011) was introduced to the field by Michael Quinn Patton in 2011. The introduction of this approach created a surge among evaluators who were looking for guidance on ways to evaluate change in complex systems. Dr. Patton eloquently described an approach to evaluation that was grounded in systems thinking and complexity science and provided a way for evaluators to manage the uncertainty and complexity of social systems. Consistent with the emphasis of his previous work, developmental evaluation stresses stakeholder involvement and the utilization of an evaluation's findings. Since introducing developmental evaluation to the field, evaluators have struggled with its application in practice, however. Constant demands for timely information that aids a system's ability to adapt and change is a challenge that requires evaluators to gain additional knowledge and learn a new set of skills. The American Evaluation Association's Topical Interest Group (TIG) on Systems in Evaluation is currently leading an effort to identify a set of principles and corresponding skill sets for *Effective Use of Systems Thinking and Complexity Science in Evaluation* (Hargreaves, Britt, & Noga, 2016). Early drafts of these principles suggest that evaluators need abilities to apply systems thinking and use complexity science as a lens to understand and analyze a program's (or programs') context and the situation to be addressed by the evaluation. They also imply the need for abilities to recognize the problematic and interdependent nature of social issues and the appropriateness of a systems approach for an evaluation's design. This set of principles is "capped off" with three principles that prevail across all approaches to evaluation, including the consideration of assumptions that underlie criteria for judging the value or worth of a program and an evaluator's responsibility to justify an evaluation's results and facilitate their use. Collectively these principles are welcome guidelines for evaluation practice in complex social systems.

SOCIAL JUSTICE AND INCLUSIVE EVALUATION PRACTICE

In the United States, it has never been more important to attend to social justice and inclusion in evaluation. The political polarization of our country is increasing; the diversity of our population across race, ethnicity, and religion has expanded; classism is more pronounced; and serious incidences of crime and violence are increasing. Consequently, local communities are forming coalitions and advocacy groups to address inequities in such areas as health care, incarceration, education, and public policy. Universities are enacting efforts to address an increase in sexual violence and racial discrimination. In the evaluation field, the American Evaluation Association (AEA) has endorsed a set of guidelines for culturally responsive evaluation practice as an important component of professional standards (American Evaluation Association, 2011). Topical Interest Groups (TIGs) on social justice and inclusion also have formed to specifically give significant attention to this topic in our field. Manuscripts and entire issues published in the association's journals have been devoted to social justice, inclusion, and culturally competent evaluation practice, such as an issue devoted to "Evaluation and Social Justice in Complex Sociopolitical Contexts" in *New Directions for Evaluation* (Rosenstein & Syna, 2015). And in 2014, the American Evaluation Association hosted its annual conference with the title, "Visionary Evaluation for a Sustainable, Equitable Future."

Local and regional efforts as well are expanding. In Wisconsin, iMilwaukee Evaluation! (http://evaluation.wildapricot.org/), an AEA affiliate was recently formed with one of its goals to "establish and maintain a pipeline for evaluators of color and underrepresented groups (e.g., low-income, LGBT, non-college enrolled youth, rural, and Spanish-speaking)." In 2015, they partnered with the nearby Chicago affiliate to host a conference specifically devoted to Social Justice and Evaluation. More recently, the Minnesota Evaluation Studies Institute chose as its Spring 2016 training theme, *Reconciling Equity and Accountability: Evaluation in an Unjust World*. Within those various contexts and events, what dialogue takes place and what does social justice and inclusion mean for evaluation practice in an age of accountability? Although an entire book could be spent on this topic, I will highlight some recent literature on social justice and inclusive practices in the field as a way to address this question.

When the terms, "social justice" and "inclusive practice" come to mind, I think of other terms, such as "equity," "fairness," and "voice." I also think of several evaluation approaches, such as participatory approaches (Cousins & Earl, 1995; Guba & Lincoln, 1989; Stake, 1967), deliberative–democratic evaluation (House & Howe, 1999, 2002), culturally responsive evaluation (Hood, Frierson, & Hopson, 2005; Hood, Hopson, & Kirkhart, 2015), utilization-focused evaluation (Patton, 1997), transformative approaches (Mertens, 2007, 2009), and empowerment evaluation (Fetterman, 1994; Fetterman & Wandersman, 2005)—collectively referred to as *collaborative* approaches (Cousins, Whitmore, & Shulha, 2012; Shulha, Whitmore, Cousins, Gilbert, & Hudib, 2016). I also think about the necessity for adequate time to build relationships with a heterogeneous group of key stakeholders, acquiring a thorough understanding of the evaluation's context, and using a set of qualitative methods that help me to gain a better understanding of the physical, political, economic, and social ecologies that embrace a program or other central unit of the evaluation (i.e., evaluand). However, as Jill Chouinard (2013) points out in "The Case for Participatory Evaluation in an Era of Accountability," the meaning of accountability is constructed as "technological" as opposed to "participatory," which creates relational, epistemological, pedagogical, contextual, political, methodological, and organizational tensions for evaluation practice.

> These distinctions illustrate that program evaluation can play a dual role, one that legitimates and is responsive to the current systems of performance measurement and accountability that is so prevalent in the public sector, and/or as a means to broaden democracy by including the voices and perspectives of the less powerful in our society and those more directly involved in the program itself. (Chouinard, 2013, p. 242)

Does program evaluation *need* to serve a dual role or can these two perspectives (i.e., technological and participatory) be married in some way? What are some useful strategies for evaluators who need to satisfy funders' requirements for rigorous and "scientific" evaluation designs but desire to be inclusive and socially responsible?

I begin by highlighting a profound and engaging dialogue that was reported in the Summer 2015 edition of *New Directions for Evaluation* as a way to articulate a strategic goal and role for evaluators. This dialogue occurred between two highly experienced and knowledgeable evaluation colleagues who had a philosophical and ethical discussion about an evaluator's role and values relative to the purpose and scope of the evaluation (Levin-Rozalis, 2015). It was particularly relevant at the time, because I and a graduate student project assistant had had a similar conversation about an evaluation in which we were involved to determine the feasibility of expanding an outreach program in a new region of the state. It was becoming increasingly apparent to us that the program as originally designed and the client's desired funding mechanism would not be an ideal or optimal fit for that region of the state. If the client wanted to expand services to that region, the program would need to be conceptualized in a very different way. Realizing that we were in a position of power and influence, how did we remain accountable to the client and funder while moving the evaluation in the direction of inclusion, participation, and empowerment? The conclusion of Levin-Rozalis and her colleague was, "As evaluators, we bear a very great social responsibility: to look broadly, to look forward, to be responsible for our actions, and as far as possible, to be sure that the purpose is indeed for the benefit of those who will ultimately be affected by our work."

For us, that meant it was important to include a range of key stakeholders, including but not limited to those who lack food, the stigmatizing ladies at the local food pantry, convenience store managers, food banks, anyone involved in transportation, local service providers (e.g., public health, social work, Cooperative Extension), political leaders, and grocers in our efforts to bring more food to these communities and engage them in decisions about what type of program would best suit their community's needs. By using participatory approaches, the program could be developed by the community, for the community it serves, and in a way that would meet their unique context and needs. With this vision and evaluation role in mind, we engaged these key stakeholders in phone interviews, online questionnaires, and face-to-face interviews and focus groups (Bakken, Wallace, & Rumball, 2016) to determine both the needs and context for the evaluation from their perspectives. We also suggested that the proposed program hire outreach specialists who had skills for grass-roots organizing and cross-sector engagement, so that food insecurity could be addressed from a systems perspective. In doing so, we were able to identify several outcomes and indicators that aligned with the roles and functions of a food outreach specialist and simultaneously supported the funders' performance measures. We also proposed that those outcomes be framed within a continuous learning loop so that communities could be more adaptive to change (e.g., seasonal job loss). One of our greatest challenges was the one-year time frame we had to conduct the study—a difficult timeline when institutional review board (IRB) approvals have to be obtained, and relationships need to be established and built to be inclusive. Nonetheless, we engaged a broad range of stakeholders to the extent possible in the time frame provided and plunged forward.

Similarly, Lapidot-Lefler, Friedman, Arieli, Haj, Sykes, and Kais (2015) performed a series of stakeholder interviews and as a result, proposed *life space maps* as an assessment tool for evaluating change in social inclusion before and after a program's implementation. With this strategy, evaluators could satisfy the technocrats while emphasizing participation. Using a conceptual framework grounded in social space and field theory, the authors created life space maps as visual representations of one's life ecologies along four dimensions: political, social, resources, and cultural (pp. 40–41). If each dimension is assessed on a "roughly measurable" scale, change could be quantified (to satisfy the "technocrats"; Chouinard, 2013). The maps also provide a way to monitor and assess improvements in inclusive practice over time. The authors conclude, however, that "an instrument for assessing the life space of individuals would be incomplete without complementary instruments for assessing and challenging the structural relationships that generates exclusion" (p. 41). Exclusion, too, can be identified through qualitative forms of inquiry, so I would advocate for more studies involving mixed methods approaches to satisfy the "technocrats" while practicing evaluation that favors inclusion.

Recently, Thomas and Parsons (2016) wrote an article about the intersections of culturally responsive evaluation (CRE) and systems-oriented evaluation (SOE). The similarities between these two evaluation approaches include such things as attention to factors outside the boundaries of a program, stakeholders' positioning within a broader context, the importance of interrelationships, and attention to multiple and diverse perspectives. What distinguishes these two broad approaches to evaluation is the way in which they are framed—CRE emphasizes cultural groups, while SOE emphasizes formal and informal social systems. They also position the evaluator in somewhat different ways. CRE emphasizes the importance of evaluators within "shared lived experiences"; whereas, SOE acknowledges an evaluator as an integral part of and potential influence on the system. Evaluation questions also tend to differ, but both approaches use qualitative, quantitative, and mixed methods forms of inquiry. Collectively, these approaches to evaluation provide encouragement for evaluators to think about a variety of cultural groups within the complex systems they study.

Merging culturally responsive and system-oriented evaluation approaches, the authors cite a useful mnemonic tool, called ZIPPER (Parsons, 2013), as a way to enrich evaluation practice (Thomas & Parsons, 2017). This acronym reminds evaluators to *Zoom* in and out of the evaluand (i.e., program) and its environment or context; *Interconnect* the parts of the evaluand and connect to other parts of the greater whole; *Plunge* into paradigms, structures, and conditions to gain a richer, deeper understanding of the evaluand; *Perceive* patterns as a way to inform inquiry or action; *Envision* and leverage energy as opportunities for understanding or changing patterns; and *Recognize* short-term, long-term, proximal, and distal results that will inform the evaluation questions and achieve the evaluation's purpose (Thomas & Parsons, 2017). I found this mnemonic to be a helpful tool for systems evaluation, so I will take a moment to raise several questions that come to mind when we think about CRE/SOE together in the context of the ZIPPER mnemonic.

In zooming in and out of a program, it is important that we go beyond the organizations and local communities in which programs are embedded and consider broader ecologies (e.g., families, the multiple organizations in which they interact, social networks) that surround programs and people and the ways these multiple ecologies are interconnected (that systems within systems idea). It is helpful to understand and zoom in on the cultural dimensions of the people for whom our programs are intended, so that we question its design and relevance. So, not only do programs become the focus of our zoom, but the people and other benefactors of our programs become objects of our inquiry in relation to the people our programs serve. As we look at the interconnectedness of a program's parts, in what ways does culture influence those connections? What cultural groups are represented? How are they represented? Who holds power and what are the group's collective dynamics? When we plunge into paradigms, structures, and conditions, with whom are they associated? Whose values do they represent? Who sets the conditions and determines the structures? And how are they formed? How do different cultural groups perceive a system and why? How do different perceptions shape their system? What patterns can we observe across these various perceptions? What perceptions bind systems change? In terms of envisioning energy, who is energized and how are they energized? For what purpose are different cultural groups energized and what factors energize them? When results are being recognized, who is recognizing them and why? Who's not recognizing the results and why? Whose results matter? What results matter? How are results recognized by various cultural groups and who deems them important? These questions provide a deeper lens for conducting a culturally responsive systems-oriented evaluation.

Reynolds (2014) further enhances our ability to conduct culturally responsive and inclusive evaluations by blending development evaluation, equity, and critical systems thinking in a conceptual framework that addresses issues of power and privilege. He begins his discourse by distinguishing between *normative* ethical traditions (value judgments) and three forms of *philosophical* ethics that reflect the "theoretical underpinnings associated with *doing* what's good (consequentialist ethics), *doing* what's right (deontological ethics), and *being* responsible (virtue-based ethics)" (pp. 77–78). He argues that developmental evaluation provides an opportunity to frame equity as "a construct or emergent property in the making" and is, therefore, less about "applying value judgements than developing value judgements" (p. 79). Developmental evaluation as a utility-focused approach, however, is subject to the domination of "clients" over "beneficiaries." Reynolds offers critical systems thinking (CST) as a way to examine power and privilege for the explicit purposes of "1) understanding interrelationships associated with a situation, 2) engaging with contrasting perspectives regarding a situation, and 3) reflecting on boundaries of such representation and interactions" (p. 81).

I found two applications for evaluation in this manuscript to be particularly useful and helpful to evaluators when working with multiple stakeholders in a complex system. First, it's not sufficient to only determine who the key stakeholders are for an evaluation or program. From a CST perspective, we also must identify each stakeholder's stake in the evaluation/program and the possibilities for improving stakeholdings. By doing so, an evaluator can learn what each stakeholder values and how to leverage their perspectives in ways that will facilitate systems change.

Reynolds (2014) also offers four sources of influence derived from critical systems heuristics—motivation, control, knowledge, and legitimacy—as one dimension of a two-dimensional matrix (Table 11.2) that accounts for various stakeholders, their stake in the evaluation, and stakeholdings (Reynolds, 2014; Ulrich & Reynolds, 2010). The other dimension of the matrix incorporates the three aspects of stakeholders just described. Using this matrix, evaluators can gain a richer understanding of the values, power structures, knowledge claims, and legitimacy held by stakeholders when assessing boundary judgments. This matrix provides a tool for giving attention to and engaging stakeholders both

Table 11.2. STAKEHOLDING ENTRENCHMENT OR DEVELOPMENT ASSOCIATED WITH A SYSTEM OF INTEREST[a]

Source of Influence	Stakeholders Social Roles	Stakes Role-specific Concerns	Stakeholdings Key Problems or Issues = tensions between idealized "system" vs. "realities" of "situation"	
Motivation	Beneficiary/Client	Purpose	(measures of success) enchantment of fixed measurable outcomes vs. managing emergence Check on values (circumscribing the system)	The Involved
Control	Decision-maker	Resources	(environment) imperative toward command and control vs. allowing autonomy Check on power (controlling the system)	
Knowledge	Expert	Expertise	(guarantor) dogma and promises of professional expertise vs. wider humility of social/ecological uncertainty Check on complacency (Informing the system)	
Legitimacy	Witness	Emancipation	(world view) righteousness and premises of "the" system vs. rights of, and consequences on, those affected Check on fundamental meanings (assumed within the system)	The Affected

[a] Adapted from Reynolds (2014). Reprinted with permission from Sage Publications, Inc. © 2014.

internal and external to "the system" when analyzing the context of a complex systems evaluation. Moreover, the underlying concepts of this matrix emphasize the importance of understanding how power and privilege influence a system and how they might be leveraged to promote equity and social justice.

Community psychologists are keenly aware of and addressing these issues in the evaluation field. In 2012, a topical interest group in community psychology was established in the American Evaluation Association to give greater emphasis to programs as strategies for effecting social change and promoting social justice (Cook, 2014; Sheldon & Wolfe, 2015). "Central to community psychology is the explicit goal of empowering those who are disenfranchised and powerless" (Cook, 2014, p. 108). Consistent with the evaluation approaches (and theories) mentioned earlier in this chapter (e.g., empowerment evaluation or transformative evaluation among others), this disciplinary focus values stakeholder engagement and inclusion as a way to "promote democratic principles of equality, fairness, and justice in deliberation and decision making" (p. 109). Cook goes on to propose 10 evaluation strategies to promote community change that "focus evaluation work toward effecting broader community change rather than merely gaining knowledge about the effectiveness of a program" (p. 110). Cook's statements reflect a somewhat narrow understanding of the evaluation field and years of research in program theory. Although recent emphases on program evaluation have focused on effectiveness in order to address our society's demand for technocentric accountability, the field of evaluation has established a variety of approaches and methods to address a range of purposes and types of questions over decades of scholarship. Nonetheless, the insights and values of community psychologists will help to propel the evaluation field's efforts toward a more just and inclusive society. Critical systems thinking combined with developmental evaluation and community psychology may be a useful combination of philosophical perspectives, experiences, and methods for systems change that tackles complex social issues. What do these trends in the evaluation field mean for evaluators over the next decade?

PREPARING FOR THE FUTURE: EVALUATION SKILLS FOR A CHANGING FIELD

You cannot nor should you ignore or abandon the knowledge and skills that you have gained over decades of work and scholarship in program evaluation. Instead, you must embrace and expand them with new or enhanced skills and knowledge that will prepare you for evaluation over the next decade or so. In other words, you must adapt to the changes that the evaluation field presents to you through ongoing learning and professional development. Table 11.3 highlights some of the most important areas on which to focus

Table 11.3. FOCUS AREAS FOR EVALUATION PRACTICE AND PROFESSIONAL
DEVELOPMENT

Practices

- Communicate and negotiate across people, organizations, and communities with different cultural norms, values, and power structures.
- Expand networks of professional colleagues so that various specializations, expertise, and perspectives inform practice.
- Maintain ongoing knowledge of the literature and advancements in the field.
- Work with teams of professionals who have complementary expertise.

Professional Development

- Ability to recognize different forms of change and select evaluation approaches that are most suitable to these various forms.
- Greater understanding of complex study designs and statistical analyses.
- Knowledge of capacity building, including coaching.
- Systems thinking, theory, and application.

this attention, in addition to complying with the professional standards and competencies that have been defined for the field (Yarbrough, Shulha, Hopson, & Caruthers, 2011).

Although most of you will not acquire an advanced level of understanding of evaluation for your professional practice, it is important to understand the knowledge and skills that are demanded of current trends in the evaluation field. By understanding these trends, you are able to recognize the limitations of program evaluation and the expertise needed to tackle the complexity of social problems and issues. Therefore, it is important that you gain a level of competence in program evaluation that will serve your purposes, yet not exceed its limitations. This book has provided you with a fundamental understanding of program evaluation and equipped you with skills and tools that will support your efforts. The next section describes other ways you can support evaluation practice in the face of these emergent trends.

SUMMARY AND IMPLICATIONS FOR EVALUATION PRACTICE

The need for sufficient time and funding to support evaluations of complex magnitude and scale is increasing. Practicing professionals must work with their professional organizations to advocate for greater funding for evaluations if we are to respond to the expanding scope and magnitude required to evaluate programs within complex systems. We also must build individual and organizational capacity for evaluation so that continuous learning and adaptation becomes embedded in the fabric of everyday work. This effort will require a shift from traditional linear ways of thinking and causal models for evaluation to systems ways of thinking and adaptive models for action. Evaluation can play a major role in assessing adaptive processes and providing information that is of use to its key stakeholders. By being inclusive and broadening the perspectives that shape our mental models of change, change can be achieved that benefits and empowers key stakeholders and facilitates a more just society. Evaluation in an age of accountability is taking new forms. You are in a key role to evaluate and inform social change over the next century.

REFERENCES

American Evaluation Association. (2011). *American Evaluation Association Statement on Cultural Competence in Evaluation.* Downloaded from http://www.eval.org/p/cm/ld/fid=92.

Bakken, L. L. (in progress). *A systems framework for collective impact: Implications for evaluation practice and research.*

Bakken, L. L., Wallace, B., & Rumball, L. (2016). *The feasibility of expanding foodshare outreach in northern Wisconsin counties.* Madison, WI: Unpublished Report.

Cabrera, D., & Cabrera, L. (2015). *Systems thinking made simple: New hope for solving wicked problems.* Odyssean Press.

Chouinard, J. A. (2013). The case for participatory evaluation in an era of accountability. *American Journal of Evaluation, 34*(2), 237–253.

Cook J. R. (2014). Using evaluation to effect social change: Looking through a community psychology lens. *American Journal of Evaluation, 36*(1), 107–117.

Cousins. J. B., & Earl, L. M. (Eds.). (1995). *Participatory evaluation in education: Studies in evaluation use and organizational learning.* London: Falmer Press.

Cousins, J. B., Whitmore, E., & Shulha, L. (2012). Arguments for a common set of principles for collaborative inquiry in evaluation. *American Journal of Evaluation, 34*(1), 7–22.

Eoyang, G. H. (2009). *Coping with chaos: Seven simple tools.* Circle Pines, MN: Lagumo.

Eoyang, G. H., & Holladay, R. J. (2013). *Adaptive action: Leveraging uncertainty in your organization.* Stanford, CA: Stanford Business Books.

Fetterman, D. M. (1994). Empowerment evaluation. 1993 presidential address. *Evaluation Practice, 15,* 1–15.

Fetterman, D. M., & Wandersman, A. (Eds.). (2005). *Empowerment evaluation principles in practice.* New York: The Guilford Press.

Gregory, A. (2000). Problematizing participation: A critical review of approaches to participation in evaluation theory. *Evaluation, 6*(2), 179–199.

Guba, E. G., & Lincoln, Y. S. (1989). *Fourth generation evaluation.* Thousand Oaks, CA: Sage Publications.

Hargreaves, M., Britt, H., & Noga, J. (October, 2016). *Principles for effective use of systems thinking and complexity science in evaluation.* Presented at the meeting of the American Evaluation Association, Atlanta, Georgia.

Hood, S., Frierson, H., & Hopson, R. (Eds.). (2005). *The role of culture and cultural context in evaluation: A mandate for inclusion, the discovery of truth and understanding.* Greenwich, CT: Information Age Publishing.

Hood, S., Hopson, R. K., & Kirkhart, K. E. (2015). Culturally responsive evaluation: Theory, practice and future implications. In K. E. Newcomer, H. P. Hatry & J. S. Wholey (Eds.), *Handbook of Practical Program Evaluation* (4th ed., pp. 281–317). Hoboken, NJ: John Wiley & Sons.

House, E. R., & Howe, K. (1999). *Values in evaluation and social research.* Thousand Oaks, CA: Sage Publications.

House, E. R., & Howe, K. (2002). Deliberative democratic evaluation in practice. In D. L. Stufflebeam, G. F. Madaus & T. Kallaghan (Eds.), *Evaluation models: Viewpoints on educational and human services evaluation* (2nd ed., pp. 409–421). New York: Kluwer Academic Publishers.

Human Systems Dynamics Institute. (2016). Human Systems Dynamics Glossary. Retrieved from http://www.hsdinstitute.org/resources/glossary-reference.html.

Kania, J., & Kramer, M. (2011). Embracing emergence: How collective impact addresses complexity. *Stanford Social Innovation Review, Winter,* 1–8. Retrieved from www.fsg.org.

Kurtz, C. F., & Snowden, D. J. (2003). The new dynamics of strategy: Sense-making in a complex and complicated world. *IBM Systems Journal, 42*(3), 462–482.

Lapidot-Lefler, N., Friedman, V. J., Arieli, D., Haj, N., Sykes, I., & Kais, N. (2015). Social space and field as constructs for evaluating social inclusion. In B. Rosenstein & H. Desivilya Syna (Eds.), *Evaluation and social justice in complex sociopolitical contexts. New Directions for Evaluation, 146,* 33–43.

Levin-Rozalis, M. (2015). A purpose-driven action: The ethical aspect and social responsibility of evaluation. In B. Rosenstein & H. Desivilya Syna (Eds.), *Evaluation and social justice in complex sociopolitical contexts. New Directions for Evaluation, 146,* 19–32.

Mayne, J. (2001). Addressing attribution through contribution analysis: Using performance measures sensibly. *The Canadian Journal of Program Evaluation, 16*(1), 1–24.

Mertens, D. M. (2007). Transformative considerations: Inclusion and social justice. *American Journal of Evaluation, 28*(1), 86–90.

Mertens, D. M. (2009). *Transformative research and evaluation.* New York: Guilford Press.

Parson, B. (2013). ZIPPER: A mnemonic for systems-based evaluation. Retrieved from http://insites.org/resource/zipper-a-mnemonic-for-systems-based-evaluation/.

Patton, M. Q. (1997). *Utilization-focused evaluation* (3rd ed.). Thousand Oaks, CA: Sage Publications.

Patton, M. Q. (2011). *Developmental evaluation: Applying complexity concepts to enhance innovation and use.* New York: The Guilford Press.

Pawson, R., & Tilley, N. (1997). *Realistic evaluation.* Thousand Oaks, CA: Sage Publications.

Porter, S. (2015). The uncritical realism of realist evaluation. *Evaluation, 21*(1), 65–82.

Reynolds, M. (2014). Equity-focused developmental evaluation using critical systems thinking. *Evaluation, 20*(1), 75–95.

Rosenstein, B., & Syna, H. D. (Eds.). (2015). Evaluation and Social Justice in Complex Sociopolitical Contexts. *New Directions for Evaluation, 146,* 1–132.

Sheldon, J. A., & Wolfe, S. M. (2015). The community psychology evaluation nexus. *American Journal of Evaluation, 36*(1), 86–117.

Shulha, L. M., Whitmore, E., Cousins, J. B., Gilbert, N., & Hudib, H. (2016). Introducing evidence-based principles to guide collaborative approaches to evaluation: Results of an empirical process. *American Journal of Evaluation,* *37*(2), 193–215.

Snowden, D. (2002). Complex acts of knowing: Paradox and descriptive self-awareness. *Journal of Knowledge Management, 6*(2), 100–111.

Stake, R. E. (1967). The countenance of educational evaluation. *Teachers College Record, 68,* 523–540.

Thomas, V. G., & Parsons, B. A. (2017). Culturally responsive evaluation meets systems-oriented evaluation. *American Journal of Evaluation, 38*(1), 7–28.

Ulrich, W., & Reynolds, M. (2010). Critical systems heuristics. In M. Reynolds & S. Holwell (Eds.), *Systems approaches to managing change* (pp. 243–292). London: Springer and The Open University.

Williams, B., & Hummelbrunner, R. (2009). *Systems concepts in action: A practitioner's toolkit.* Stanford, CA: Stanford University Press.

Yarbrough, D. B., Shulha, L. M., Hopson, R. K., & Caruthers, F. A. (Eds.). (2011). *The Program Evaluation Standards: A guide for evaluators and evaluation users* (3rd ed.). Thousand Oaks, CA: Sage Publications.

INDEX

Note: Page numbers followed by *f, t,* and *b* indicate figures, tables, and boxes.

contribution *vs.* attribution, 77, 204, 205
control variables, 144
convenience samples, 98–99
convergent validity, 122
Cook, J. R., 220
Cooperative Extension professionals, 20
Corbin, J., 171
correlational designs, 80, 90
cover page, in written reports,
    190–191, 191*f*
CRE (culturally responsive evaluation),
    216–218
Creswell, J. W., 171
criteria, in everyday evaluation, 5
critical systems thinking (CST),
    218–220, 219*t*
Cronbach's alpha, 122
cross-over effects, 105
cross-sectional study designs. *See* one-
    shot study designs
cultural competence
    in evaluation planning, 54
    as evaluator skill, 26–30, 29*b*, 30*b*
    in transformative approaches to
        evaluation, 45
culturally responsive evaluation (CRE),
    216–218
culture, 28–29, 54
Cynefin Framework, 207, 207*f*

data
    cleaning, 139–141
    managing, 182–183
    storing, 133–137
    tracking, 136–137
data, missing, 139–141, 141*b*
data analysis
    demographic information and, 134,
        135*f*, 135*t*
    post-hoc, 10, 157–158
    qualitative (*See* qualitative data,
        analyzing and interpreting)
    quantitative (*See* quantitative data,
        analyzing and interpreting)
databases, designing, 133–136
data collection methods
    accuracy and reliability of information,
        132–133
    aligning with evaluation questions,
        114, 115*t*, 193, 193*f*

checklists and rubrics, 126, 127*f*
data tracking and, 136–137
defining credible evidence, 114–116
existing sources, 131
interviews and focus groups, 123–125
maps and drawings, 126–129, 128*f*,
    130*f*, 131*f*
observations and video-recordings,
    125–126
photographs, 129–131
psychometric tests, 120–123, 121*b*
sampling methods and, 108, 109*t*
surveys, 116–120
types of, 97
data sources, 97–98, 133, 134*f*
data visualization techniques, 194,
    194*f*, 197
debriefings, validation through, 181
decision-oriented evaluation
    approaches, 42–43
deductive approaches, 80
deductive coding, 177, 177*f*
deductive thinking, 170
demographic information
    in databases, 134, 135*f*, 135*t*
    in surveys, 116–117
dependent variables
    defined, 83
    level of measurement, 144
    statistical tests and, 142, 142*t*, 159,
        160, 161–162, 163*t*
    types of, 142, 142*t*
descriptive statistics, 142,
    145–146, 145*t*
developmental evaluation, 213, 218, 220
Developmental Evaluation (Patton),
    204, 206
Dillman, Don, 21, 116, 117
dimensions, in coding process, 178
discrepancy-based evaluation
    approaches, 37
discriminant validity, 122
dissemination of evaluation findings,
    197, 199–200
distribution, skewed, 145, 148, 150*f*
Donaldson, S. I., 41
double-barreled survey items, 117, 118*t*
drawings, 129, 197, 199
dynamical change, 207, 208, 209
dynamic change, 207, 208, 209